Insidious Competition

Other Books by Richard Telofski

Fast Food for e-Business Marketers

Dangerous Competition, Critical Issues in eCompetitive Intelligence

Conehenge, The Story of a Jersey Schlub

Insidious Competition

The Battle for Meaning and the Corporate Image

Richard Telofski

iUniverse, Inc.
New York Bloomington

Insidious Competition
The Battle for Meaning and the Corporate Image

iUniverse books may be ordered through booksellers or by contacting:

iUniverse
1663 Liberty Drive
Bloomington, IN 47403
www.iuniverse.com
1-800-Authors (1-800-288-4677)

Copyedited and proofread by Nena Weber.

Original cover concept by the author.

ISBN: 978-1-4502-2908-1 (pbk)
ISBN: 978-1-4502-2910-4 (cloth)
ISBN: 978-1-4502-3043-8 (ebk)

Printed in the United States of America

Library of Congress Control Number: 2010907571

iUniverse rev. date: 6/10/2010

Dedicated to Florence,
who first impressed upon me the value of human interaction.

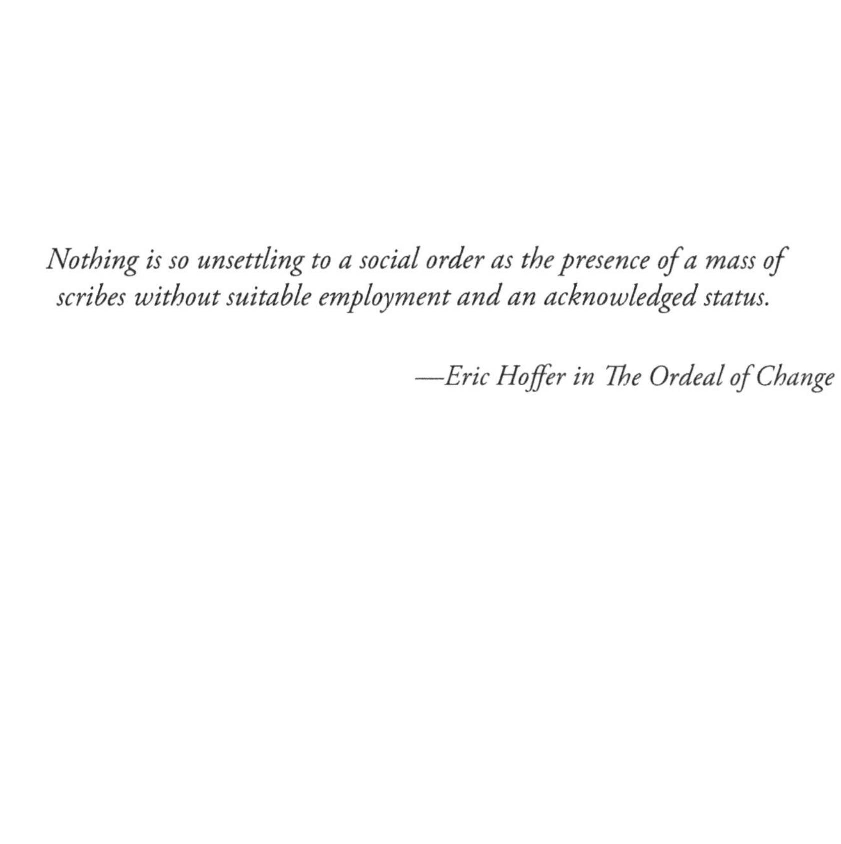

Nothing is so unsettling to a social order as the presence of a mass of scribes without suitable employment and an acknowledged status.

—Eric Hoffer in The Ordeal of Change

Contents

Section Two: The Principles of Propaganda and their Application

Section Three: Attack Classes and Types of Insidious Competitors

List of Tables and Figures

Introduction: Just What Is Insidious Competition?

"Workers of the world unite."

Many people believe that the line you see above is the opening line of *The Communist Manifesto.* This line is actually not the opening line of that classic work, but it is the opening line of this book, *Insidious Competition – The Battle for Meaning and the Corporate Image.* Don't become confused. This isn't a book about communism. I'm not a communist; far from it. I write that opening line not as a call to action, but as a statement of fact. "Workers of the world unite," a present tense statement of fact representing what is happening in the online world today. Perhaps a better way of making my point is to convert that statement into the present imperfect (passive) tense.

"Workers of the world are uniting."

By "workers," I mean all of us; the people who work every day to put bread on their tables. That's pretty much everyone.

And by "uniting" I mean "uniting online." People are uniting online to talk about almost every topic imaginable. Those workers, those people, those "everyones" are uniting on the social web, an area of the Internet reserved for virtual social interaction. Blogs, social networks, mini-blogs, etc. became mainstream around 2005 and, as we'll discuss later on in this book, people have been flocking to those sites to discuss every imaginable topic under the sun. And within some of those topics, somebody, somewhere across the globe on an inexorable 24/7 schedule is discussing your company, its image, and what it means to them.

When people discuss your company, some of them are talking truthfully and some of them are speaking falsely. Some of them have legitimate comments and complaints and some of them like to talk trash just because they can. Some of them have an agenda and some of those agendas are hidden while other agendas are not. Some of them don't have an agenda, but just want other people to react to what they say and some just want to vent and throw garbage on your company's good name.

As a competitive intelligence and strategy analyst, I study the behaviors of the "atypical" and "non-traditional competitors" that my corporate clients now face in social media. I am very familiar with what people do to damage the image of the corporation for which you work, as well as how and why they do it. During the past several years in my "travels" across the social web, I've seen this kind of bad behavior pick up speed. More people are doing it each day. And as more people do it each day, they are building upon a collective work about your company or other companies. They read the trash talk left by others on various social sites and then they add to it. They pile on. Each subsequent person puts another brick in the wall that hides and obscures what your real company image is. As more people enter the social web and become familiar with how to use social media tools, what you want your company's corporate image to mean gradually fades in the collective consciousness. Outside of your control, your corporate image subtly changes day by day. Your corporate image drifts in the minds of the public. Your corporate image becomes redefined. My discovery of this new problem is what led me to write this book. I wrote this book to help you. And, you need to read this book to help you solve a problem that is not going to resolve itself.

This book is written primarily for those who have the responsibility of creating, maintaining, and improving the image of a company, large or small, or of a brand of a company. Those who make their living in public relations, corporate communications, marketing, the "c-suite," issues and crisis management, competitive intelligence, and/or social media will draw useful insights from *Insidious Competition*. But, before you and I discuss this new problem, a problem laid out in detail from here through the back cover, you will need to shift your thinking a bit. So that you can come away with a better understanding of this insidious threat to your company, so that you can recognize how truly dangerous this new business threat is, and so you can acquire the necessary knowledge and skills needed to meet this new problem head-on, you will need to shift your thinking in terms of what "competition" is.

The people who contribute to this image drifting, to this brand redefinition, are actually "competitors." Yes, they are competitors. They are "atypical" or "non-traditional competitors."

You must think of them in this way.

Your direct competitors, the companies in your industry who sell products or services similar to those which your company sells, reposition what your company image means. They do that each day. In promoting their own product or services, your direct competitors, either directly or indirectly, communicate to people what your company does or does not do, in terms that favor them and not you. In the mind of the collective marketplace, your direct competitors are active in forming the image of what your company means. Those competitors, in effect, attack your image. And, in its marketing and corporate communications programs, your company does its best to counteract those attacks made by your direct competitors. Correct, yes?

So, how is what your direct competitors do any different from what these "workers of the world," these non-traditional competitors, do when they attack your company image from within social media?

Do you think that people using social media don't have as much power as your direct competitors? And therefore, those people in social media should not be a cause of concern? If so, you're wrong and we'll discuss this issue.

Do you think that what people say in social media just isn't trusted or regarded as important by those who read social media? And therefore, those social media conversations should not be a cause of concern? If so, you're wrong again and we'll discuss that issue, as well.

Do you think that social media is not a significant communications environment? And therefore, social media should not be a cause of concern? If so, yes, you're wrong again and we'll discuss why later on.

Do you think that social media communicators are not as clever in their communications strategy as are your direct competitors? And therefore, those social media communicators should not be a cause of concern? By now, you should know the answer to this one, too.

Compared to what your company does to fight the image attacks mounted by your direct competitors, does your company do as much to counteract the image attacks that non-traditional competitors create against your company in social media?

If not, then you must read the rest of this book.

You must read the rest of this book because now, in the era of social media, your company image is, or can become, the victim of *insidious competition.*

From Webster's New World Dictionary:

insidious - adj. *- proceeding in a gradual or subtle way, but with harmful effects* **-insidiousness n.**

Also from Webster's New World Dictionary:

competition **- n. -** ***the opposition*** **- competitive adj.**

Thanks to social media, there is a significant opposition to your company's corporate image; opposition that is conducted cleverly, gradually, subtly, and with harmful effects that progress over time. And if you don't take at least as much action against it as you do against your traditional opposition, your company's ability to succeed may be impaired.

Your battles, your "war" against insidious competition, won't be easy. Fighting for the meaning of your corporate image here in the information-age involves dealing with threats that are more diffuse and ambiguous than traditional threats.[1] Indeed, these types of ambiguous attacks may be the most difficult information-age attacks against which to protect. Bruce Schneier, a well-known crypto-analyst and computer security expert, in an Internet newsletter talked about this very type of attack back in October 2000.

Bruce said then that there are three types of network, or information-age, attacks. The oldest is the type of attack that targeted computer hardware infrastructure, the wires, the computer, the electronics. The second oldest is the type that targeted the software that drives that computer infrastructure. Attacks of this sort are the domain of what we have come to know as the computer "hacker." In this book, you and I are not concerned with either of these types of attacks. But pertinent to our discussion here in *Insidious Competition*, Bruce said that the third type of attack, a "semantic attack," is targeted at the way humans "assign meaning to content." He referred to how people tend to believe what they read and perform very little due diligence in ferreting out the truth about the written material which they consume. While alluding to the human link in the computer network as the weakest point in the whole system and referring to the dissemination of questionable information and people's tendency to believe it, Bruce pointed out that now due to the rapid dissemination of that information via computer networks the problem of a "semantic attack" is more serious than ever before. He said that it is a problem which is more critical than the "hacking" attacks of hardware and software.[2] Hardware and software attacks have discrete targets which can be directly defended. However, the target of the "semantic attack" is much more ethereal and ephemeral. And, unlike the computer hacker who must possess specific skills to mount his attack against hardware or software, the "semantic" target may be attacked by anyone who has access to the Internet. This characteristic makes the "semantic attack" the most difficult type of information-age attack to repulse or against which to defend.

This, the arena of the semantic attack, is where I believe business will fight an important battle in the coming decades. Because of the pervasiveness, ease of creation and access to "information" on the social web, business will fight for what its corporate image means. This *"Battle for Meaning and the Corporate Image"* against an insidious opponent will be just as important, or perhaps more important, than the wars you fight against your direct and more traditional competitors. It's always the foe that you don't see that is the most deadly.

You can't turn the other cheek on this one. You can't appease this new type of attacker, this non-traditional competitor, and just hope that they go away. They won't. You can't allow their ideas and accusations about your company reputation to go unchallenged because ideas and accusations that are allowed to exist become "true." And they live forever on the Internet.

Here in *Insidious Competition*, we will discuss many concepts, facts, and theories that will help us define just what insidious competition really is. This will be a lot of work. But we need to undertake this work because this opponent is new. This insidious opponent has been created by the new communications environment, social media, which grows more powerful every day. No competitor like this has existed before. And because a competitor of this nature has not existed before today, has not been recognized until today, nothing has been written previously about what or who this non-traditional competitor is, or how it operates, or why it is a threat, or how to counter the type of threat that comes from this new competitor. There is no prior model to build upon, so we must create one in this book. We will build this new model because it is vital to the development of our ability to fight this new type of foe, the insidious competitor.

Here is a description of the journey we will take to build this model.

In Section One of *Insidious Competition* we will discuss "The Elements of Social Media Danger." There in Chapter One, entitled "Social Media Has the Power, Baby," we will discuss in detail how social media sets up an environment that has the power to enable your new foe. We'll learn about the

Six Uncontrollable Factors in a Business Environment and how Social Media has become the Seventh. Then in Chapter Two, entitled "There's a Crowd in Them There Social Media," we'll discuss tribes and communities and crowds. Much has been written about social media communities. Well, you and I will see how those communities really aren't communities after all, but how those communities are really much more like crowds. And where you have crowds, you have crowd behaviors. This is where the wheels start to come off and The Battle for Meaning begins in earnest.

Still in Section One, from there we go on to Chapter Three, to discuss what I have coined as "The Five Factors of Insidious Competition." You can't be an insidious competition warrior without knowing about and understanding how crowd behaviors foster the Five Factors that drive your insidious competitor, driving them on the inside and empowering them on the outside. Chapter Three asks us to do some heady thinking, but we won't slow down our mental processes after Chapter Three. Quite the contrary. In Chapter Four, with the long title of "The Battle for Meaning, Reality Repackaged . . . and Liability Be Damned," we get even heavier and we will talk about the nature of reality, which is the essential element underlying The Battle for Meaning. We will talk there about how reality is created and what happens when reality creators lose a sense of responsibility because there is no liability attached to how their reality is packaged.

Now, having discussed the first half of this book's subtitle, *The Battle for Meaning*, we'll head into Chapter Five which is entitled "The Ephemeral Image," where we'll discuss the second half of this book's subtitle, *The Corporate Image.* We'll talk about how vital to your company its corporate image is and how that image can be the first victim in The Battle for Meaning, making the second victim your company's revenues, and the third victim possibly your own livelihood.

Rounding out Section One and our discussion of The Elements of Social Media Danger will be an even more intensive discussion of how reality is created and, in particular, how people come to know what they know. In Chapter Six, entitled "Solipsism & Epistemology or The System of Knowing," we'll delve deeply into how people learn. We'll discover there that what people learn, or what they know, is how they see reality. And we'll learn there the basics of the critical process of how insidious competitors "diddle" with the meaning of your company's corporate image. You can't be an effective insidious competitor warrior without knowing how the foe constructs an attack. Chapter Six will help you obtain this skill.

Once we understand the process of how the insidious competitor diddles with meaning, we then move on to Section Two entitled, "The Principles of Propaganda and their Application." Now, knowing the critical process of meaning, here we will see in Chapter Seven entitled, "The Principles of Propaganda," how the insidious competitor applies the process of meaning within the principles of propaganda. We will see in this chapter how insidious competitors apply those principles, both consciously and unconsciously, from within the environment of social media. And we will also see here how some principles of propaganda support the environment of social media itself. Chapter Seven will also show you how insidious competition organizes itself. All of this is important intelligence in being able to understand and combat this new, 21st century business foe.

We'll then move on to Chapter Eight, "The Four Tools of the Insidious Competitor." In this discussion, you and I will uncover the actual mechanisms through which the insidious competitor leverages the principles of propaganda, and by which meaning is diddled.

We won't stop there.

Next in Section Three, "Attack Classes and Types of Insidious Competitors," we'll move from the foundational theory and toward the more pragmatic. There in Chapter Nine, "Dangerous Days Are Trending Nearer," we remind ourselves about the nature of the threat we are facing and then go on to discuss in Chapter Ten, "Classifications of Competitive Attacks," the six classes of attacks that can be perpetrated by an insidious competitor. We discussed "semantic attacks" briefly above, and in Chapter Ten we will discuss semantic attacks in much more detail and come to learn that information-age attacks have many more dimensions. A good understanding of attack classes is essential to being able to later form an effective counter-strategy.

Then we will begin our multi-chapter discussion about the specific classes of insidious competitors out there on the social web. First up is Chapter Eleven, "The Reality Benders." This insidious competitor is characterized by those foes in social media who disseminate misleading or one-sided information. Within this competitor class we will find three types of insidious competitors. They are Tagging Terrorists, Mommy Bloggers, and NGOs/Activists. In that discussion we'll talk specifically about why each type is a threat, what tools each type uses, their organization and attack classes, and we will also see some specific examples.

Next in Chapter Twelve, "The Nasties," we'll discuss a class of insidious competitor quite different from the Reality Benders. Whereas the Reality Benders propagate one-sided information, The Nasties disseminate false information from false sources. In other words, *they lie.* Thus, the name "Nasties." We will see one type of insidious competitor in this class. That type is Foreign Governments & Their Agents. We will discuss why they are a threat and talk about their organizational form, their attack class, and their tools.

After an intense discussion about The Nasties, we'll talk about something a little more "friendly." In Chapter Thirteen, "The Friendlies," we'll discuss four types of this class of insidious competitor, which are Customers/Clients/Consumers, Employees, Activist Stockholders, and Labor Unions. We'll talk about why each of these types is a threat, the tools that each type uses, their attack class, and their organizational form. Some examples of The Friendlies are given in that chapter. Why do I call them "friendly?" Well, it's because each type is associated closely with your company, but yet has an agenda different from that of your company. Are they really "friendly?" I suppose that's a relative word. You'll know more after you read Chapter Thirteen.

Chapter Fourteen, "The Digital Pirates," follows. These are the people who "borrow" your corporate intellectual property and forget to give it back. In Chapter Fourteen, we will discuss only one type of insidious competitor in this class. That type is known as the Culture Jammer, and in our discussion we will talk about why they pose a threat, their tools, their attack class, and their organization. We will see some very interesting examples there, as well.

Moving on to Section Four, "Strategies & Tactics Against Insidious Competition," we'll lead off with Chapter Fifteen, "Suggested General Strategies & Tactics Against Insidious Competition," and discuss just that, general strategies and tactics. In this chapter, we will discuss both proactive and reactive strategies and tactics. And we will review previously discussed concepts, such as the Five Factors of Insidious Competition, the Principles of Propaganda, and Solipsism & Epistemology, as parameters under which these general proactive or reactive strategies can be considered.

As we leave Chapter Fifteen, we will begin to learn how to apply our general strategies and tactics specifically against each class and type of insidious competitor, taking each one in turn. To do this, we'll lead off with Chapter Sixteen, "Suggested Strategies & Tactics Against the Reality Benders," where we will see examples of how the strategies and tactics might be applied against each of the three types of insidious competitor in this class. In the discussion we'll consider specifics such as the type of tools each uses, as well as their attack classes and organizational form.

Then comes the shortest chapter in *Insidious Competition*. In Chapter Seventeen, "Suggested Strategies & Tactics Against the Nasties," we'll have a bit of a different discussion. Why different? Well, you will just have to wait until you get there.

Following in Chapter Eighteen, "Suggested Strategies & Tactics Against the Friendlies," we'll discuss some examples of strategies and tactics that might be applied against the four types of insidious competitors in this class and, in doing so, we'll talk about how each type's attack class, organizational form, and tool usage may enter into the strategic/tactical selection.

Then, Chapter Nineteen, "Suggested Strategies & Tactics Against the Digital Pirates," wraps up our section on strategies and tactics. In Chapter Nineteen, you and I will talk about how strategies and tactics might be applied to the one type of insidious competitor found in this class and we will consider this competitor's unique characteristics.

Finally, the Conclusion, "Your Battle Starts Now," brings us to the wrap-up and to your departure from our exploration of insidious competition. Your own battle for the meaning of your corporate image then awaits.

* * *

As I've said previously, I believe this fight, this Battle for Meaning and how it impacts your Corporate Image is an important one. And as you read both the facts and the theories contained within *Insidious Competition*, you will learn more and more why I believe this and, more importantly, *why you should, too.*

The Battle for Meaning is one that is about fighting lies and misrepresentations. For you as a person working for a company that has fallen victim to these lies and misrepresentations, this book's intent is *not* to help you create lies or misrepresentations in return. This book's purpose is *not* to assist you and your company in creating and implementing strategies and tactics that are illegal, immoral, unethical, or shady. So charlatans, please look elsewhere. You will not find your answers within these pages.

If your company has performed improper behaviors only to find itself "insidiously competed with," well, then your company needs to "fess up." Because by not doing so, the insidious competition will only grow and may reach a point at which abatement is impossible.

But if you work for a company that is among the majority of companies which are honest and law-abiding, then this book will be of interest to you. This book is intended to assist companies of good character and integrity in battling those who have wronged it.

Now, please continue with your reading of *Insidious Competition.* I will be honored if you do so. I hope you enjoy your reading as much as I enjoyed the writing.

Section One:
The Elements of Social Media Danger

Chapter One:
Social Media Has the Power, Baby

What makes social media a competitive threat that is different from the other types of competitive threats that business people face? Well, how about to start with, it's *insidious*. And, it's *competition*. Let's go back to our Webster's Dictionary to remember that "insidious" means "proceeding in a gradual or subtle way, but with harmful effects" and "competition" means "the opposition."

Yes, social media has the power to compete with you for the meaning of your corporate image – just like any traditional competitor. And what makes the threat from social media so *insidious* is that, as of this writing, the threat is just *not being taken seriously.*

Taken seriously it should be because social media are being regarded as a significant communications method. This is attested to in a study by Universal Mc Cann, a reputable research company and a subsidiary of the Interpublic Group of Companies, Inc. In that study it was found that:

- We trust strangers online almost as much as we trust a face-to-face recommendation.
- We would much rather trust a stranger than a celebrity, by a long way.
- We trust a stranger over any paid-for communications or advertising.
- We trust a stranger in a regulated environment like reviews (social tools) on a retail site such as Amazon or an auction site like eBay.[3]

So, social media are important communications methods, not just something for your kids to play with.

As I write, marketers are experimenting with, and discovering, how social media can be used successfully within their marketing promotions mix. But what business people are not considering nearly as much is that if social media can be used to **promote** products and services, if it has that kind of power (and the Universal Mc Cann study, among others which we will see later, says that it does), then alternatively it can be used to **demote** or damage the image of products and services – and yes, even your corporate image. Yes, social media has that kind of power.

And that power is going to be used both in unexpected ways and by unexpected persons and entities. Not the usual suspects of competition. Not necessarily the "direct competitor" who sells the same products and services as your company does. No. These *new competitors* don't want to sell your customers, clients, or consumers a comparable product or service. These new competitors want to sell your customers, clients, or consumers a competing *image* of your product, service, or your very company. An image of your company that is not as flattering as that which you work hard to maintain every business day and certainly not as flattering as the image on which your company was built and which is integral to your company's continued and future success.

But wait, I feel like I'm getting ahead of myself. And when I check my book outline I find that yes I am running ahead of where I should be at this point in the book. Let me slow this discussion of the new competitor down a bit. I'll come back to that later more fully. For right now, let's just look at the traditional competitor, the "non-insidious competitor," the one that is smack dab in front of your nose every business day, the one that can be easily recognized, the one on which businesses concentrate when someone utters the word "competitor." Let's talk about the traditional competitor from within a framework that you may recognize – *The Six Uncontrollable Factors in a Business Environment.*[4]

When I was in business school, I had this framework pounded into my head on a regular basis. It's basic, yes, as you will see. But it's very helpful in gaining an understanding on how to approach business problems every day. When I taught in business school, I did the same with my students. Hey, let no good deed go unpunished. Think of it as a tradition. But more than that, consider this basic framework as a necessity in order to think straight about what you and your company are doing. After all, you are responsible to shareholders, be they public or private.

As its name describes, the framework says that, basically, there are six "uncontrollable" factors in any business environment.

The Six Uncontrollable Factors in a Business Environment

- The Customers
- The Government
- The Economy
- The Competition
- The Technology
- The Independent Media (commonly known as Mainstream Media)

These are the factors that impact what we, as business people, do every day. If any one of these factors contributes a negative influence to your business, well, we call that a "threat." Whatever your business problem happens to be on any given day, you can use the framework to trace it back to one of these influences to understand how to categorize the "threat" and, most importantly, to develop strategies and tactics to handle the problem.

Some examples follow.

- When inventories on a particular style of product or a particular color begin to increase, that's an indication that consumer preferences may be changing - The Customers
- When it takes longer to develop a new product because new regulations require more reports to be filed with authorities, that's an indication that the folks in the state capital or in Washington, D.C. have been working overtime. - The Government (As info, when I say "working overtime," I'm just using that as an expression. I don't really mean to say that they're actually working overtime. I used to work for the government. Believe me. They don't work overtime.)

- When your finance department has difficulty arranging funding for a particular activity, that's an indicator of a problem in the financial system. - The Economy
- When a directly competitive company comes out with a new product, that's a competitive threat to all the other companies who sell similar products. - The Competition (i.e., the traditional competitor)
- When those direct competitors discover a new technology for use in manufacturing or as a feature in a product or service, that's an opportunity to perhaps reduce costs and increase market penetration. - The Technology
- When independent media publish stories unfavorable to a company's new product introduction, that's a negative impact on sales and perhaps a death knell for the new product. - The Independent Media

Try as you might, you won't have *total* control over any or even one of these factors. All the other factors that impact a business, which cannot sub-classify under any of these six factors, are controllable. But these little uncontrollable buggers are what give you a job. These little buggers give your company problems and that's why your employer hires you. To try to solve, or at the least to mitigate, the problems, read that as "threats," created by these six uncontrollable factors is the reason you collect your paycheck. All of the threats generated by these factors can affect not only the specific functional activities of your business but these threats can also, at least indirectly, affect the general reputation of your company. And companies take great pains to prevent, mitigate, or control any damage to their company's corporate image.

So won't paying attention to the framework of ***The Six Uncontrollable Factors in a Business Environment*** help you protect and grow your business?

The threat to business that we're discussing in this book, this *insidiously competitive threat,* is unprecedented in business history. Think of it like this. Think of this threat of *insidious competition* as if the "uncontrollable" factors of Customers, Technology, and Media have morphed together into a **seventh**

"uncontrollable" factor – Social Media. No, it's not the same as the sixth factor, "The Media." This one is different. Much different. Why?

Well, first of all, social media is comprised mostly of individuals, like you and me, and not of groups of newspapers, magazines, TV and radio stations, etc. as is "The Media." Second of all, social media is based on human *interaction*, the multi-directional messaging of those individuals. "The Media" is based on reporting, unidirectional messaging.

There has never been anything like social media. And social media, and the threats it can generate, go to the core of human communication; it hits and lives within the human soul. Yes, this threat is different. This threat relates directly to that stuff that we crave to have and will do almost anything to get - interaction with another human being. The desire for that interaction is an immutable force. In other words, the desire for human interaction is unstoppable. Think about it. An unstoppable force, one born of human nature, up against an ephemeral image that is your brand or your company's reputation.

Who do you think will win?

Take-Aways from
Chapter One – Social Media Has the Power, Baby

Just one: Social media is now the seventh uncontrollable factor in the business environment.

Deal with it.

Chapter Two:
There's a Crowd in Them There Social Media

We've all heard a lot about "social media communities." There's a community for this, a community for that, and so on. I live in a community and have lived in many communities during my life and I'm not referring to the town in which I live. For me, the town in which I live is a place; it's not a community. But I belong to other communities in which I interact with other humans, and whether or not your town is your community, if you are human, you likely belong to communities, too. But what I see in social media is not a community. Read on.

Tribes vs. Communities vs. Crowds

The way many of us are in the process of interacting and uniting is via the Internet. We are "workers of the world" and we are uniting. We're uniting within that worldwide interconnection of computers that was originally constructed for academics and government officials to exchange files of information, the contents of which would bore most of us to tears. But through the rise and maturity of the Internet, from its birth as a project of DARPA (the American Defense Advanced Research Project Administration), through the dot com boom of the late 1990s, through the dot com bomb of the early 2000s, to the advent of social media in the middle of the first decade of the 21st century (can't we just call that decade, for sake of simplicity, the "Ones?"), everyday folks have been adapting the Internet for their own purposes, most of those purposes for good, some of those less so.

Adaptation is something living things do very well. From plants to ants to bears to hares, living things adapt to their surroundings and among all the living things that adapt to their environment, humans are probably the leaders in this practice. What makes us the leaders in the adaptation process is that not only do we have the ability to adapt to the environment around us, but we also have the ability to adapt the environment around us to us. And the part of that environment that is very pertinent to the discussions in this book is the Internet. We humans have not only created the Internet, but have along the path of its life adapted it to serve some of our most basic as well as some of our most unimportant needs and desires. One of the most basic needs to which the Internet has been adapted is the need for social interaction. The human is a social animal, after all, with origins in a tribe or pack culture, where a tribe or pack is defined as a hierarchical group of people with common interests. From your experience in life, I think that you would agree with me when I say that, in general, humans like interaction, especially with those who think and act similarly. That's why solitary confinement is used as a punishment, and it's why "time-outs" work for modifying most kids' behaviors. I know that time-outs worked on me when, after some unsatisfactory behavior of mine, my mother would sit me down in "the chair."

I got "the chair" my fair share of times when I was a kid. And at that time, the only meaning the phrase "time out" had was when a sports team called one on the field. When I was a kid, time outs weren't a term that was applied to child rearing, but my mother knew the value of applying one to her children. I would swear that she learned this from watching hockey games, but I know that my mother was not a hockey fan. No, she instinctively knew the value of a well-applied "time out" and that it could make a point and teach a lesson that a swift swat on the bottom could never communicate. And I received my fair share of those swats on the bottom, too. But the swat on the bottom wasn't nearly as effective with me as was "the chair." The swat was over too quickly and did not deny me for very long that which my juvenile human spirit craved, "interaction." To me, the lack of interaction was the greatest punishment my mother could mete out. And she did. In fact, she even "amped it up a bit" by sitting me in a chair, in our living room, with my toys on the floor, and the television turned off not more than eight feet in front of my nose. What was really only ten minutes felt like ten days. I could not stand the lack of interaction and involvement and I would toe the line pretty quickly. We humans crave interaction, and we'll do a lot of things to avoid not having it!

Because we crave that interaction so much and because it's "hard-wired" into our psyches, when a new technology comes along that can be used to increase interaction, that basic need, we jump on it. Interaction is enabled by communication. And communication, of course, is achieved via many forms. The stone tablet, papyrus, moveable type, the pony express, the telegraph, the telephone, fax, e-mail, and now social media, are all communication technologies that humans have employed to stay in touch, to keep that much desired interaction going, avoiding that feeling of being parked in "the chair." The human adaptation processes that morphed the Internet into its current configuration, which some folks call "Web 2.0," yielded a type of virtual interaction started in the 1980s with the electronic boards, places where people could post and read messages. Boards morphed into Usenet (the forerunner of today's social networks) and forums which started popping up in the late 1980s, enabling people to "congregate" online and express their opinions on various topics.

The congregation that took place, in the virtual world as in the physical world, was around topics of common interest. When writing my outline for this book and in my preliminary thoughts about insidious competition which would be developed, augmented, and written in *Insidious Competition*, my first inclination was to think of the online assemblages, which we now commonly refer to as "communities," as online tribes. I started to think about those online groups as tribes because: 1) it's so fashionable to use such primal terms to describe various phenomena in today's social media. You aren't "in" in the business of social media unless you use such terms. And because: 2) in 2008, the media guru named Seth Godin published a book entitled *Tribes*, about which much of the social media world went gaga, even though Seth's book is not exclusively about social media. So, to an extent, I too succumbed to some of the pop culture with which social media is inextricably entangled and thought that online groups must indeed be like tribes. Now, not all of my thinking was swayed by the pop culture influence, which can be so, so enticing. Some of my thinking about those online groups as tribes was based in sound sociological theory. Employing that theory, I thought of those online groups as tribes because tribes are groups of people organized around a common interest. Certainly, I thought, that the masses of people who "congregate" on social media sites have a common interest. Whether it's a hobby, a problem in search of a solution (or even a solution in search of a problem), a fetish, or just an idle curiosity concerning a passing thought, social sites are usually devoted to one central theme, a common interest. But when I thought about it more deeply, it occurred to me that people swarming around a social site *really aren't tribes.* Here's why they aren't.

Per Webster's Dictionary, tribes are hierarchical groups of people organized around common habits or ideas. (Yes, I know I'm using the dictionary as the basis for a discussion in sociological theory, but it's more succinct and efficient than using a sociology textbook definition. And since *Insidious Competition* is a business book and not a long, dry, boring, academic discourse in sociology, let's just roll with it.) Fundamentally, tribes are organized around a common interest, or more accurately stated, they are organized around a common *purpose.* To achieve that common purpose, there must be a leadership to direct the group (i.e., a hierarchy) just as there is in a pack of dogs, for example.

Tribes and communities do have much in common. Both have hierarchies. But online groups, those things most of us call online "communities," seldom, if ever, have a leadership. In my mind, this difference, that of an online community not having a leadership, was driven home while I was reading the blog article, "Follow the Herd. How Behaviors and Stories Spread Through Online Crowds." [5]

The blog post author, who claims to be a neuroscientist and is known only to the world as Patrick, opines that online communities such as those at Digg.com and StumbleUpon.com are not really "communities" at all. He says that online groups are crowds. "Ah-hah! Yes, this man has a point. Leaderless online communities are really more like crowds. That's the label I've been seeking," I thought as I continued to read on.

Patrick reminded me that two of the factors that separate communities from crowds are that communities possess both leadership and a common purpose. He's right, communities do possess those qualities. Patrick maintains that online groups do not possess leadership and common purpose. He says that online groups are crowds. Yes, I agreed with him that online groups are more crowd than community. But being someone who never lets a good thought, even my own, become stale in pursuit of fresher and better ideas, I began to think further about this concept of leaderless online groups. I thought, "Is Patrick really correct in saying that online crowds lack leadership and a common purpose?" I'll address this question in a few moments. But before I do, let me briefly depart from this line of discussion and tell you something that popped into my mind as I was writing this and which should be said now before we go any further.

Patrick's article was extremely interesting and raised many intriguing questions. But being that the blog article was, in effect, anonymously authored, I think it must be approached cautiously. This article and its argument would have carried much more weight, more authority, if the author had supplied some biographical information, including a full name, so I could have vetted him for use as a more reliable source. Because anonymous social media/web sources and their potential dangers are something I'll discuss more fully later in this book, when you reach that point in this book I don't want you having the idea that I'm being hypocritical and saying that, well, Patrick's anonymous source material is fine but other anonymous source material is not. I question the authority of his material, although it actually may be adequate. But what I don't question is his opinion, which is that online groups of people are not communities, but instead are crowds. So now, with that issue of sourcing addressed, let's rejoin the previous line of discussion and go back to the issue of crowds.

Many of my social media colleagues like to call groups of people on social media sites "communities" perhaps because it sounds better than calling them a "crowd." If the label sounds good, then my colleagues can more easily persuade their clients to undertake social media marketing projects, generating fees. Certainly it's better to say to your client, "Let's establish a brand community," instead of saying "Let's establish a brand crowd." "Community" sounds cuter, more warm and fuzzy, more friendly, more like, "Hey, this is gonna generate us some cash." (And don't get me wrong. There's nothing wrong with generating some cash. I subscribe to the capitalist idea behind the famous quote: "No one eats until somebody sells something.")

"Crowd" sounds brash, unmanageable, and uncontrollable which would fit well with the currently chic and fashionable exhortations for brand managers to "lose control of their brand" by marketing via social media. But come on, what brand manager actually wants to lose control of their brand? What brand manager wants to go for lack of control as his or her employment objective? The world is chaotic enough as it is. If brand managers yielded to the social media intelligentsia crowd (pun intended) and lost control of their brand, why would their employers need to keep employing them? The brand manager's company could just save an expensive salary and let nature take its course in managing their brands. Using misnomers is not a good way to start out in the problem resolution process that is business. But to revisit some rhetoric from the 2008 presidential campaign and to employ a standard American cultural cliché, "You can put lipstick on a pig, but it's still a pig." So call it a community if you like, but it's still a crowd.

Now, let's get back to that question I posed a few moments ago, "Is Patrick really correct in saying that online crowds lack leadership and a common purpose?"

Crowd. First, let's take Patrick's assertion that a crowd has no common purpose.

Webster's says that a crowd is "a group of people having something in common." Yes, the dictionary again, but it's reliable and on-point and not an anonymous source, and by using it we see that the people in a crowd do have something in common. Well, use your head. Of course, crowd members have something in common. Why else would they come together? Think of any crowd that you have ever been in and on the most basic level there was something that you had in common with every other person there. The purpose of the crowd may have not always been an outcome to be effected by the crowd, such as in a protest demonstration or a picket line. The purpose may have been just to achieve something on an individual level, like being in a crowd at a concert, where the individual members of the crowd want to be entertained, or a crowd of people walking down a street, where the individuals in the crowd simply want to get from point A to point B in the most efficient manner given the physical circumstances presented. So, yes. The individuals in a crowd, and the crowd taken collectively, have a common purpose. Now, second, let's move on to Patrick's assertion that a crowd doesn't possess leadership.

Again from Webster's, it says that the word "crowd" is "applied to an assembly of persons . . . and may suggest a lack of order, loss of personal identity, etc." Okay. So based on Webster's definition, which I deem a reliable source as would most people, I can agree with Patrick here. Crowds differ from communities in that a crowd is a leaderless, less organized group of persons than is a community. There is no leadership in a crowd. And that more accurately describes what we see on social sites. From what I've just discussed here, you can see that online groups are a hybrid between community and crowd. Online groups have common purpose among their members, as does a community, but are leaderless like a crowd. Because of the nature of online groups and how we've come to regard them as a great "sea of anonymity," I would have to say that the more prominent of these two forms would be the "crowd." Lack of leadership and the loss of personal identity factors, providing inherent anonymity, are big, very big factors in social media. And I'll come to explain throughout this book how those factors contribute to very dangerous, no *insidious*, competition for today's businesses.

So let's sum up what we have so far regarding groups of people online. What we see online is a virtual crowd with something in common, but they are a leaderless, faceless group of people, with a lack of order, and with little or no personal identity.

Okay. So, It's a Crowd.

In *The Crowd* by Gustave Le Bon, one of the first psychological enquiries into crowd behavior, the author says that "in crowds it is stupidity and not mother-wit that is accumulated." I like that. Gustave [6] also says that the effect of a crowd will be:

1. To make the individual feel invincible, allowing him/her to yield to instincts which, if alone, the individual may have "kept under restraint."
2. To make the individual submit to the contagion of the crowd, sacrificing personal interest for the collective interest of the crowd.

To put this in common language, what Gustave means is that we as fallible humans get caught up in the excitement, we feel deep emotions, and we "go along with the crowd." You've heard that expression. You probably heard your parents say not to do this. (Mine did. Although, I didn't get "the chair" for doing so.) You've felt these emotions. Because I'm human, I've felt these emotions, too. Those emotions are often visceral and primitive. Although you may like to think of yourself as unaffected by crowd behavior, very few, if any of us, humans are completely immune to its effects.

This is thought-provoking stuff and I'm going to hit you with one more thought-provoker before I pull all of these thought-provoking thoughts together into a final thought-provoking definition of "online crowds." Alvin Toffler, the guy who wrote the seminal work on society and culture entitled *Future Shock,* posited in *Powershift* that the "crowd" was the first mass medium, sending messages from the "ruled" to the "ruler." [7] Fascinating stuff. Imagine. A sender, the crowd, is also the medium. A media paradigm which conjures up mental images of the French Revolution, with throngs of people storming the gates of The Bastille, with quips from Marie Antoinette like "The peasants are revolting," or "Let them eat cake." These mental images suggest that, because their rulers weren't listening or didn't care or both, these peasants had no other communications resource to employ and used the "crowd" as their petition. What a strange paradigm, one that we see at several points in human history. One that today seems far-removed. Or is it really very far-removed? Do we still see this first mass medium being used today? Has it been reprised perhaps with different people and different crowds playing the roles? We can apply Alvin's idea of the first mass medium to the situation of social media's use today, as everyday people try to communicate with companies that make the goods and services that these everyday people buy every day. The "ruled" are the customers. The "rulers" are the companies who serve them.

Alvin Toffler also thought that in addition to the *messages* that crowds sent via the medium of the crowd itself, the *size* of the crowd was also a message in that it communicated the *importance* of the message. Recall the Mc Luhan adage, "The medium is the message." Very apropos here, don't you think? Message quality and quantity are important in reaching the desired communications objective. But in addition to the size of the crowd sending a message to the ruler, the size of the crowd also sent a message to the "ruled," a sort of "intra-crowd communication." Alvin says that that message to the ruled is, "You are not alone." [8] This idea of intra-crowd communication, the idea of not being alone, and its effect, is very important to our discussion of social media's creation of the non-traditional and insidious competitor because this idea supports the property of invincibility that Gustave Le Bon proposed. If people in groups, with no leadership, with somewhat of a common purpose sense that they are not alone, and that feeling is amplified by the size of the group, which may get progressively larger, then they may feel that feeling of invincibility.

So, now let's tie all of this foregoing discussion together and go for a final definition of a crowd.

A Final Definition of Crowds

Based on the previous discussion, you and I can see that crowds contain the following six factors, and are thereby defined. We can see crowds as groups:

1. With common interests,
2. With leaderless organization,
3. That are bathed in anonymity,
4. That use their size to amplify their message to the "ruler" and to the "ruled,"
5. That make individuals feel invincible and powerful,
6. That manufacture behavioral contagion, causing those powerful-feeling individuals to perform instinctual behaviors, which the individuals believe will be in support of group interests.

Now, here comes the fun part, although I'm not implying that the foregoing hasn't been fun. If you've read this far, then you must have had some enjoyment out of it.

You and I have already identified online groups as crowds. Let's push this knowledge a bit further (Remember. Never let a good idea go stale.) and compare the Final Definition of Crowds, with its six factors, to social media so that we may get a more robust description of the social media environment and learn even more about that online environment's characteristics.

Comparing the Final Definition of Crowds to the Environment of Social Media

1. Common Interests - Social media users generally organize around a "collective interest" in that they congregate on sites where there are subjects that attract and appeal to them. Their collective interest is, at least on the surface, that they seek and contribute information, building what's been come to be called in the vernacular "collective intelligence."

2. A Lack of Formal Organization - Social media users generally lack formal organization, usually with no leader, although there have been cases, such as political campaigns, where those users operated in a formally organized fashion.

3. Anonymity - Social media users are, or can be, bathed in anonymity. There is no need or requirement for correct identities to be conveyed within social media. (This can be at once both exciting and particularly annoying.)

4. Message Amplification - Social media "gadgets" exist, and users remind other social media users to employ these gadgets, to spread a message, helping that message to go viral, gaining a larger audience, enlarging the crowd, amplifying and increasing the importance of the message in the minds of the receivers.

5. Invincibility and Power - Do social media make people feel powerful? I suppose that could be a subjective question. Why don't we get an opinion from a reliable source?

The book, *Groundswell*, a treatise on the rise of the use of social media in business, contains a great quote regarding the question of power: "The Internet allows people to draw strength from each other . . . to connect to each other, to feel unafraid, and to be powerful." [9] And the anonymity feeds that feeling of power. Anonymity breeds a disregard for responsibility. No responsibility? Say whatever you like.

History and literature are rife with examples of the abdication of responsibility due to power. Some examples are: Hitler, the Roman Empire, Teapot Dome, Enron, Animal Farm. The list is sadly endless. The way people within the social web feel "absolute power" is, of course, quite different from the ways in which individuals in these examples established and felt their absolute power. Yet differences in methods of power creation do not diminish the feelings of power nor the exercise of that power. People are people. It's human nature. We've seen it happen far too many times. When people get together, a power base forms automatically and, as the power grows, the people holding it become more confident. As their confidence grows and as they succeed they start to forget the rules, cut corners, and violate moral and ethical standards. If the powerful fear no "reciprocity," or loss, if people feel "immortal," then rules generally fly right out the window. It's the ugly side of human nature.

Think of this concept simply. If as a result of your actions you are likely to be identified, you are more likely to obey moral, ethical, and legal limits.

That's why bandits wear masks to a stick-up. Anonymity and irresponsibility are directly related.

So, do social media make people feel powerful? Yes. Social media can make people feel powerful and the anonymous nature of social media can lead to a greater sense of power.

Thus far, in comparing the Final Definition of Crowds to the social media environment, we can see a match along five out of the six factors as shown above. But, the sixth factor is more of a toughie to match up. Recall that Number Six is:

> *Crowds manufacture behavioral contagion, causing those powerful-feeling individuals to perform instinctual behaviors, which the individuals believe will be in support of group interests.*

All right. Never let a good idea get stale. To see if we can get a match up, let's explore Number Six a bit further.

Contagious Crowd Behavior

People usually start out behaving in a manner that is consistent with the way society expects. We all learned, well most of us did, how to do this starting at an early age. Remember "the chair." And yes, sorry. The sociology theory is back again, but I'll keep it basic and not amp it up to a level that makes you think that this part of the book is being written by some sociology professor who wears a long beard and sandals and features a poster of Ché in his office.

As I said, most all of us were socialized to behave in the way society expects. It's called socialization and it's part of what makes a society functional. But there are conditions, both personal and social, that cause individuals to act in an anti-social manner. And one of those social conditions arises when you have strength in numbers, multiplied by the cloak of anonymity. It's under these conditions that the wheels can start to come off. Peoples' basic instincts come out. Goodbye, Mr. Superego and Hello, Mr. Id. Let the instincts all hang out. That's when irresponsibility, which you and I discussed a few moments ago, comes out to play.

So, we can see where a situation of strength in numbers and its attendant anonymity can lead to instinctual behaviors. Now, let's compare this instinctual behavior situation to the social media environment.

A person may come to a social site, a blog perhaps, expecting to contribute in a civilized fashion, and perhaps even under his or her own name. Think about this. Feel this. Imagine this. Recall that you've probably experienced this very situation. But after reading the main post and perhaps a dozen comments under the main post, and perhaps becoming incensed by those comments or the main post, the contagion and the group-think kicks in and from deep down in the darkest of your dark Id comes the most primal of a response via your fingertips, and under a false name. Does this seem familiar? If you've spent even a little time reading blogs, you'll recognize this scenario.

Indeed, in a television interview on the Charlie Rose program, writer David Denby alluded to this type of scenario saying that in blog posts the emergence of negative comments or abusive language is almost "algorithmic." David said that this type of behavior is so formulaic that you can almost calculate how many comments it will take until the commenters from hell emerge.[10] This "piling on" behavior is enabled within social media, especially if the character of an organization (read that, for purposes of this book, as a "company") is being disparaged. As public relations experts Eric Dezenhall and John Weber said in their book *Damage Control*, "If the accused (sic) character is in doubt, mob rule kicks in." [11] It's an "Id Pile On" and it reaches deep into the darkest regions of the human psyche.

So yes, going back to the comparison of the last of the six factors, from the Final Definition of Crowds, to the environment of social media:

> *6. Crowds manufacture behavioral contagion, causing those powerful-feeling individuals to perform instinctual behaviors, which the individuals believe will be in support of group interests.*

We can see that the sixth factor fits well into a description of the social media environment.

Per what David observed, above, about the property of "piling-on," the social media crowd causes contagion and elicits instinctive, Id-type behaviors. And based on what Eric and John said about mob rule kicking in when it's time to "kick the hell" out of an accused whose character is in doubt, like people are often wont to do to a company, social media participants would feel that they are in support of the group interests in the beating up of the accused. Crowds are notorious for this.

Social interaction allows us to draw strength from each other, within groups of our choosing. The Internet, because it's a tool, a tool that we humans have adapted to our communicational and interactive social needs, amplifies, leverages, and increases our ability to draw strength from each other. The Internet breaks down the geographic distances which would otherwise dampen the exchange of opinions and allows us to find similarly minded individuals that we wouldn't have otherwise been able to locate due to the restrictions of distance. The Internet is a tool that allows us to increase our social reach with all the advantages or disadvantages that go with those connections. The Internet allows us to be part of a virtual crowd.

Thus, here we are now at the part of the book where we start to realize the inherent danger to business that comes from social media. From what you and I have discussed so far, we now have a basic foundation upon which to build a better understanding of that danger.

Take-Aways from Chapter Two – There's a Crowd in Them There Social Media

1. Humans crave interaction.
2. Social media is more of a crowd than a community.
3. Crowds manufacture crowd behavior, which can lead to the crowd supporting crowd interests (i.e., not your interests), with a lack of formal organization, via anonymous identities which breed irresponsible actions.
4. The crowd behavior will be unmerciful against any organization whose character is questioned. Crowd behavior is a major influencing factor within social media interaction.

Chapter Three:
The Five Factors of Insidious Competition

So, through all the discussion about tribes, communities, and crowds, you and I can now see that it is crowd power that people are able to draw upon. The contagion in the online crowd, the yielding to instinct to support the collective crowd interest, the appearance of Mr. Id, the anonymity of the social media world and its attendant irresponsibility with all the potential for misuse that that implies, create the very environment that enables the non-traditional type of competition that is the subject of this book, *Insidious Competition*. Now, naturally the subject of *insidious* competition is of grave concern to me. That concern should be quite clear given the fact that I have written this book about the subject, a book that, quite frankly, at the time of its publication is the only one that addresses this exact topic. The threat to modern business from the insidious competition existing within the social web is more dangerous than any competition posed by traditional competitors. To understand the nature of this new type of competition better, and to empower ourselves to build counter-strategies against it, let's develop a framework through which insidious competition can be more thoroughly examined. The first four elements of this framework draw heavily upon, and crystalize, the concepts that we have discussed up to this point.

I'll call that framework the **Five Factors of Insidious Competition**, because without any of these five factors insidious competition would not have the potency it has, nor would it be a lurking competitive force capable of eroding the image and vitality of the modern corporation.

Here are the **Five Factors of Insidious Competition**:

1. Anonymity of the social media environment.
2. Individual power drawn from that anonymity.
3. Contagion that amplifies that power.
4. Yielding to instinct to support the collective crowd interest.
5. Individual disdain of institutional power.

Please remember these five factors. Anonymity, power, contagion, instinct, disdain. You and I will be using them frequently throughout the remainder of this book.

In the previous discussions about tribes, communities, and crowds, especially those within social media, I've already covered the first four factors of anonymity, power, contagion, and instinct and have discussed their supporting concepts in detail. You should, by now, have a very good understanding about how and why those factors foster and support insidious competition. But "individual disdain of institutional power" is a new idea in our discussion so far. So let's learn more about this disdain of institutional power and its implications for the modern corporation.

Disdain of Institutional Power

Let's go back to the book *Groundswell.* The authors of this key work about the employment of social media for commercial purposes present an idea that should come as no shock to any of us: the idea that "people have always rebelled against institutional power." [12]

Duh. Again. History is rife with examples.

The American Revolution, which some folks say continues even to this day being that the Constitution was written as a living document, which can be changed to protect the people from an overbearing government.

The Bill of Rights, which puts the individual above the institution that governs the people.

The French Revolution. You and I touched on this one during our discussion about crowds. The people didn't like cake all that much. Instead of merely cake, the people wanted more from life and without the institution of royal government controlling what those people got from that life. The people could choose freedom or they could choose the cake. They didn't choose the cake.

The American Civil War, which when you come down to it was about states' rights and rebelling against the larger institution, the federal government.

The First World War. The Great War. The War to End All Wars.

The Second World War.

And these are just the highlights.

Look into your own soul. That's the most important test we should apply here.

How do you feel about an institution having power over your life? Do you wake up in the morning thinking about how government and corporations will provide for your every want and need? Making all your dreams come true?

This feeling of institutional disdain has been around, well, probably ever since men and women first established organizations. And it's likely this sentiment will continue into the future. Given social media, with its virtually intrinsic anonymity creating the potential for individual power and the contagion that amplifies that power, and with its ability to also create an environment making it easy to yield to the instinct to support the collective crowd interest, this fifth factor of anti-institution sentiment certainly doesn't bode well for corporations. Corporations. Those very institutions upon which we have traditionally "relied" for accurate information about which goods and services to purchase to solve the problems of our everyday lives.

"We will stop falling for people who think they can put something over on us," an allusion to the influence of corporate promotion, says trend spotter Richard Laermer. [13] So, assuming that we're not going to sequester ourselves to caves, make our own soap (if we would even need soap when we're living in a cave), and eat roots, bark, and beetles for extra protein, on whom, and what, should we rely for information if we are to eschew corporate messaging about products and services? Where would people turn for information about what goods and services would satisfy their needs and wants? How about turning to their "friends?" Or other individuals who could be made into "friends?"

It's been known for a long time that "word of mouth marketing" is far more powerful than traditional advertising. Think about it. Who likes to be "told" what to do by a faceless, big organization? Who likes to be told what to buy by a large corporation when that large corporation might be leaning toward self-interest? Who believes "big business" transparency statements, which cannot be clearly articulated often because of the very size of the corporate structure and its attendant need for the message to go through an almost infinite series of committees, marketing minds, and legal reviews before it comes out as a watered-down, almost unrecognizable version of its original form? (If you've answered "me" to any of these questions, please e-mail me at Richard@Telofski.com because I'd really like to know more.)

The disdain of institutions gets into worse territory than just a sentiment. For more on this thought let's jump to Michael Strangelove, author of *The Empire of Mind.* In that book, Michael said that, corporations today face the start of a much decentralized communication system whose members revolt against commercial messages, regard meaning as public property, and have a disregard for private property.[14] Ouch. It's not just the negative sentiment that is a problem. There is a larger problem at hand. That larger problem is *the battle for meaning,* a battle sparked by negative sentiment and its fomentation within social media.

People dislike corporations. No. This isn't a news flash. It's common knowledge, periodically supported, by the way, by the traditional media. The why isn't important right now, and anyway the reasons are so far-ranging that they would make, and do make, subject matter for many other books. Let's look at a few examples.

In the first chapter of *Media Unlimited,* Todd Gitlin lays out a case for how the average American lives in a "torrent of media." [15] Again, this is pretty much common knowledge. You and I both live it. But let's think about what's being said within that media torrent. Within the media are far and wide-ranging sentiments against business, particularly big business, in general. Think about the following movies:

- The Rainmaker
- A Civil Action
- Erin Brockovich
- Silkwood
- Wall Street
- Norma Rae
- Network
- The Alien Trilogy

All of these movies portrayed "big business" as the overarching villain against individuals or, as this "struggle" between company and human was characterized in the book *Damage Control*, "a vulnerable victim pitted against an arrogant or incompetent villain." [16] These portrayals represent archetypal narratives to which human beings can relate. Because there are so many narratives that reflect this theme, you can probably go on to name many more. In movies where business is involved, can you name many, or any, films that don't portray big business as a problem, as a villain? How many films have you seen where the company plays the hero?

As I write this chapter, there is one particularly relevant example of anti-business themed communication that is being discussed widely. The "Protect Insurance Companies PSA" is a video appearing on the social web. "Protect Insurance Companies" is an ersatz public service announcement (PSA) crafted in and bathed in satire. The video features several celebrities from television, screen, and music "bemoaning the fact" that insurance companies will be damaged as a result of a government-run health plan. The celebrities implore you to take pity on the poor insurance company executives and their families as their lives will be negatively affected should government-run health care become a reality. (I write this chapter in the midst of the debate.) The tone of the video is snarky. (We'll learn more about snark later in this book.) The point of the video is obvious, especially when one considers that the video springs from the left-wing, pro-government health care, political action group, MoveOn.org.[17] On the day of my writing about "Protect Insurance Companies," the video had tallied over 2.5 million viewers on its main site, FunnyOrDie.com, with over 800 comments. So, popular it is and widely does it spread its satirical message about the "evil" corporation. In communications of this type, it is the drama which is paramount and not the facts.

According to a USA Today article, "Why Health Insurers Make Lousy Villains," health insurance companies are members of an industry which is one of the least profitable in America today. "Overall, the profit margin for health insurance companies was a modest 3.4 percent over the past year, according to data provided by Morningstar. That ranks 87th out of 215 industries and slightly above the median of 2.2 percent. By this measure, the most profitable industry over the past year has been beverages, with a 25.9 percent profit margin," says USA Today.[18] Never let the truth get in the way of a good satire. (We'll come back to this adage later when we discover the nature of reality.) Despite the facts, painting big business as the villain in any argument persists.

The same sort of "business as devil" theme is portrayed in many television dramas as well as in mainstream, network news broadcasts, which are television dramas of a different sort. Currently, as I write this section, "corporations" are being demonized in the mainstream media as being the culprits of the economic downturn starting in 2008. In the mainstream news, we repeatedly see government officials pointing "fingers of blame" at large corporations as the culprits of the recession. (It often seems to me that when the economy is good, politicians take the credit, but when the economy is bad those same politicians point the finger of blame at big business.)

Do you expect this to change? Will people suddenly or even gradually start to adore their electric utility? Or the company who makes their kids' cereal? Or the business that provides their cable TV signal? Or the company that makes the shoes that go on their feet? Or any company for that matter? None of those seem very likely, do they?

The myth of the corporation as devil just gets perpetuated, rightly or wrongly, and that myth can, and does, get easily transferred into social media. And from there, the devil theme just rolls and builds like a snowball on a steep hill, accumulating everything in its path, and damaging corporate reputations in the process.

Given the other four of the **Five Factors of Insidious Competition** (anonymity, power, contagion, and instinct), the potential for social media to carry, multiply, and distort a message, influenced by the fifth factor of institutional disdain, does not bode well for the creation, maintenance, or control of the *corporate image*.

As was pointed out in the Ad Age article entitled, "Comcast Must Die," Mark Twain is credited with the quote, "Never pick a fight with a man who buys his ink by the barrel." This is an allusion to 19th century technology. Today we can make a similar 21st century parallel, as did Bob Garfield in that landmark article about Comcast, Dell, and AOL, saying "never get in a dispute with someone with access to a computer" [19] and, I would add, who is mad enough and persistent enough to make your life "hell." This idea of making someone's life hell reminds me of an old episode from the 1980s TV series, "Miami Vice." (The TV series. Not that wreck of a movie that they based on the TV series.)

I recently saw that episode in reruns. In the episode, the main character Sonny Crockett, a police vice detective, was questioning a reluctant source of information. The source was not as forthcoming as Sonny would have preferred so Sonny said to the source that he (Sonny) would "clear my desk of all my other cases and make your life a living hell." (Indeed, I have used this same approach with some companies with which I have dealt when they have treated me in a way that I perceived as less than fair. The approach has worked and I'll have to credit Sonny for the inspiration.) Sonny would be mad enough and persistent enough to get what he wanted. If he had had a blog, he probably could have cut in half the time required for that task. Or maybe not, Sonny could be pretty persuasive with just a scowled countenance, a .45 caliber automatic hanging from his underarm, and the option to throw some "skell" in the "pokey" overnight until the "skell" reconsidered his position.

The same ideas apply to today's social media participants. They don't have .45s hanging from their underarms. Well, maybe some do, but I hope that most don't. But "mad enough, persistent enough, net-savvy even somewhat enough" individuals, while boosted by the crowd-inspired power, electrified by the contagion, driven by the resulting instinct, and augmented by the anonymity in the social media crowd, can escalate their general dislike of institutional power into a nightmare for any given company. They can "clear their desks of all their other cases" and make the life of an institution, and by extension the lives of those who work there, a living hell.

If that doesn't qualify as a threat against corporate image management, then I don't know what does. And if the *corporate image* is the basis upon which the company operates, and it is, then truly all companies are at risk.

* * *

So there we have it, a framework through which insidious competition may be more thoroughly examined. That framework is called **The Five Factors of Insidious Competition.** As a quick reference for you, I have included Table 3-1, The Five Factors of Insidious Competition, which you see below.

Table 3-1, Five Factors of Insidious Competition

Factor	Explanation
1. Anonymity	Social media doesn't require that participants are correctly identified.
2. Power	The anonymity can lead to a corruption of ethical behavior, making users feel powerful.
3. Contagion	Power corrupts. Social media users are susceptible to this infection. And it spreads like a virus.
4. Instinct	Powerful-feeling individuals perform behaviors which they instinctively believe will be in support of the crowd's collective interests.
5. Disdain	Deep-rooted dislike of institutions is amplified and perpetuated by the other four factors.

What makes non-traditional and insidious competition "competition" is that people are competing for the *image of the corporation* and are doing so online, within the social web. Please note that here, in *Insidious Competition*, I am not including the legitimate complaint about a company. Certainly, the company needs to be aware of such things. But it's not the considered criticism of a product or a service, which may indeed enable the marketers of that product or service to improve their offering, that should worry management. It's not the balanced argument which contributes to reasonable discourse that threatens the corporate image. No. It's the antithesis of these, coming from within social media, that *threatens the corporate image.* It's the innuendo, insinuation, spin, implication, hint, overtone, undertone, aspersion, or allusion to the inferiority or wrongdoing of a company and/or its products or services *falsely* created within social media that supports the threat of *insidious competition. Insidious* because these innuendoes, insinuations, spins, implications, hints, overtones, undertones, aspersions, or allusions proceed in a gradual and subtle manner to harm the corporate image, repeatedly, gradually, and incrementally, over time. The danger and its effects are not noticed until it is too late. What this process constitutes is a distortion of reality, or *a battle for meaning.*

If we are to understand and attempt, at least, to manage *insidious competition* and to win that *battle for meaning*, then we must have the foundation for understanding that competition. We now have a good start on that foundation. Yet, we need to work harder to build our footing in this area. In the next chapter we will continue to build this foundation by starting an examination of the "construction of reality" and we will get back to that comment I made in the previous paragraph, the comment about "a distortion of reality" and "the battle for meaning."

Take-Aways from
Chapter Three – The Five Factors of Insidious Competition

In this chapter, we discussed a framework through which we could better understand insidious competition. This framework consists of the Five Factors of Insidious Competition.

1. Anonymity of the social media environment.
2. Individual power drawn from that anonymity.
3. Contagion that amplifies that power.
4. Yielding to instinct to support the collective crowd interest.
5. Individual disdain of institutional power.

Chapter Four:
The Battle for Meaning, Reality Repackaged . . . and Liability Be Damned

Screen names and the free-wheeling, open nature of social media today create an online air of anonymity, inviting irresponsibility and a trashing of the rules, along with the trashing of any target of the writer's even slightest instinctual discontent. Those targets can be ideas, people, institutions, governments, or companies. Within social media the opportunity exists for average people to choose a target and to, in effect, "repackage" the reality of that target, *changing meaning* in the process.

Previously, before the Internet crept its way into everyone's homes, way back there in the olden days prior to 1992, back when things were more "real," this privilege of "reality packaging" and *meaning change* belonged to those with the financial resources to support the communications effort necessary to achieve such things. The mainstream media, large corporations, and governments were generally the only entities who could repackage and define reality for us on a large scale.

No longer. Now everyone with an Internet connection can play in this game.

Average persons can, and do, get together online, in the social web, and using inexpensive tools, tools which are not difficult to learn how to use, which are easier in fact to operate than a car, collectively define, or redefine, reality as they like with meaning held in the balance.

Facing every day can be, for some, a challenge. For others, it's no contest;

it's as simple as "falling off a log." But whichever outlook you may share with other members of society, you'll probably agree that many of us go about our daily lives thinking and feeling that reality is a constant, an absolute. Feeling secure in that belief we conduct our lives accordingly. We need a reference point. We plan on and forecast, to a reasonable degree, a certain series of events with particular outcomes. (We do all this even though an old adage, which according to a Google search is largely attributed to Yogi Berra, goes, "Forecasting is very difficult, especially when it involves the future.") We act and behave according to our expectation of those events, so our in sync behaviors will obtain for us the maximum benefit. We presume that other people, with whom we interface either directly or indirectly on a daily basis, will have the same reference points, based in a "common reality."

However, truth be known, reality is a tricky thing. Really tricky. Would that it were, but reality is not an absolute. This problem, this aberration of the very truths that we consider to drive our days, is partly what contributes to people having different opinions on the same subject. It's why we look at someone "like they're from Mars" when we discover that their viewpoint on a given topic of mutual interest is entirely different from our own. The genesis of that difference is based on perception. And because perception is subjective, and because perceptions are at least partially manageable, perception can be modified to change reality. There's a saying that goes "you can't change the past, but you can change the future." Reality lives in the past, but grows in the future. Growth has not occurred yet, so reality's future can always be changed. Reality's future can be increased or decreased, or altered in many ways. So, therefore reality can be changed.

There have been many who have defined the "keepers of reality" as the traditional mainstream media, or as we know them, newspapers, magazines, television and radio news. Now, we can debate from now until the moon crashes into the Earth, which I'm sure we all hope will not be soon, about how "accurately" the mainstream media has projected reality. But the fact remains that to have a view of what is happening around us, there needs to be a reference point. And since we can't attend to every event that may affect us, we need to have an intermediary do that for us. We could say that those intermediaries are "agents of common knowledge."

In modern American society, and in the societies of most Western countries, those agents have customarily been the traditional, mainstream media. So, it has been to those reference points, those agents of common knowledge, those "objective" sources of the traditional media, for better or for worse, which we have turned over the past decades, seeking a window into what is real and into the events that do or could shape our lives. But as many of us already know, currently those agents of common knowledge, those "keepers of reality" are under siege. Oddly, and from within the context of the discussion at hand, they are not so much under siege for their portrayal of "reality" as they are for a retention of readers or viewers or listeners. Their audiences are dwindling. As people view, listen, and read less of those mainstream "reality references," our perceptions of what is real fragment. (I will show you some figures later on that demonstrate the demise of traditional media.) As those traditional media decrease, reality becomes more scattered, less concrete, more abstract.

This won't come as any surprise to anyone paying attention to, ironically, the traditional media. Those traditional media have been reporting paradoxically for quite a while now that instead of getting information from traditional media sources, many Americans, and people of other Western nations, are now turning to the Internet for their information. However, the fact that we can believe that this is common knowledge is quite interesting. Because if the traditional media are reporting the decline of their own importance in reporting reality, wouldn't their decline become known by progressively fewer people?

Instead of thinking in terms of a conundrum about how the mainstream media is reporting their own demise, let's just go with the idea that the mainstream media is becoming less significant in terms of total media. As David Denby, who I mentioned previously, wrote in his book entitled *Snark*, while referring to the demise of the mainstream media reporting reality, the "authority of agreed upon facts and central narrative of the world could dissolve," creating what he called a "future dystopia." [20] A future dystopia seems like something in which I wouldn't care to participate. I despair because we haven't seen any information that indicates that this trend toward Denby's future dystopia is going to reverse any time soon, or even at all.

So what does all this heavy-thinking mean? Well, let's trot out Michael Strangelove again and discuss a thought of his that he revealed in *The Empire of Mind*. He said that the allowing of all voices an outlet via the Internet weakens the "hegemonic construction of reality." [21] Huh? Simply put in less academic language, he means that we're losing the centrally located, "objective," liability-fearing, repository, reference points of reality. Michael's theory is in direct contrast with one about which we'll hear later, a theory from The Mackenzie Institute; one that is very trendy. But for now, let's just concentrate on the problem that reality is being diluted. And as I said before reality is becoming less real. Less objective. More subjective. Not that reality was ever really truly, concretely objective. But now it is becoming rapidly even less so.

What's causing this? It's what Michael just said. The Internet, and by extension, social media.

Now, that's not to say that there wasn't an active campaign to alter the face of reality prior to social media getting a strong foothold long about 2004 or 2005. There always have been campaigns to control or change reality and meaning. Within modern society the players in that game have usually been public relations firms, representing corporations, or politicians who ostensibly represent the "people" but more accurately probably represent their party or even themselves. However, now because of the pervasiveness and ease of use of social media tools, anyone can play in the repackaging of reality and the dilution of meaning.

People need training and a license to operate a motor vehicle. The reason for this is that the improper operation of a motor vehicle can result in injury, destruction, or death. To operate social media tools, no similar training or license is required yet I maintain that injury, destruction, and "death" can be caused through the usage of social media. Social media (blogs, forums, social networks, vlogs, plogs, splogs, photo-sharing sites, mini-blogs, etc.) enable anyone with a pulse to either "report" or opine about reality and have that message shared with countless others, from only a few to a few million. Indeed, social media are employed in this manner. Let's look at some numbers describing how social media are used.

A survey was performed by the public relations firm Ruder Finn listing reasons that U.S. Internet users gave for going online. Here are some of the results:

Connect with others - 92%
Discuss - 76%
Be part of a community - 72%
Opine - 62%

Influence others - 56%
Activate support - 52%

Now please understand that the survey was to discover the reasons for going online, which doesn't necessarily mean using social media. But the results shown above indicate, no, scream the usage of social media. These results show that people aren't just popping online to check stock quotes or the weather, or to find out what's playing tonight down at the local Bijou. No. These results are about interaction and social discourse.

One of the most interesting findings of this survey was that half of young adults, aged 18 to 29, went online "specifically to rage against a person or an organization." [22, 23] Half! I suppose that they've got that disdain factor of the Five Factors of Insidious Competition down pretty well. This finding is especially significant because social media skews young. As we know about youth, having been young ourselves and having had young, impetus friends during that time, youth is apt to say things against business because doing so is rebellious, considered cool among their peers, and I suppose part of the process of finding oneself. The more outrageous the statement, well, the more cool you may be perceived. Have you ever heard of a young person saying, "Hey man. That industrial manufacturer in the next town is so cool, I hope they start selling t-shirts so I can wear one to school." No. What we hear from them is usually quite the opposite. And statements from them about businesses are usually based in emotion, not reason, resulting in an emotionally charged atmosphere on the social web when it comes to the discussion of companies. (Sit tight. I'll come back to this idea of an emotionally charged atmosphere when I discuss propaganda three chapters from right here.)

Reality and *meaning* are under threat, and one of the things that determines their fate *today* are the perceptions experienced within social media.

For individuals, previous to the existence of social media, connecting with others, discussing topics of interest, being part of a community or a crowd, opining, influencing others, activating support, and raging against people or organizations were communication activities that depended on being in the physical presence of others (meetings, conferences, conventions, demonstrations, parties, etc.). Or, if not in the physical presence of others, these communication activities depended on using media that required an expense, either in terms of money or time or in the number of persons who could be reached with one message, and were thus inefficient and restrictive in effectiveness (telephone, mail, etc.). Of course, individuals could co-opt mass media into opining, influencing others, or activating support concerning their positions, but that process was "iffy" and required talent that most individuals did not possess and/or skills that most individuals could not invest the time or the money to acquire.

For mass media, previous to the existence of social media, the creation of "reality" was carefully crafted through an investigative/research process and was compulsorily hedged against any adverse consequences just in case that "truth" wasn't actually "true." Mass media organizations producing such "reality" messages were well aware of their responsibilities and their potential liabilities, and they put processes in place to reduce running afoul of libel and/or slander laws. They were and still are largely, but not wholly, successful in mitigating damage from liability claims. From a business perspective, under which mass media operate, risk reduction is always preferable to damage control and fire extinguishment. Under these restrictive risk reduction processes, the chances and ability of individuals being able to use mass media for their own personal influence and personal agenda were and are small.

But that concern for liability doesn't exist with today's participants in social media. Any person with a pulse can and does use social media to say whatever he or she wants to say and however he or she likes to say it. Of course, that's what free speech is all about, saying what you want, when you want, how you want, why you want, where you want, etc. That's great for the First Amendment freaks out there. But it's not great for us reality freaks in here. This is not to say that I am advocating the total sacrifice of free speech in favor of "reality speech." Let's call that "truth." Yet the fact remains that in America, and in most other nations around the globe where free speech and expression are encouraged, one is not allowed to shout "FIRE" in a theater when no fire exists.

In today's social media, participants wanting to connect with others, to discuss various topics, and to be part of a crowd (although they would rather call it a community) can and do post under their own name if they so choose. When posting under a real name, displaying a sense of responsibility, liability enforcement would be more easily realized. But social media also enables people to post under an alias, a handle, or as it's known in social media land, a "screen name." (The screen name enables that pesky anonymity property I discussed previously - remember the Five Factors of Insidious

Competition? Can you imagine the people who we have traditionally regarded as the "keepers of reality" communicating anonymously?) Call the alias what you like, it offers any person with a pulse an opportunity to participate in the *repackaging of reality.* Unlike voting, where a person gets to contribute to the construction of reality with only one vote per election, any person can post his or her reality-bending, meaning-mangling vote an *infinite* number of times under one, two, three, or an *infinite* number of different screen names.

So what we can see here is *reality* and *meaning* being manufactured by "votes of opinion," sometimes hyperbole, sometimes innuendo, and often via snarkiness. (I'll discuss snark in more detail later.) The real danger, with which to be concerned in the construction of reality, is the intentional blurring of fact with opinion. And within social media, distinguishing between fact and opinion is not always apparent to the reader. One can often be disguised or confused for the other, either intentionally or simply through an inability to communicate clearly, which unfortunately is the often the case for the many rank amateurs with which social media overflows.

Is social media starting to sound like a dangerous environment yet? One that can be very hostile to business?

I believe your answer would be "Yes" when you reread those figures from that Ruder Finn study and check out their entire study online.[24] Seems we've gone past the "tipping point," as Malcolm Gladwell would put it.

And I suppose your answer would be "Yes" if you believe that people take social media, or more precisely the content of social media, seriously. Watch out because it appears that we do.

Indeed, recall that back in the beginning of Chapter One, in the Universal Mc Cann study, we saw that online users trust each others' recommendations and opinions almost as much as they trust face-to-face opinions.[25]

Feeling the danger yet? No?

All right, then. To more fully explain the danger, I'm going to take a brief break from the discussion of the *repackaging of reality* and the *mangling of meaning.* I know we've only scratched the surface and I am going to return to this topic soon.

But before I do return to this topic, for you to more fully understand the danger that we face, we'll need to discuss a subject which is critical to the essence of modern business. That subject is the "brand," that critical asset that companies nurture for their economic survival.

When we return to the topic of reality repackaging and meaning mangling, we will do so within the context of how it can affect the "brand," (and by extension the corporate image) because a brand is highly dependent upon reality, and the construction thereof.

Take-Aways from Chapter Four – The Battle for Meaning, Reality Repackaged . . . and Liability Be Damned

1. The differences people hold in reality and meaning are dependent upon their personal perceptions.
2. Perceptions, because they are subjective, can be modified to change reality.
3. The "Keepers of Reality" are dwindling, resulting in a fragmenting of perceptions, their attendant realities, and a fracturing of meaning.
4. Social media are used by millions to connect with others, discuss opinions, and influence many. The perceptions made within social media influence reality and meaning.
5. In the manipulation of meaning within social media, fears of liability run lower than within traditional media.
6. Meaning can be manipulated anonymously and *infinitely* repeated within the social web.

CHAPTER FIVE:
The Ephemeral Image

As I said at the end of the previous chapter, let's take a bit of a breather. Here in this chapter we're going to discuss something a little more mundane than reality construction. Let's do something pedestrian like discussing what a brand is. Yes, I know it's a subject that's somewhat over-discussed. On my bookshelves, I have about ten books dedicated to the subject of brands and branding. Over-discussed the subject of the brand may be, I will first need to make a few points just in case some readers haven't read as much as you and I may have read about the definition of a brand.

What is a Brand and How is It Threatened?

"A brand is a person's gut feeling about a product, service, or company," says Marty Neumeier in the book *The Brand Gap.* "Each person creates his or her own version of it. While companies can't control this process, they can influence it by communicating the qualities that make this product different than that product. When enough individuals arrive at the same gut feeling, a company can be said to have a brand." [26] I think you now see why I have preceded this chapter with a discussion of *reality repackaging.* Indeed, why.

The brand is so all-important to a company because the corporate image is dependent upon the integrity of a consistently communicated brand image. A brand is a communications device through which a corporate image is built. Without a consistent brand image, the corporate image is in peril. Without the corporate image, the company is dead in the commercial water.

We are in the "Brand Image Era." Or at least, we're *still* in the brand image era. Successful companies have found that brand image or company image is more of a factor in selling products and services than are the features of the products and services that they are trying to sell.[27] So much for "building a better mouse trap." What's critical is communicating that you do have a better mousetrap. And why is that? Because, per marketer Ted Levitt, "Expectations are what people buy, not things." [28] People expect products and services to solve a problem whether that problem is to fix their toilet that is running and keeping them awake at night, or to earn more return on their investments so they can have a secure retirement, or to make them more attractive to the opposite sex so they can get . . . well, you know. (That's an eternal problem.) The brand must communicate that expectation of problem resolution, that "guarantee," if you will, and the brand must communicate that expectation quickly. I said at the beginning of this paragraph that "we're still in the brand image era." Did I mean to imply that the brand image era might go away at some point? In 2001, I thought it might.

In 2001, I wrote my second book entitled *Dangerous Competition.* In the chapter entitled "Brands Moribund," I posited that due to the decrease of information asymmetry, enabled by the Internet and its robust search capabilities, brands would soon not be needed to identify quality offerings.[29] Well, here we are almost a decade later and brands are still very much needed. Perhaps even more so.

Presently on the Internet, brands still serve their function to instantly communicate quality, setting themselves above all the questionable offerings that abound in cyberspace. And as we all probably know, there are many, many questionable offerings abounding in cyberspace. Search technology hasn't evolved to the point that I thought it would by now. When I wrote *Dangerous Competition*, I believed that by the end of this decade, search technology would be so highly refined that it would be able to identify quality offerings from junk without the need of brand identification. So far, I am wrong about that. As I write *Insidious Competition*, there is still one more year left in the decade since I wrote *Dangerous Competition* and I suppose that it is possible that search technology may still live up to the prediction I made about it in 2001. But I won't hold my breath while waiting for those improvements and, so far, no search technology seems to be capable of obsoleting brands. Brands moribund? No. Brands flourish. *Still.*

There it is. A brand is a collection of thoughts, images, and expectations regarding the quality of a product or service. How delicate. How fragile. How fleeting. How *ephemeral.* When I think about this concept, I'm reminded of astronomers I've heard speaking on the Discovery Channel or the National Geographic Channel when they warn us about the fragility of the Earth, floating in a sea of black chaotic space, a sitting duck for an errant comet or meteor. One that, if it hits the Earth just right, could wipe out human civilization in an hour. A civilization that took billions of years to evolve and that could be wiped out in a time that would be infinitesimally smaller than the cosmological blink of an eye. I'm also reminded of a business quote by Warren Buffet, "It takes 20 years to build a reputation and five minutes to ruin it." Sort of a business parallel for that cosmological doomsday scenario.

So, now do you see how reality repackaging can devastate a brand? And with it the corporate image which depends upon the brand for support? Are you now beginning to understand how easily this can be done from within social media, a communications environment that is essentially accessible by anyone?

The brand marketers set out to create a certain brand image, but if it gets "diddled" in social media, well, obviously that makes the job of the brand marketers, the communicators, all that much more difficult. And when the brand image is "repackaged," so is the corporate image of the company owning that brand. That company's brand marketers are then, in essence, *competing* with social media users for the definition of the brand, and with it the definition of their corporation's image. Insidious competition, enabled by social media. Protecting your company's brand image, and by extension its *corporate image*, is a very new challenge in today's world of social media.

A company does not have to be "active" in social media for this challenge to arise. Even if a company does *not* promote its products or services via a social media marketing program, that company is still susceptible to the threat of insidious competition. If a company sells something, and if they didn't they wouldn't be a company, then they are a potential target of insidious competition. People, in social media, will always talk about goods and services, and brands, impacting corporate images as they do. The threat is far-reaching, global, and potentially devastating to the progress of organized commerce.

And if a company chooses to be "active" in social media, to promote their products or services not only through traditional communications channels, but also through social media marketing programs, they may be increasing their risk even more.

We should keep in mind that in this time of social media, brands are no longer only connected to products and services. Brands are now also connected to individuals. The standard concept of a celebrity is something that could be classified as such. Celebrities represent their own brand, which stands for a service, with all of the expectations that come with that. And when those celebrities disappoint and don't live up to expectations, it affects and tarnishes their personal brand image. But what I am specifically referring to here is a more direct connection between the brands of products and services produced by a "regular" company and the image of an individual, a non-celebrity, an individual who at the outset is not very well-known, an individual who represents those products and services for that company. I'm referring to the "brandividual."

What is a Brandividual?

A brandividual is a person who simultaneously represents a company's brand and their own personal brand from within social media.[30] This method of brand communication, and by extension corporate image communication, is unique to the new environment of social media and is an central element of any corporate social media marketing program where a company *actively* and intentionally uses the environment of social media to promote its products or services.

Within social media, the brandividual acts as a champion for their employer's brand while raising and developing their own profile and notoriety within social media. The two entities, the company brand and the individual, (along with the corporate image they support) then become intertwined, at least in the minds of those who participate within social media. And those social media participants help contribute to the building of the brandividual's identity and strength. Such a scenario can be a boon for brand marketers (i.e., the company), who by lending a human face to its brand can help position that brand in a more natural and transparent way, relating to the average person, the average customer, more easily, and thereby hopefully increasing sales. This is one of the things that social media is good at. Yes, it can be a boon if everything goes well.

There is a danger in a company pursuing the business tactic of brandividual as its "face" because things don't always go well. By using the brandividual method in its marketing program, the company increases its risk of having its brand image, and along with it its corporate image, attacked. By going the brandividual route, the company gives social media users two targets, the brand and the brandividual. The brand is always out there subject to attack, as I said, whether your company participates in an active social media marketing program or not. That's now just an ever-present cost of doing business in the age of social media. But when your company does participate in an active social media program with a brandividual at its core, then there is increased danger. The danger lies specifically in what people on the social web may say about a brandividual. Or should I say not about the individual personally, but rather about the "brand" (also to be read as "the company" and its corporate image) that the brandividual represents and which has become one with the brandividual. And that danger is fueled by the potential of a brandividual gaffe that can be made online. Easy to do. As the saying goes, "you can't please everyone all the time."

There's a cliché that the public likes to build up a public personality just so they can later tear them down. I think rather that it is more the press, the mainstream media, who actually do the building of the public personality, the creating of the drama to which the public attends. Yet, it seems, as Eric Dezenhall and John Weber put it in *Damage Control*, that this cliché really represents an overly simplified view of what the public really wants. Eric and John think that what the public really wants is to have "a sense of control over our icons. We want to have played a role in making them. If we have a hand in their success, it's not a threat because we are psychic shareholders. When that success, however, ceases to have anything to do with us, resentment kicks in." [31] Can you see how this idea, as put forth by Eric and John, would pertain directly to social media brandividuals? Brandividuals cannot exist unless others have participated in making those brandividuals become the champions they are perceived, and known, to be as experienced on the social web. Because of the supposed open and transparent nature of social media, the audience of a brandividual would feel like they are a part of the brandividual's life – almost as if they themselves have touched celebrity.

Brandividuals are not professional celebrities. But they do play the part of a celebrity from within the social web. Yet, I'd hazard that most, if not all, of them have had little or no training or previous experience at being a celebrity.

And as we as a society have seen, at least since Hollywood began to manufacture celebrities wholesale, many celebrities are just not emotionally equipped to deal with the notoriety that comes with celebrity. The same idea can apply to the brandividual, probably even more so because they don't have a Hollywood PR machine backing them up. If this same idea, the fragility of celebrity, or the celebrity's inability to deal with fame, does apply to the brandividual, then, in this age of social media rapidly becoming a significant new method of communication, it puts the company employing the brandividual, and its brand, at an even greater risk of insidious competition.

For the company employing the brandividual, caution would be advised. If the brandividual does anything that could cause the least amount of resentment within his or her audience, and again that's easy to do, the brandividual, and the company brand which the brandividual represents along with the inevitably attached corporate image, are all in jeopardy.

When a company employs the brandividual method of promotion in a social media marketing program, they compound the risk that their brand and, along with it, their *corporate image* will have its meaning "redefined" by social media users. Having the brand is a necessity and its meaning can be attacked by insidious competition. But having a brandividual in the communications mix just increases the risk to that "ephemeral image."

The Preservation of the Brand Image

So, now knowing more about what a brand is and how critical its maintenance is to the corporate image, you can now see how the anonymity, power, contagion, instinct, and disdain (from the Five Factors of Insidious Competition) that exist in the world of social media can put the brand or the brandividual or both at risk. One wrong statement by a brandividual, or one statement about a brand or company from a social media user made or taken "wrongly," and the company's brand and the corporate image could be irreparably damaged. Once the "wrong" message is "out there" it lives forever on the ***worldwide*** web.

The ephemeral image, that reputation so critical to the success of a "brand" or "company" and the preservation of its *corporate image*, must now learn how to defend its meaning in the new, uncontrolled, and dangerous environment we now know as "social media."

What does the preservation of that vital brand image come down to?

Does brand image preservation depend on what the brand owner says about the brand in "traditional" media and promotional tactics? Does brand image preservation depend on what a brandividual is saying on a daily basis? Not exactly. Brand image preservation depends on something even harder to manage. Remember from earlier in this chapter:

> *A brand is a person's gut feeling about a product, service, or company. Each person creates his or her own version of it.*[32]

Brand image depends on what people hear or read about the brand. It always has, pre-Internet or not. So that hasn't changed. But what has changed is that now, unlike ever before in commercial history, opinions about almost anything are available from within social media, 24/7/365, on a global basis, for hundreds of millions of people to experience and perceive. Brand image is now not only at the mercy of each person's own gut feeling based on what they heard from the company's brand message, but it is also at the mercy of each person's own gut feeling as influenced by the others within social media who have knowingly or unknowingly *repackaged reality*, thereby potentially *changing meaning*. Those "realities" and "meanings" of what the brand is, and its dependent *corporate image*, are influenced by solipsism and epistemology.

Solips and epis . . . whaa?

Take-Aways from Chapter Five – The Ephemeral Image

1. Each person creates his or her own version of a brand image.
2. Branding communicates an expectation of problem resolution. Brand images are based on those expectations.
3. Brand images are delicate.
4. The brand image is the foundation of the corporate image.
5. Brands are even more important on the Internet than in the physical world.
6. The brand image is subject to change by millions of people on the social web, and so is the corporate image by extension.
7. Brandividuals as company image representatives are highly vulnerable to attack by insidious competitors.
8. Brand, and corporate image, meanings are influenced through solipsism and epistemology.

Chapter Six:
Solipsism & Epistemology or The System of Knowing

Okay. We've discussed the brand. You now know that the brand is vital to the support of the corporate image. You also now realize that the corporate image and the brand on which the corporate image depends are very susceptible to redefinition from within social media, and that their "realities," their "meanings" can be repackaged by anyone with a pulse, from anywhere on the globe, at any time. Thus, the heart of this threat of insidious competition is in the manipulation of meaning. You now need to know more about meaning.

So at this point in our discussion, it's time to take a more in-depth look at how reality is packaged and how meanings are made. As an insidious competition fighter you will need to know this because knowing this goes to the core of how the insidious competitor conducts its attacks on your company's corporate image.

Reality packaging and the *meaning* of the *corporate image* are subject to the processes of solipsism and epistemology.

Yes. I introduced these terms at the end of last chapter. And at the risk of sounding all professorial, academic, and potentially pretentious, I used them anyway.

Solipsism and epistemology are subjects I studied in my introductory philosophy class in college. Perhaps you did as well. At the college I attended, which was a "petrie dish" for lawyers, most students didn't get through their first year without taking some sort of philosophy course, learning how words worked, and learning how to manipulate those words, the essence of good lawyering. Well, I wasn't pre-law, as were most of my philosophy classmates. But I was a communications major. (Later, learning that communications majors don't make a lot of money, I decided to join the business world and earned an MBA.) As a communications major, learning about words and how their meanings worked was extremely important, and in that philosophy class I was in good company. I learned much from the professor and from my classmates who went on to become the butt of the lawyer jokes that we all tell daily.

Now, I'm just an average kind of guy. I'm not interested in manipulating words and their meanings. However, I am interested in the issue of how others do that. I want to be able to communicate this complex issue, critical to understanding, to all the readers who are likely to have different backgrounds and levels of knowledge. So, let's try to reach across those various levels of knowledge and get to the core of the issue and explain it in simple, interesting, and easily digestible ways. The terms solipsism and epistemology may be known to you. If they are, then that's great. If they aren't, then let's just agree right now that every time I say either or both of those two words you'll think the term "system of knowing."

From Webster's New World Dictionary:

solipsism - n. - *the theory that the self can be aware of nothing but its own experiences* -solipsistic adj.

Or as the philosopher D.W. Hamlyn would say, when we perceive something we have knowledge and we can only perceive something when we have experiences.[33] Let's put this same idea more simply. As another philosopher named Will Rogers once said, "All I know is just what I read in the papers."

Yes. This is some of what philosophers spend their time doing. Thinking thoughts such as these. But you can see that those identical thoughts can be complex, like Hamlyn, or home-spun, like Rogers. Yes, this is part of philosophy; well, actually, epistemology to be exact. And solipsism is a subset of epistemology.

Epis -whaa?

Epistemology Comes Alive

Again, from Webster's New World Dictionary:

epistemology - n. - *the theory of the nature, sources, and limits of knowledge* -epistemological adj.

In other words, how do we know what we know? (Or, you may read that as the "system of knowing.")

For a period in my life, I was an academic and made my living from the halls of knowledge. Once when teaching a freshman course in macroeconomics I had just completed a lengthy lecture about monopoly and oligopoly. I concluded by asking the class if there were any questions. I knew that there were. I could tell by the puzzled faces I saw before me. (Was that a testament to my teaching skills?) One student raised his hand and said, "Yes. I have a question. What's epistemology?" I thought, "Hmmm. This kid is either a class clown or he just came from a confusing philosophy class prior to economics. Or, perhaps both." Anyway, I fielded the question by first saying that epistemology is not a subset of economics but instead is a discipline of philosophy. But, I continued, we can still use the epistemological approach to understand what was just presented in the lecture. Then, digging back in my mind to my undergraduate philosophy classes, I explained to him and the class that epistemology is the system of knowing what we know. That we are only a sum of our experiential knowledge. Tying it into the lecture I had just delivered, I explained that the class' understanding of monopoly and oligopoly was now based upon my lecture, their reading assignment, and the synthesis of the two through class discussion. I added that their understanding of that material would remain so until a different set of experiential knowledge was had by them.

The kid was stunned. I think he thought he would just trip up an economics lecturer with a non-sequitur and gain a good laugh in the process. Well, there was a good laugh when he posed the question. Now that I think about this incident from years ago, the fact that there was a class-wide laugh hinted that many in the class must have had at least an inkling of what epistemology was. Otherwise, no one would have laughed. They thought it was funny. I thought the question was funny, too. Yet, the joke led to an enhanced discussion of how we know what we know, and how we should take great care in selecting and exposing ourselves to sources of information so that we not only gain a proper understanding of monopoly and oligopoly, but of any category of knowledge that we pursue. I suggested to them that they came to college to learn about economics rather than trying to learn about economics by, say, hanging out at a bus station. They chose the correct source of information, the best experience, for the knowledge that they sought. And the same idea holds true for understanding reality, in general.

All right, then. Synthesizing all this by jumping back to last chapter's discussion of brands, how do we know about a brand and its dependent *corporate image*? How do we form our knowledge of that *corporate image*? What system do we use to know? Easy. Via our own limited sources and from our own experiences. Let's look at this whole solipsism and epistemology and Will Rogers thing like this.

Experience >>> Perception >>> Knowledge

We experience something. We perceive something. We have knowledge of what we just perceived. Simple. Happens every day. All the time. We're not even aware of the process going on inside our heads. What we know is a direct product of what we have perceived based on what we have experienced. Paraphrasing Will Rogers, all I know is just what I read in the papers, or in blogs, or in magazines, or in books, or hear from others, or see on TV, *ad infinitum*; name your own communications medium. What Will Rogers was really talking about was based in solipsism and epistemology, but he brought a down-home flavor to it and placed it on a level of understanding for everyone. I prefer the Will Rogers' approach.

If you don't know who Will Rogers was, go dial him up on YouTube.com. You'll enjoy this American entertainer and social philosopher from an America we knew before World War II. His approach to things was straightforward, considered, and simple. But not so simple that it lacked perspicacious insight. I wish I had thought of the Will Rogers approach when I was explaining epistemology to the economics student because after a while the class started to glaze over even more than during the lecture about monopoly and oligopoly. Now I know better. I experienced the situation. I perceived the class becoming bored. My knowledge will further inform the way I approach similar circumstances. Our knowledge is a sum of the perceptions from our experiences.

The Dearth of News and the Death of Reality

The Will Rogers technique would have been the best explanation for that economics, turned philosophy, class. But is that technique the most relevant today? Today using the Will Rogers' quote to explain the system of knowing would be somewhat off-target because Will used the idea of newspapers to explain how he creates his sum of knowledge. Newspapers (and mainstream news organizations in general) are particularly relevant to our discussion here of how we know what we know relative to our experiences. Newspapers and other traditional media are key to our understanding of being confused today about what we "know."

All I know is just what I read in the papers.

Will's approach is too early 20th century-centric for today, because we as a society are reading less and less from newspapers and are therefore experiencing much less "objective reality." (Remember, as discussed back in Chapter Four, I am referring to "mainstream media" as being "agents of common knowledge" and providing "objective reality.") Why? Well, the reasons for newspapers' decline notwithstanding, or forming any sort of circular logic in this discussion, simply put, collectively there are fewer newspapers around today than in the 1920s and the 1930s when Will Rogers was reading them. This decrease in newspapers has only recently accelerated with newspapers seeing their greatest declines during the last half of the first decade in the 21st century. All the while the usage of social media has increased during that same time period, insinuating itself into the process of how people get their "news." In fact, fewer people are getting news, at all. In an article titled "The Rebirth of News," which appeared in The Economist, it was stated that since 1999 the percentage of Americans aged 18 to 24 who read or view any news has dropped from 34% to 25%.[34] Is it any wonder? Even if some of them were inclined to read news, newspapers are simply dropping by the wayside, decreasing anyone's chance of reading them.

As mentioned back in Chapter Four, "The Battle for Meaning, Reality Repackaged . . . and Liability Be Damned," I said that I would show you some data about the demise of traditional media. Well, here it is. The following list tells the story of what's happened recently to the survival of, and the prospects for, the major common body of knowledge repositories of "our reality:"

- The Seattle Post-Intelligencer - This paper published its last print edition on Tuesday, March 17, 2009. An article on the paper's Web site said that the newspaper would become a completely digital news product.[35]
- The Minneapolis Star Tribune filed for bankruptcy in January 2009.[36]
- The Philadelphia Inquirer and The Daily News filed for bankruptcy in February 2009.[37]
- The Rocky Mountain News (Denver) closed on February 27, 2009.[38]
- The Tucson Citizen ceased its print edition and moved reduced operations to its Web site.[39]

The list of print editions which are as dead as the trees which went into the paper on which those print editions were formerly printed goes on and it's one that will likely continue after this book is published, and after you finish reading it.

Some of the above list was cited from a New York Times graphic and article titled, "Bad News for Newspapers." An examination of this graphic, about the health of major American newspapers, shows that most, in fact almost all, demonstrate a circulation change of between 0% and negative 20% in the time period from third quarter 2005 to third quarter 2008, with most falling in the negative 10% to negative 20% range.[40] This isn't good news for newspapers, or the people who work at them, and it's not good news for news, either. Precisely I mean that it's not good news for the news business or the "reality" which they stewarded. Now, I'm going to bring all this back to solipsism and epistemology, or the system of knowing, but the trip won't be quick.

The point here in this discussion is that the future for printed newspapers doesn't look good and, I think, the expectations for "reality" look no better. With newspapers dying, you're going to have trouble experiencing, perceiving, and knowing. "Hold on," you say, "the newspapers and their stewardship of reality won't go away. Newspapers will just put their operations online. The news is still the news. Reality can still be established, maintained, preserved, and defended. It'll just be *presented differently.*" Yes, that's true. The newspapers can go online; many have and others will do so. Yet, let's think about that key adverb there which is "differently." Potentially very differently. Now, in electronic, digital formats, the news can be presented so *differently* that, in many instances, one does not even have to go to that online newspaper site to get information from that newspaper. "Huh?" you question. "You mean I don't even have to go to a news site to get news from the news organization that presented it?" Yes, you read that right. The digerati among my readers know this already, but the newbies don't. So for the newbies, an explanation.

Digital content is mashable, which means that it travels more easily than a crooked congressman on a thirty day, tax payer-fueled European junket. What do I mean by "mashable?" "Mashable" is an Internet term referring to content that can be taken from various sources and combined to form something quite different from its original form. (There's that word "different" again; this time it's an adjective.) This idea of mashability has been around for awhile and it's part of what complicates the business model of Internet content providers, news organizations especially. Clay Shirky is a well-known Internet consultant and author who posted a blog entry which contained this quote.

> *Back in 1993, the Knight-Ridder newspaper chain began investigating piracy of Dave Barry's popular column, which was published by the Miami Herald and syndicated widely. In the course of tracking down the sources of unlicensed distribution, they found many things, including the copying of his column to alt.fan.dave_barry on usenet; a 2000-person strong mailing list also reading pirated versions; and a teenager in the Midwest who was doing some of the copying himself, because he loved Barry's work so much he wanted everybody to be able to read it.*[41]

In 1993, this sort of problem was somewhat unique. Digital content like cartoon strips, editorials, columns, etc. were taking a walk and appearing far and wide across the Internet, nowhere near where they were originally published. The intellectual property and copyright attorneys were salivating. Now, almost twenty years since this dilemma was hatched, we know these problems of "digital drift" are common and almost as widespread as dirt. Perhaps you even contribute to the problem. Yes, the trouble was uncommon in 1993 and it represented a problem with which the newspapers would have to deal. And they dealt with it tactically. But they forgot to look at the dilemma strategically. The larger problem was staring newspapers smack dab in the face. They just didn't see it.

Because seeing into the future is always difficult, unless you have a swami at your side, for the newspapers back there in the early 1990s it was difficult to predict the future ramifications as a result of digital drift. The problem of digital drift exists because digital content travels easily, much too easily if you ask its creators; not easily enough if you ask its consumers. Digital content is digital. It's not physical; it's just 1s and 0s; it's electrons that are either there or not. And with the availability of the Internet, it was easy for anyone to ship it anywhere, whether they "owned" that content or not. So here then was a situation where there was far too much opportunity for people to read a newspaper's digital story *on someone else's site*, whether the appearance of that story on the other site was authorized by the news organization that created it – or not. If the news story can be viewed on a "foreign" site, then the organization which created it won't get the benefit of selling the advertisement that supports that content's creation and distribution in the first place. "Information wants to be free" is the retort that's heard across the Internet in response to complaints about digital drift. Well, information itself might want to be free, and that exhortation is certainly stylish from a pop culture perspective, but the people who create and distribute that information, worthwhile and vetted information that is, don't work for free. I'll guess that you don't work for free, either.

Going a step further, you don't even need to view the story on a "foreign" site; you can capture the story's RSS feeds from your favorite news organization and view them in a news reader of your choice (Google News, News Gator, Yahoo News, etc.) right on your desktop. Or, even more easily, simply receive the RSS feed for the news story of your choice right into your e-mail software and minimize (or even eliminate) those pesky ads that the news organization puts on their site so that they can finance their presentation of your reality. When these things happen, the financial model that supported print versions, and which the newspapers have recently tried to extend to their digital versions, falls apart in our online world; and so the producers and repositories of that common body of knowledge that we have come to know as "reality," those who **vet** the "truth" under the pain of a potential liability suit, disappear.

In the print world, the ad (and the revenue the ad equals) are inseparable from the news, and the attendant reality, that is being presented. The news story appears next to an ad, physically, on the same page. Oh sure, one can rip a news story from the pages of a newspaper, separating the story from the ad next to it, and send the story to a friend, with your notes in the margin. In so doing, the friend doesn't see the ad and his or her eyeballs are not counted among those for which the newspaper is charging the advertiser. But the frequency of this happening with "printed format" is small compared to its frequency of happening with digital format because ripping out a story and mailing it to a friend just requires "too much work." The process is inefficient. Too much input for the amount of perceived output. However, in the digital world "ripping" out that story is much, much easier. Copy the story onto your computer's clip board. Insert it into your e-mail program, and perhaps write in a comment or two, click the "Send" button, and it's on its way for your friend or family member to enjoy (or not) at someone else's expense. Digital drift. Separation of content from its supporting revenue. In the digital world on a news organization's site, the ads (and the revenue the ads equal) are easily separated, giving advertisers much less incentive to spend their ad dollars on those sites. Those ad dollars can be more easily spent by the advertiser on other media, where the tendency for digital drift does not exist, where the advertiser can be more assured that their advertisement will actually reach its intended audience.

Now, talk about drift. You may think that I've drifted a bit away from the title of this chapter, "Solipsism & Epistemology or The System of Knowing." But I haven't. What we are discussing here are the practical applications of the solipsistic and epistemological process within social media and the Internet in general.

Solipsism and Epistemology Corrupted

Regarding solipsism and epistemology, what can result from the situation of digital drift? The answer, I hope by this point, is obvious. The answer is an infection in the system of knowing, a *corrupted* solipsistic and epistemological process of knowledge. An infection in the process, as we have come to know it, of experience-perception-knowledge with all the effects that can be imagined upon the accompanying construction of reality.

Say all that you want about information wanting to be free, but when you come down to it, that slogan is just a rhetorical mantra. This motto has been taken up by an elite intelligentsia, and their hanger-on crowds, who have not considered the consequences to business, consequences in the form of insidious competition from social media; and they have not ultimately considered the consequences to the lives of those that those businesses affect. If we as a society want a repository of reality that is of high quality, meaning that the information in the repository is vetted and correlates as highly as possible to actual occurrences, then we must remember that having such a social institution will cost its members money. And those members to which I refer are you and me and everyone else. Without such a paradigm, our opportunities to experience, perceive, and know "reality" will decrease. The number of news organizations will decrease because they will receive less and less revenue, resulting in fewer writers, writing about fewer issues, and leaving us with less "liability-fearing fueled objectivity." As they shrink they will abdicate the "creation of reality" to someone else who is good at mashing up what's left. Some of those people would be folks such as bloggers, independent individuals, with relatively less "liability-fearing fueled objectivity," who often use opinion or innuendo or even raving lunacy as a stand-in for reality and to attract readers. Solipsistic and epistemological processes will be fouled with that which is not "real." That is the scenario that can result; that is the scenario that is resulting. And this scenario manifests itself in the business environment as insidious competition.

I'm not blaming the bloggers, for example, for using these tactics to attract readers. They want readers. Why wouldn't they? Certainly bloggers didn't invent this strategy to affect the solipsistic and epistemological process of experience-perception-knowledge. They're just building on this strategy which was pioneered by others in other media. They're just "standing on the shoulders of giants who have preceded" them. Here's a quote from SocialMediaToday.com:

> *Alternative reality has turned out to be a decent business model. On any given night, you can surf between raving lunatics on MSNBC and raving lunatics on Fox and come away with the impression that we are living in a world in which facts are mere debating points, to be won or lost by those who make the loudest or most persuasive arguments.*[42]

If you take the preceding quote seriously, along with all that I have put forth in this chapter so far, you will understand that the dearth of news contributes to the death of reality. What people appear to be absorbing now is not news, it's content. There's a big difference between the two.

It's About the Drama, Stupid.

The human mind likes to think in terms of a dramatic narrative, a story. This preference has been engrained in our individual and collective psyches from an early age. I don't mean since we were two years of age, although most of us appreciated a good story at that time in our lives. The early age to which I refer is more like since the Stone Age or the Bronze Age. From before and after those times, early man in his social groupings told stories as a method of passing on a cultural identity, as a way of imparting quotidian information needed for survival, and as a coping mechanism for dealing with the way nature changed around them and affected their daily lives and welfare. The verbal story was their main communication mode and format. Since that time we have come to absorb in our social and cultural consciousness a preference for a "good story." We all know, either consciously or unconsciously, the elements of a good story. A villain, a victim, a problem, a hero, a conflict, a resolution, a victory. When we watch a movie, a play, or read a novel, we look for these elements and are disappointed if they do not appear in the proper order or if they do not assume the level of quality and depth that we would prefer.

Stories help bolster our ability to deal with our world and overcome our own individual challenges. The Bible is filled with them. Stories are a solipsistic and epistemological process. They help us experience through a "model," perceive, and know. Some stories which we have read, seen on the screen (small or large), or have experienced on the stage are "true." Others are "based on a true story," while others are, of course, just plain untrue.

A family member of mine is a very good story teller. With great pleasure, I'll listen to her recount the events of a family get-together. But occasionally, her version of "true events" departs from mine. Not materially. She doesn't change the outcome of the story, but her departures color the story line differently from that which I have perceived. I've asked her about this tendency to depart from the true story line and her response is "Never let the truth get in the way of a good story." (We touched on this idea back in Chapter 3.) Talk about departure. The integrity of her solipsistic and epistemological process, her system of knowing, departs from mine. Many, if not all of us, experience this problem in some way.

A moment ago, I mentioned content vs. news. There is a big difference between content and news. Content, especially opinion content when presented in the dramatic format with all the elements of a story, exploits the human instinctive need and preference for a story and becomes subject to disallowing the truth to get in the way of a good story. Pure, fact-based, objective news does not exploit the instinctive human need and preference for a story, preferably a "good story." Pure, fact-based, objective news is not a story. It's a statement. News is the presentation of facts, for interpretation by the receiver. And it doesn't tickle our primal fancy for a story. Simply put, it's not fun.

The experience, perception and knowing of that which is related to us via pure, objective news requires work, brain work, which is something that many folks like to avoid. Conversely, opinion, loaded with the elements of story, is something that is more fun to experience and perceive and possibly absorb as our own "knowledge." Doing so feeds our psychic jones. The death of the newspaper industry and of objective news organizations in general, along with the call for "free" information, only speeds an opinion fueled reality, enough of which our thirsty psyches cannot get.

Burkart Holzner, a philosopher, in a seminal epistemological work entitled *Reality Construction in Society* said, "The diversity in his own modes of reality construction is . . . directly linked to the scope of diversity of epistemic communities." [43] Yes. I know. It's "Huh?" time again. Philosophers are often difficult to understand, especially the ones who wear beards and work in universities. In my opinion, they and other academics will often (why am I saying "often" when what I'm really thinking is "pretty much always") write in an obtuse fashion, using esoteric words, just to see who can out-obtuse and out-impress the other academics that are all within, sadly, only their own epistemic communities. The result of their approach is that instead of imparting useful information to the broader society, they only achieve very small readerships and less-than-flattering opinions among that general public which they should be attempting to help. To simplify the "Huh?" time, let's just try to keep in mind the Oklahoman, mid-20th century philosopher, Will Rogers, and his mantra "All I know is just what I read in the papers" and let's adapt it to Burkart by saying "All I know is just what I experience and perceive in my epistemic communities." Okay, I made it as simple as possible to here, now let me try harder.

Please remember that at this point in our discussion, newspapers and their "objective" realities, are effectively out of the reality equation. Right now, here, in this book, in talking about the social media world, we're dealing in communities, err, uh, crowds. Remember the tribes vs. communities vs. crowds argument from earlier? Here's where we combine some of what we learned about crowd behavior, in Chapter Two, with what we've learned about reality re-packaging and changing meaning, in Chapter Four.

Besides being a "gobblety-gook," esoteric mouthful that academics may be using just to impress other academics, and in the process alienate folks like you and me who might just benefit from their learned insights if only stated more simply, just what is an epistemic community? In the work I referenced above, Burkart gives examples of epistemic communities as scientific communities, religious communities, work communities, or ideological movements. As in those examples, since communities, or crowds for that matter, are as we previously discussed social units containing people who share common interests or goals, I think we could broaden and simplify Burkart's explanation and safely say that epistemic communities are social units not only with common interest, but also with common features that we can all recognize and on which we can all agree. A common lexicon, common terminologies, and/or common social roles are all socially agreed upon, or "constructed," within the group. It's through these "constructs," or commonly shared features or tools, that the members of the group experience, perceive, and know. Here they act together as a "crowd." One member adopts the reality the others have "suggested," and in doing so takes on a crowd behavior. Sounds like most online communities, or crowds, that I've ever known. The online groups each and all have their own distinct set of words or symbols (lexicon), ways of expressing those lexical elements (terminologies), and members who assume various functions or positions within the social interaction of the group (social roles).

Whether or not the gravitation toward online groups of common interests causes the death of news or vice versa is not a critical issue to our immediate discussion. What is important to the discussion of *insidious competition* is that traditional, mainstream news is dying and that people are migrating to online groups. And what is also critical to our discussion of *insidious competition* is that the gravitation toward online groups of common interest contributes to our obtaining our reality there, rather than from the vetted repositories of that common body of knowledge that formed our "reality" in pre-Internet days. Interpreting Burkart, we would construct our own reality based on the diversity (i.e., the range of perceptions) to be had within the online groups we frequent.

If, in our media futures, we become even more inundated with opinions, or subject ourselves willingly to opinion and the dramas on which they base themselves, because that is all that is left, our reality creation will depend upon the manufacture of opinion and drama rather than fact. That's most of what we'll experience; that's most of what we'll perceive; so that's most of what we'll know. If that is true, then the threat to the corporate image is high. Very high. If that is true, then insidious competition will run rampant.

Very high indeed, because the corporate image would then be at the mercy of definition by the epistemic groups in which we participate, either by choice or through default, and it will be those groups which will play a significant part in forming our own realities. Now, don't pooh-pooh this theory. Don't think that an occurrence of this type would take such a long time that the effect would be scarcely noticeable or critical to the examination of an insidious competitor's effects. Such a process could happen more quickly than we realize. How likely is it that people would be subjected to these online epistemic, dramatic "realities" which could change corporate image perceptions in short order? When you consider that the average American now spends 32.5% of his or her "media day" on the Internet,[44] it seems that we can consider it very likely that these changes can occur rapidly.

The Nine Elements of Social Media Danger to the Corporate Image

Synthesizing what we have discussed so far, especially that from Chapter Three - The Five Factors of Insidious Competition, Chapter Four - The Battle for Meaning, Reality Repackaged . . . and Liability Be Damned, Chapter Five - The Ephemeral Image, and here in Chapter Six - Solipsism & Epistemology or The System of Knowing, you and I can see at least nine elements of danger to the *corporate image* from within social media. The danger exists:

1. because the Five Factors of Insidious Competition (anonymity, power, contagion, instinct, and disdain) are supported within social media,
2. because just about anyone with a pulse can access social media,

3. because the ephemeral brand image itself is so critical to the creation of the corporate image and thus the success of the modern corporation here in the brand image era,
4. because of the possibility of a brandividual meltdown and its repercussions on the corporate image,
5. because of the ongoing demise of the repositories of reality,
6. because of the instinctive human thirst for a good dramatic story,
7. because of the sharing of certain interactional tools by which we come to "know" things via a group,
8. because we will become increasingly more dependent on those groups, online, for our reality construction in the future, and;
9. because the brand and its dependent corporate image depends so vitally on the integrity of the solipsistic and epistemological process (the system of knowing) which, due to the previous eight reasons, can be easily corrupted within social media.

All of these Nine Elements of Social Media Danger to the Corporate Image are important for the insidious competition fighter to realize. But, it is element number nine, the integrity of the solipsistic and epistemological process (the system of knowing) within social media, that we must consider as the most important here in *Insidious Competition*. This element of danger is the one that can be most directly controlled by the insidious competitor. The other eight elements are conditions or circumstances that exist with or without the insidious competitor. The insidious competitor merely needs to operate within those other eight elements and exploit the ninth element in order to be effective.

Going Forward

The statistic above, the one about Americans spending 32.5% of their media day on the Internet, says that we'll have the potential of spending at least a third of our media day experiencing opinions on the Internet. This is quite a sea change, quite a shift from what social man, as we know him, has previously encountered. But does that mean we'll necessarily believe what we experience and perceive there? Will the most critical element of danger, the easy corruption of the solipsistic and epistemological process from within social media, be absolute in its effects? Will Will Rogers be correct from within a 21st century frame of reference?

Within the context of our discussion here in *Insidious Competition*, the level to which we believe what we experience and perceive (i.e., the level to which the content becomes "knowledge" forming our realities and defining our meanings) depends upon the integrity of the system of knowing. In the next chapter, we'll discuss propaganda which is the principle that can affect the integrity of the solipsistic and epistemological process and which is used by the insidious competitor lurking within social media.

Take-Aways from Chapter Six – Solipsism & Epistemology or The System of Knowing

1. Solipsism and epistemology comprise a process producing reality and meaning. The process looks like this: Experience >>> Perception >>> Knowledge
2. There is a dearth of news causing a death of reality.
3. Digital and drifting content is contributing to the financial decline of the liability-fearing agents of common knowledge, the keepers of reality.
4. Content is not news.
5. Unvetted digital content is assuming the role of the agents of common knowledge. Digital content has fewer fears of liability claims.
6. Digital content is susceptible to a corrupted solipsistic and epistemological process, producing mangled meaning.
7. Content is drama. Drama is preferred to news and it substitutes for news which is absorbed by millions of social media users.
8. Epistemic communities will fragment reality perception and distort meaning.
9. There are Nine Elements of Social Media Danger to the Corporate Image. The most significant in terms of understanding the insidious competitor is the ease of corruption in the solipsistic and epistemological process (i.e., the system of knowing) from within social media.
10. Insidious competitors use the principles of propaganda to corrupt the solipsistic and epistemological process.

Section Two:
The Principles of Propaganda and their Application

Chapter Seven: The Principles of Propaganda

In order for insidious competitors to manifest as threats, in order for them to truly carry out their potential economic damage, then there must be a way for their ideas to be applied, a way for those ideas to be transmitted, a way for those ideas to take form. Those applications, those transmissions, those manifestations require a tool. Tools give form and shape to ideas. In social media, the tools of the insidious competitor enable the *changing of ideas* and the *mangling of meaning.* They directly attack the solipsistic and epistemological process (the system of knowing) which is used to define The Ephemeral Image. And in a business context, this means that these tools can be used to re-package reality, effectively redefining the *corporate image.*

As with all tools, there are underlying principles that support their effectiveness and the same is true for the tools employed by insidious competition. And for insidious competition, the perfect tools are grounded in the principles of propaganda. Let's look at Four Tools of Insidious Competition, which are literally at the fingertips of the insidious competitor. They are:

1. Mutant Conversation,
2. Social Engineering,
3. Hip Chat, and
4. Snark.

Now, you might be thinking, "Hey. Not so fast, Richard. The tools that insidious competitors use within social media are really stuff like blogs, mini-blogs, social networks, forums, splogs, plogs, or vlogs. After all, if I was going to be an insidious competitor, which I assure you that I am not, those are the tools that I would use."

If you're thinking that, then stop thinking that right now. Right now. Especially that part about you not being an insidious competitor. Many of us are insidious competitors whether we know it or not, as you will come to discover later in this book when we discuss the types of insidious competitors. You might find yourself somewhere in those lists.

Don't think that the blogs and social networks, etc. are the tools of the insidious competitor. Think this instead.

In the world of insidious competition, blogs, social networks, video sharing sites, and all that stuff that people are increasingly using every day, almost to the annoyance of everyone around them, are not tools. They're venues. Yes. Venues.

Venues in which tools based in the supporting principles of propaganda are applied. Yes. I can see where you might think that blogs, social networks, etc. would be called tools. You would think that because we frequently read in articles about social media that these aforementioned things are "social media tools." And yes, things like blogs and other social media venues may well be considered "tools" by social media marketers. If social media marketers want to call those things tools, well, that is up to them. Though, I think that they are missing the larger, more strategic point; an important point which might actually help them become more prudent marketers. For business, the critical issue in social media is the *solipsistic and epistemological process that takes place within social media*. And remember, as we have come to learn, the solipsistic and epistemological process within social media is very different from the one we have come to understand in the world of mainstream media. So, it's the *system of knowing which results in the creation and interpretation of meaning* that's important, not just the usage of blogs and other venues of social media.

Blogs or other such venues simply provide the "forum" (no pun intended) in which the solipsistic and epistemological process of *meaning creation* takes place. And *meaning* is actually what is under attack by insidious competition within social media. What does The Ephemeral Image mean?

That's the question that insidious competitors want to raise in the minds of social media users. That question is the essence of what makes insidious competitors, well, "competition." They want to compete for your corporation's *ephemeral image*. The *ephemeral image*, that image so critical to the success of your company. That's what insidious competitors want to change. The meaning of The Ephemeral Image is their target and later in this book, when we discuss the types of insidious competitors, we will explore some of the reasons behind this competitive battle for the corporate image.

Remember the Four Tools of Insidious Competition – Mutant Conversation, Social Engineering, Hip Chat, and Snark? Whether or not ***all*** types of insidious competitors are fully aware that these tools apply the principles of propaganda, the fact remains that they do. And these are the instruments, the visible applications, the tools that are being used to apply propaganda in the insidiously competitive battle for meaning. As with any tool or device, the effectiveness of it depends upon its foundation, or the principles upon which it is based. For instance, the effectiveness of a screwdriver (the type you get at a hardware store, not the type you get at a bar) is dependent upon the principle of the wheel and axle. If it was not for the fundamental principle of the wheel and axle, a screwdriver could not function. The same comparison is being made here. The effectiveness of the insidious competitor's tools depends on the foundation upon which it sits, its principles.

So, if we want to combat this non-traditional and insidious competitor, then we must know more about the usage and application of the tools of this new type of competitor. We can improve our understanding by knowing more about the principles behind those tools, the principles of propaganda. To achieve this goal, a true understanding of propaganda must be had. Thus, to combat the insidious competitor we must not only understand the Nine Elements of Social Media Danger, which we summarized in the preceding chapter, but we must particularly understand how the Four Tools of Insidious Competition are applied against the ninth element, the integrity of the solipsistic and epistemological process, the system of knowing, on which the vitality of the corporate image so vitally depends, and we must understand the principles that support the tools.

Now, let's discuss those principles, the principles of propaganda, to lay the foundation for our discussion of the four tools: Mutant Conversation, Social Engineering, Hip Chat and Snark, in the next chapter.

Think About Propaganda Differently

Before we begin this discussion of propaganda, there is one thing that I would like you to do. The choice is, of course, yours, but I think you might enjoy the following discussion on the principles of propaganda to a greater extent and get more out of it if you would not think of propaganda as a negative. Don't think about jack boots and goose-stepping whenever I mention the word "propaganda." Just put that out of your mind now. Change that perception. Doing so will increase your knowledge about how propaganda is applied by the insidious competitor. Please do not think of propaganda as a negative or a positive. Think of it simply as a set of principles which influence a process, a solipsistic and epistemological process, a system of knowing. I've done this. When I first studied propaganda, I found that taking this approach helped me increase my understanding of the principles.

Now, as my piano teacher used to say, "Let's begin."

In July 1999, The Mackenzie Institute, a Toronto think-tank, wrote on its Web site about the NATO bombing taking place in Serbia. The Mackenzie Institute cited that military action in Serbia was the first "extra-national conflict" in which all involved parties used the Internet to advance their own perspectives on the conflict. The Institute goes on to opine that "Like everything else humanity has ever produced, it (the Internet) will have an influence on the course of warfare." [45]

In case you have forgotten what things were like when this Mackenzie Institute article was posted, the Internet, and many of the impacts from it, were in full swing. During that heady time of '99, it seemed that every day brought the announcement of the start-up of another dot com company, or another dot com stock IPO, or new highs on the NASDAQ, or an e-mail from your friend recommending a site that "you've just got to check out, dude." Back then, the dot com boom was riding high and everyone knew that the Internet was not "the next big thing," it WAS the big thing. The Internet, or more precisely the common, everyday and/or commercial usage of the Internet, was probably the biggest thing we as a society had seen since the Wright Brothers shot their airplane across a beach in North Carolina, ascended into the air, and changed the course of human existence forever. And at the time of '99, I thought that the Internet would probably be the biggest new thing we'd see for the rest of my life and for the rest of the lives of my contemporaries. I still think that.

As The Mackenzie Institute pointed out in that post, obviously the Internet is a communications device. The Internet is unique in many ways; if it was not, there would not have been so much hubbub about it. One of the features that makes the Internet unique is that it is at once a device of mass communication *and* one of individual communication. And the Internet is virtually limitless, especially with wireless Internet available. The Internet and everything on it is globally available. Never before has a communications apparatus, one available to the "common person," been so ubiquitous. The Net's potential for distributing messages, both true and false, is unparalleled in human history. Lucky us to be on the planet at this particular point in human progress. And the Internet's potential for distributing propaganda, be it of a political nature, which was the focus of The Mackenzie Institute article, or of a commercial nature, which is the focus of this book, can be devastating. Remember how delicate is The Ephemeral Image, so dependent upon the solipsistic and epistemological process.

As a sidebar to the Institute's article as cited above, they also said, "As the Internet continues to grow and expand, it may be the ultimate antidote to propaganda. Let's make sure the whole world becomes plugged in." I understand what they mean. Their call-to-action sounds, on the surface, all new age and progressive and oh-so 21st century and egalitarian and very hunky dory. Now please don't think me a regressive, but I couldn't disagree more. Let me come back to this disagreement later in Chapter Nine. First, let's take a look at just what propaganda is by examining its principles.

I just love Webster's dictionary, in its various versions and editions. You've probably noticed by now that I have been using the dictionary a lot in this book. You really cannot go wrong by using the dictionary when you need some support to make your argument. Why? Well, when a passage from a scholarly article or a book, for example, is used to help make an argument, it seems that the source itself is more often than not "arguable." Using such a source doesn't "slam dunk" your argument and help put away your opponent decisively. In fact, many times it just helps confuse your argument.

But the dictionary, that's something on which everyone agrees. We all accept it. Who argues with the dictionary? It provides a *common body of knowledge*. The dictionary increases the probability of slam-dunking your case. So here goes. I'm going to use the dictionary again.

From Webster's New World Dictionary:

propaganda - n. - *widespread dissemination or promotion of particular ideas, doctrines, practices, etc. to further one's own cause to or to damage an opposing one* -propagandistic adj.

Doesn't this sound like something that could be of great use in a commercial setting? In business?

Rhetorically, yes. Well then, let's dig a little further, excuse me, let's dig a lot further into what propaganda really is and how we can recognize it. After that discussion and based on that discussion, I'll let you have my definition of propaganda which will serve as the foundation for exploring propaganda on the Internet, specifically within social media, and even more specifically within the context of the supporting principles of the four tools used by the insidious competitor within social media.

In its post, as mentioned above, The Mackenzie Institute cited the classic work in propaganda, authored by Jacques Ellul and titled very simply, *Propaganda*, and subtitled *The Formation of Men's Attitudes.* This is a really great book. When I first came upon this book, one of the first things I liked was its title. One word. Crisp. Clean. Concise. Cogent. To the point. *Propaganda* is a classic work in the theory of communication. I've had this book in my library for quite a while, since I read it as a college sophomore taking my first course in communications. As I said, one of the first things I liked about this book was its to-the-point title. Alas, I can't extend that same compliment to the writing style within the book itself.

Propaganda is somewhat "thick" in its 1965 writing style. "Somewhat thick?" What am I saying? The style is very, very thick. Get out your machete. But if you can stay with it, slashing through the academic genre within, and the occasional thirty-plus line paragraph (Yes. Thirty lines. On page 7 of my edition there is a 39 line paragraph.), then *Propaganda* can greatly enlighten you on the basics of general communication. That is where this book shines. The book forces the reader to think about propaganda differently. The book forces the reader to think about propaganda as a general communication process, a persuasive process, a solipsistic and epistemological process, a system of knowing. That's what I truly enjoy about this book.

There are other works on propaganda, of course, and in our discussion of the principles of propaganda, you and I will discuss works by Douglas Walton, Baruch Hazan, Jay Black, and Nancy Snow. And because Jacques Ellul, one of the originals, is not the be all and end all in the study of propaganda, these other experts will help us add to Jacques' seminal thoughts and will also help us examine not only the environment in which propaganda can be used, but also the forces within the messages that employ the principles of propaganda.

When reading here about propaganda, please keep in mind that most of the experts cited have a primary focus in the area of political communication. My focus in *Insidious Competition* is in the area of communication for business purposes, but because we are discussing persuasive communication we can still use some of these ideas of propaganda as an outline and guide for the points I'm making in *Insidious Competition*.

The Seven Principles for Successful Propaganda

After reviewing, condensing, integrating and thinking about the classic work of Jacques Ellul and the works of the other aforementioned experts in propaganda, I have gleaned seven principles that I believe need to be in the propaganda environment or in the propaganda message itself, in order for the propagandistic message to be successful. Those principles are:

1. Person & People
2. Totality
3. Organizational Unit
4. Goal Orientation
5. Societal Basics
6. Temporal Focus
7. Veracity

Now let's go ahead and discuss these principles from within the context of social media and with regard to the insidious competitors inside social media, as well as with regard to their battle for the meaning of your *corporate image*.

1. Person & People

Jacques Ellul says that, to be successful, propaganda needs to address both the individual *and* the masses *at the same time*.

This, at first glance, seems curious. Why would he say this? It appears to be almost contradictory. But it is not. Jacques explains his reasoning by saying that the individual is of no interest to the propagandist because "as an isolated unit he presents too much resistance to external action." [46] Very interesting. And this makes sense from within the context of social media.

Jacques puts forth the idea that propaganda looks to reach persons who are participants in a group, meaning those that possess common interests. The propagandist wants to target individuals in a group because, per Jacques, the group is bound together by emotionalism, impulsiveness, and excess, and as such they are considered as not being "alone." He says that the propagandist profits from the process of the diffusion of emotions through the mass and that the propagandist leverages this group relationship and dynamic, using it to exert influence on each individual and ultimately the group.[47] Yikes! This sounds so much like the environment of social media that it's almost scary. This idea of Jacques' indicates that an environment like social media is ripe for the growth of a propagandistic message. Especially so, given our earlier discussion of groups. Consider those thoughts while thinking about social media.

As I said a short while ago, social media is both a tool of mass communication *and* one of individual communication. It is "mass" because its public messages can be read by anyone with access to the Internet. Yet social media's communications are also individualized because:

1. Social media communications are often addressed to persons taking part in a group of common interest (the featured topic(s) of the blog or social network) and, as such, are somewhat specific and not general in nature; and,
2. Because a feedback loop is provided (e.g., the comments in a blog), a conversation can be created between the site author and each reader, individually. (In reality, a conversation between the author and each reader is probably impractical, yet it is possible.) "Commenters" may even address each other, providing ample opportunity for sub-currents of propaganda.

Voila. Individualized communication via a "mass" medium.

Concerning comments that are made on blogs and social networks, many are created in an air of emotionalism and impulsiveness which are borne of the nature of the social medium itself which is anonymous, free-wheeling, open, and candid. Note that Jacques said that the emotionalism and impulsiveness are key to the success of the propaganda. The group atmosphere is a property in exerting influence on the individual. As we saw earlier in *Insidious Competition*, the Five Factors on which insidious competition stand are anonymity, power, contagion, instinct, and disdain. All of these Five Factors help to support the emotionalism and impulsiveness that Jacques says are necessary for propaganda to be successful. Think about that.

Think about that again because this is an important point in understanding the essence of the insidious competitor. Jacques' ideas about propaganda addressing the individual and the masses at the same time, along with the idea of the targeted group being bound together by emotionalism and impulsiveness, are directly on point to what we have discussed so far in *Insidious Competition*. In particular, the most salient point that I want to hammer home here is what Jacques says about the propagandist leveraging emotionalism and impulsiveness. Going back to Chapter Two, this is directly related to at least one of the elements of the Final Definition of Crowds, number six specifically. Remember:

> *Crowds manufacture behavioral contagion, causing those powerful-feeling individuals to perform instinctual behaviors, which the individuals believe will be in support of group interests.*

If you believe, as I do, that behavioral contagion is rooted in emotion, then here is where Gustave Le Bon's theory about crowds meets at least part of Jacques Ellul's theory about propaganda. And they dovetail. Nicely.

Jacques is describing an environment which is much like social media. And we didn't even have social media when he wrote his book in 1965. So, Jacques couldn't draw the parallels, but I can. Social media addresses the individual from within a group, where emotionalism and impulsiveness abound as supported by the Final Definition of Crowds and by the Five Factors of Insidious Competition.

So, Person & People, the individual and the masses, are present in the environment of social media making social media a good venue within which propaganda may function successfully.

2. Totality

The title of this second principle makes me think of it as something taken from a Hitlerian or Stalinian manual. Totality. Seems so onerous. Please try to ignore that feeling. As I mentioned at the beginning of this chapter, think about propaganda differently. I know that you will get more out of this part of this book if you can just put away those images of totalitarian regimes, even though *1984* was a great book. I have. And I have benefited from it.

Jacques discusses the idea of *total* propaganda. What I believe he is getting at in that idea is that, for propaganda to be effective, because different media have different effectiveness rates, the propagandist must send his message through different media. In other words, the propagandist must use more than one channel. But Jacques also emphasizes that the propaganda message(s) must be the only one(s) received. Okay. Seems reasonable.

Jacques mentions that the media to be used should be "the press, radio, TV, movies, posters, meetings, and door-to-door canvassing." [48] Keep in mind Jacques wrote his book in 1965, so, of course, no Internet related media would be mentioned. He is talking about what we have come to call the "traditional media" and we've already seen in our previous discussions what's starting to happen to that.

Now, if Jacques says that for propaganda to be effective the message must be *total* across various media, then I suppose I can't count on the principle of Totality to support the tools of insidious competition as they can be used in social media. Or can I? Remember. Never let a good idea go stale. Let's think further. Consider this question.

What is *total*?

Jacques published *Propaganda* back in 1965.

1965. That year seems like centuries ago in terms of what we, as a society, have been through since then.

That was before the "crapola" hit the fan in Vietnam, before the RFK and MLK assassinations, before men first walked on the moon, before Watergate, before the Nixon resignation, before the oil embargoes, before terrorism affected America, before neo-conservatives, before neo-liberals, before Monica's blue dress, before a lot of things that fragmented the American culture and changed the course of human history. I remember those times and I remember before those times how the American culture was not as fractious as it is today. Back in those days when Jacques was writing about total propaganda, Americans were less irascible, less testy, less obstreperous, and less short-tempered than they are today. Americans were relatively more united and less factional. Correspondingly, by my recollection, the messages in media were more balanced, less polemic, less skewed, and I would even go so far to say that, as a result, those message were less insipid as well. This evaluation is subjective, as would any evaluation be of this type. And it's true that although I was a kid at the time *Propaganda* was written, I was an unusual kid. Unusual in the sense that I paid attention to things on television that other kids didn't even know existed, like the daily news show. I couldn't get enough of Huntley and Brinkley. I was a news junkie before the term ever hit the vernacular. Let me provide more perspective.

My memories of news go back to around 1965. And based on my memories of news broadcasts at that time I can say, using a quote I've already used in this book, that "Alternative reality as a decent business model" had not much occurred to anyone then. I grew up in the metro New York City area, when we had only seven television channels. Seven. Yes, believe it. That's all. And that was in the New York City market, the media capital of Planet Earth and of the known media universe then as now. I shudder to think how many channels they had available at that time in Omaha. No wonder folks in that section of the country went to bed earlier, there was nothing on the tube to tantalize and distract them.

I recall that back in those days, when people selected from their much smaller media menu, what they got was a more middle-of-the-road experience-perception-knowledge viewing diet than what is being offered up today. There were fewer choices of medium, and because there were fewer choices, in order for the broadcasters to capture the widest audience, they had to make each of those program choices middle-of-the-road, and with little topical diversity. Broadcasters then did not have multiple media channels through which to skew programming in one direction or the other and collectively capture a market large enough to impress advertisers. So by default, and ironically through the limited availability of media channels, the media experience I had then, and its resulting perceptions, was more "balanced" than what we see today.

Here comes an understatement. Today things are quite different. I'll use a solipsistic model to explain my knowledge.

I no longer live in the metro New York City area. I've moved a bit south. Currently, I live in between two major media markets, New York and Philadelphia. On my cable television system, I have about 1,000 channels from which to choose. That's about 993 more television channels available to me than when I was growing up. This is only the "tip of the iceberg" when it comes to describing the more fragmented media selection I have now. Forms of communication exist today that did not exist when I was a kid. Such as Sirius Satellite Radio, from which I have hundreds of "streams" to choose. Then, of course, there is always the Internet. I spend much of my work day on the Net, far more than the previously quoted 32.5% of the media day. So in cyberspace I have literally millions of Web sites at my fingertips. There are many communication formats available now, that were not available before. You get the idea.

In today's highly fragmented media menu, we can choose immediately from whatever subject matter fits our mood or *our interpretation of reality.* Do you lean to the political right or to the left? There are news sites, social sites, cable channels, and magazines to meet the needs of either of those leanings. Do you think that space aliens walk the Earth or perhaps that we are actually descended from space aliens? There are social media sites for that, as well. Think that Elvis Presley and Michael Jackson aren't really dead and that they are living the reclusive life on a South Pacific atoll or tending bar, while in disguise, at a singles resort in Tahiti? Are you a JFK assassination or 9/11 conspiracy theorist? Just Google up your social site of choice and join a discussion that can last you from here to the next millennium.

So I think where Jacques was referring to total propaganda in a media environment that I see as more limited in selection and more middle-of-the-road topically, effectively balanced, and which no longer exists, we need for our discussion about insidious competition to reconsider total propaganda from within today's fragmented media environment where topical choice not only exists but is overly abundant, overly encouraged, overly hyped, overly criticized, and just downright totally unnecessary. When you look at the total media environment that exists today, you will see much topical diversity, with sources on any given subject running the entire breadth of the imaginable spectrum. But human nature being what it is, if we are given a choice, we're almost certain to concentrate on those things that interest us.

Humans exhibit a tendency to concentrate on the same subjects over and over again and make the same selections over and over again. Think about how you have radio stations preset on your car radio. Think about how on your DVR you have it set to record a program at the same time every week. Think about how on your weekly trip to the supermarket you tend to go up and down the same aisles in the same manner, choosing pretty much the same products week after week. Think about how when you were taking a class, where there was no seating assignment, you would sit in the same seat week after week. Over and over, with little to no deviation. We derive comfort from this type of repetitive behavior. Habits and routines simplify our lives. We, as human animals seeking psychic satisfaction, tend not to reject an opportunity to attain psychic satisfaction. *And in our media selection we will tend not to sample evenly from the overwhelming media diversity that now exists.* After all, there are only twenty-four hours in a day, and we need to sleep a good chunk of those. No, instead of sampling across the media spectrum, seeking balance and diversity, we'll concentrate on what we like. It's the same innate inner force that keeps many of us from eating a balanced diet each day. Think I'm wrong? Consider how many obese Americans you see every day.

If we choose to "junk out" on our preferred media/reality choices the same way we do with our food, then we'll receive the same messages over and over. If we choose to concentrate and limit our "diversity" within the scope of our "epistemic communities," as I discussed in the previous chapter, then we'll have essentially the same experiences repeatedly, with the same perceptions repeatedly, with the same knowledge permeating our brains repeatedly. *That's total propaganda.* Total propaganda American style. Freedom of choice. Freedom of information. Freedom to delude ourselves. Freedom to fatten our distorted realities via our own insatiable appetite for the familiar. Call it "pull propaganda" or "*propaganda by choice*."

It's commonly accepted in marketing circles that more and more people every day are abandoning traditional media in favor of the Internet. Earlier in *Insidious Competition*, we saw sources that support this assertion. But cited sources aren't really necessary because this transition in American, and even global, society is really common knowledge now. I've not seen any studies recently, or at all, that say that people, anywhere on the globe, are abandoning Internet media in favor of the traditional media mentioned by Jacques. Can you imagine that headline?

"40% of American Population Abandons Internet and Returns to Radio"

That's not going to happen, my friend.

So what does all this mean in relation to Totality?

What this means is that Internet media will progressively become, while this trend continues at least, a higher percentage of the fragmented, specialized, skewed, epistemically parochial, media *total* that people absorb on a daily basis. Indeed the study I cited in Chapter Six said that American adults now spend about one-third of their media day online.[49] Imagine this.

People will be using, increasingly, a medium that, as I established above in Person & People, is ripe for the development of propaganda. And with the human desire for "propaganda by choice," a self-imposed Totality, social media will provide a venue where propaganda can take hold, breed, flourish, and do its work. As people's use of Internet media increasingly occupies a greater percentage of their overall daily media consumption, they will become more and more susceptible to the influences of the propaganda that they themselves choose, *as it exists, or will exist, in social media, corrupting the integrity of the system of knowing, intensifying the battle for meaning, aiding insidious competitors, and threatening your corporate image.*

Frightened yet? Read on.

3. Organizational Unit

This principle in effective propaganda deals with the idea that there is an organization and/or collection of organizations that create and control the propaganda effort. Here I will build upon an idea of Jacques'. I'll call that idea "cell agents." This one really smacks of visions of *1984*, but as I counseled up front, let's try not to let our imaginations run away with us. My label of a cell agent comes from Jacques' idea where he suggests that the function of a large propaganda organization could be replaced by a series of agents who organize parts of society, persuading those parts of society to follow the message being propagandized and to pursue the actions of the propaganda being espoused.[50] Jacques? Are you kidding me? This one is so eerily like social media, it just makes me want to shudder. Yes. There does need to be a certain degree of organization for the creation and control of propaganda.

Yes, organized indeed. Nancy Snow said that propaganda is "institutional in nature" and is practiced by groups such as "corporations, government agencies, religious groups, terrorist cells, or social movements." [51] Her identification of terrorist cells is especially relevant to our discussion here, given the idea I just introduced - propaganda cell agents. Nancy says that propaganda is institutional in nature, but she extends that nature from the largest organization right down to the smallest of organizations. The smallest, such as a cell or even a social movement, could contain as few people as two, or even one. And perhaps small is where we should begin our observations of the organization principle of propaganda as it applies to insidious competition.

To understand the organization principle of propaganda, small might be a good place to start because, for the most part in the United States, we don't have large propagandist organizations creating and transmitting messages against companies. (There are some non-profit groups who do this, though. Some NGOs and certain well-organized activist groups in the environmental, animal rights, and health interests pursue an agenda against businesses and are aided by propagandist messages. We'll discuss NGOs and activists later in this book, learning more about how they can be *insidious competitors.*) To begin our understanding of propaganda organization, what I want to discuss here is the smallest of organizations that Nancy mentioned, small groups like the social movements and other forms of cell agents that can form intentionally or opportunistically within social media, and endure for who knows how long. To get to the heart of the cell agent idea and how effective even the smallest of organizations can be in social media, let me discuss two forces of nature: cosmos and chaos.

These classifications are my way of demonstrating to you that there can be two general forms of propaganda organization out there.

Cosmos and Chaos

Webster's says about **cosmos** that it is an **orderly** system and about **chaos** that it means **disorder**. Opposites. But not totally opposite when it comes to organizing systems, that is if you believe chaos theory. Both views indicate organization, just of different types.

Supporters of chaos theory say that from disorder comes order or that chaos evolves into cosmos. A basic example of this concept would be the fact that you're sitting here reading this book on Planet Earth. Earth is part of a relatively orderly solar system, a solar system which at one time was chaotic. The fact that you're not a melted blob of primordial stew swirling around in space emphasizes the validity of chaos theory. And those same forces that Mother Nature used to put together the universe, the galaxies, the solar system, the planets, the continents, and you as well as me, are most certainly found in at least the majority of other things that you can think of, especially if those things are considered a "system." One of those things I'm thinking of is human groups, which are systems, and the ways in which they function and organize. Another author had the same thoughts. Margaret Wheatley, an educational consultant, said it well, "If nature uses certain principles to create her infinite diversity, it is highly probable that those principles apply to human organizations." [52] (If any of you readers work in a large, chaotic organization, then you'll understand what I'm getting at.)

Do you see where I'm heading?

There are two forms of organization, formal and informal.

If chaotic occurrences do create cosmic systems, which I'm inclined to believe that they do simply because I'm sitting here writing this book that you're reading, it would mean the following about propaganda and social media.

As we discussed back in Chapter Two, in comparing the Final Definition of Crowds to the Environment of Social Media, social media users are generally a leaderless group, usually lacking formal organization. With chaos theory in social media, I am talking about a force that would organize people, spontaneously, but would do so *informally* by using natural forces.

We might not see this type of chaotic formation as an "organization," per se, but if there is a pattern there, a pattern which facilitates behavior, then it is an "organization." Remember what I quoted David Denby as saying back in the Crowd Behavior section of Chapter Two. He was talking about the "bad behavior" exhibited in some social media groups and said that its development was almost "algorithmic." In other words, there is a pattern there, a regular pattern that facilitates behavior, good or bad – an "organization." And while no one *apparently intended* for that bad behavior to happen – it did anyway. The forces of human nature, a subsystem of Mother Nature, kicked in and took over. Crowd behavior. No *apparent* rhyme or reason. *Apparent* is the key word there. Hidden forces are always key *and* they are always present within social media groups. Remember our Five Factors of Insidious Competition – anonymity, power, contagion, instinct and disdain? Can you see the possibility for groups of people sharing a common interest within social media to *chaotically* organize, informally, affected by the Five Factors, coalescing, speaking out and demanding change and/or satisfaction against any injustice that was *experienced, perceived, and known* and therefore taken as "reality" by the members of the group? Never mind if the perceived injustice was ever considered by any system of jurisprudence to be, in fact, valid. "Reality" becomes reality based on experience, perception, and the resulting knowledge.

So the influence of social media can be related to the "realities" of the business world. With the power of social media to attract like-minded individuals, in a "propaganda by choice," and involve them in a conversation, and with social media's global reach, a simple and singular propagandistic message, evolving from the thoughts of the group's members, could compel the group to organize *chaotically* against a company to persuade that company to change its message or its behavior or even its management. We'll see an example of this later when we talk about The Motrin Incident. In The Motrin Incident there was nothing wrong with the product - some people just didn't like an ad for the product and those people organized chaotically, from within social media, to bring pressure on the company which resulted in the ad being withdrawn. Jacques says that propaganda has the most effect on people when they are "alone" in a group.[53] Yes, indeed that worked in The Motrin Incident. Thus, it would follow that a propaganda message would have its best chance of success if launched from within a group, even if that launch is chaotically organized.

If a propagandist cell agent, or a small social movement organization, *formally* insinuates itself into strategically selected discussions within social media, seeking to take advantage of the naturally-occurring, snowballing, chaotically-organizing, informal, forces available there, that agent or social movement can leverage chaotic forces and cause significant, if not devastating effects, on the *corporate image* of their "target." We'll see more examples and learn more about this later.

Those are my thoughts about chaotically organized propaganda. But what about cosmically organized propaganda?

Chaos and cosmos are opposites. Whereas with chaos there is little or no attention to a *specific form* of organization (informal), with cosmos there is great attention as to a *specific form* of organization (formal) (e.g., a team, a squad, a task force, a coalition, etc.). In propaganda transmission in social media, both the chaotic and cosmic forms can exist. In social media, as mentioned two paragraphs ago, a cosmic form ("a propagandist cell agent, or small social movement . . .") can leverage the chaotic form, the crowd, for its own purposes.

These are exciting ideas and ones about which we'll need to know if we are to counter insidious competition effectively. We will further explore these ideas of cosmically and chaotically organized propaganda groups later in *Insidious Competition*, seeing how they can corrupt the system of knowing and threaten the corporate image.

4. Goal Orientation

In his discussion on propaganda, Jacques talks about orthopraxy. Fancy word, but what does it mean?

Orthopraxy is the practice of the correction of defects. This word is generally used as a medical term but Jacques brings it into his discussion about the principles of propaganda and uses it to mean that the propagandist has a goal for action in mind. Jacques says it does the propagandist no good just to influence someone's attitude. To be successful, the propagandist must be focused on eliciting an action, so that the action will correct a "defect," at least a defect as defined by the propagandist. The correction of the defect is the objective, while the called-for action is the tactic.[54] This idea of action is reinforced by what Nancy Snow referred to as "agenda-driven." She meant by this that propagandists have a purpose in mind.[55] Propagandists want to elicit some sort of reaction, or "action" in response to their efforts. Douglas Walton talks about the same idea.

Douglas puts forth the idea that propaganda is a "goal-directed discourse."[56] I believe that what Douglas means by "discourse" is that the propaganda recipient would make an action in response to the propagandist's message. Message, then response, which would be a discourse, an exchange. As Douglas says, propaganda is aimed at getting a response or, like Jacques' idea of orthopraxy, a goal for an action. Or more simply put, a "means to an end."

So as it relates to business, what could this "means to an end," or action, or tactic be? What could be the company "defects" that either cosmically or chaotically organized propaganda groups, manifesting themselves on the social web, would want to correct? I think you know the answers to both these questions. As I posed those questions, your conscious mind was probably flooded with likely answers, many of which are all too commonly known to us in today's society. But let's discuss them, anyway.

As defined by the propagandist at whose mercy your company may lie, those "defects" could range from something as mild and as general as "ignoring consumer concerns" to something more nefarious, egregious, and specific such as "exploiting child labor." Other real or perceived defects, as defined by the propagandist seeking to compel your company to change, might include things like:

- Disregard for animal rights, although the company follows regulations in this area.
- Manufacturing practices that abuse the environment, although the company conforms to and exceeds all environmental laws where it operates.
- Products that contain alleged carcinogens or other compounds believed to be, either correctly or incorrectly, health hazards.
- Contributory actions toward "globalization" which some groups believe exploit third world labor.
- Legitimate product or service problems.
- Or, just plain lousy service (which, due to entropy or just simply Murphy's Law, every company is bound to provide, to some degree, at some point in its corporate life).

I could go on listing "defects" which the propagandist may claim. And the listing of those defects, the designation of which is most often subjective anyway, would likely take half of this book for me to do. You'd probably prefer to make your own list. If you do, please allow plenty of time.

My point is that because the definition of a defect is often subjective, or in the eyes of the beholder, the list could be never-ending and there will never be an end to the list of real or perceived "defects." So there will always be people making a call to action, asking for orthopraxy.

What would be the calls for action a cosmically or chaotically organized propaganda group in social media would be likely to make? Again, the list could be endless. Regarding negative actions, read that as "threats" against a business, how about these for starters?

- Informal calls for boycotts. These abound on the social web.
- Petty, bullying grumbles about products blogged by consumers just because they can.
- Requests for product changes. Remember the factors of power and disdain?
- Issuing complaints against a company with no connection to an actual product or service problem (see "The Motrin Incident" later in this book). Calls to remove "offensive" ads.
- Creating class warfare (in the form of video and text messages) between the perceived haves (people who run companies) and the have-nots (people who don't run companies, i.e., pretty much everyone). Instinctual disdain. Calls to lower profit margins via contributions to social causes.
- Making objections to corporate employee/officer remuneration. Calls for reductions.

All of these calls for actions are also statements of grievances and they also serve as the generation of more propaganda. People issuing these grievances could be considered to be cell agents, numerous, witting or not, issuing complaints as tactics to further an objective, and not just for the sake of spouting off. The contagion takes hold and many social media users would react to support "calls to action" to correct the "defects." There would then be more propaganda generated. Within social media, propaganda propagates. In the atmosphere of social media, cosmic or chaotic generators of propaganda know that their messages will be absorbed and regenerated by the supportive group in which the messages are forged. Making more propaganda is more easily achieved compared to actually going out and doing something, taking real action aimed at a real objective.

But all of the above negative actions can, of course, manifest themselves on the bottom line of a company, a major orthopractic result hoped for by a propagandist cell agent. Not only would the members of the social media group (in a blog, social network, or Twitter, etc. venue) who create the propaganda, and the resulting propaganda created by the original propaganda, take their economic votes (their purchases) elsewhere, but so might casual readers of these messages. More orthopractic outcome for the cell agent.

Once content is on the Internet, it lives there pretty much indefinitely.

And it's out of the control of those who are its subject, or target, or victim depending upon how you regard the nature of the propaganda. Casual readers who will be attracted to these posts through a search on a keyword or an idea unrelated to the central theme of the propaganda will be influenced, at least to some degree, by the propaganda. Experience. Perception. Knowledge. Since this stuff is out there forever, insidious competition against your company's corporate image could live indefinitely. Long after the insidious competitor typed their last keystroke in the corruption of the system of knowing aimed at *your corporate image*, economic votes could go against a company if the negative messages are not countered with positive messages.

5. Societal Basics

Nancy Snow said that propaganda is strongly oriented toward ideology.[57] And to my way of thinking, ideologies are often deeply rooted within the very core morals and ethics that support society. In other words, the success of the propaganda hinges on that to which society is committed. Indeed, Douglas Walton touches on this idea when he says that "the argumentation of the (propaganda) proponent is based on the commitments of the (propaganda) respondent." [58] The propaganda respondent's, or the audience's, societal or social basics must be considered when propaganda is to be employed. Jacques goes into more detail in discussing this critical principle of propaganda.

Regarding this principle of Societal Basics, Jacques' idea said that the successful propaganda message must be formed by using methods and arguments understood by the target audience. Going into more detail about his idea, Jacques states that successful propaganda messages must be built upon, or address, four sociological presuppositions common to all societies and upon several myths which support the struggle in daily life.[59] (Jacques calls them "myths" but from his explanation it seems to me that by calling them "values" they can be more clearly understood.) Those sociological presuppositions and myths, or as I call them, values, are summarized below.

Four Sociological Presuppositions

1. The overarching aim in human life is happiness.
2. Humans are naturally good.
3. History develops along a path of endless progress.

4. Everything is matter. (This one we could take to be a bit "New Ageish" and therefore vague and confusing. But from Jacques' further explanation, I interpret this idea as meaning that materialism is important because it relates to the attainment of happiness as a fruit of labor.)

The "Myths" or Values Supporting Daily Life

1. Work – Valuing work leads to the foundations of all of the presuppositions shown above.
2. Nation – Love of nation protects the evolution of progress.
3. Youth – The protection of children leads to society's progress and to people's happiness. And that because humans are naturally good, they can't not protect children. Children will be allowed to develop and further the society.
4. Hero – All challenges can be overcome, progress will be attained and happiness achieved.

Per Jacques, when these presuppositions and values are considered by the propagandist, so that the message is constructed from within those frames of reference, the message is likely to be successful and the desired action, the targeted orthopractic outcome, will be taken.

Merci, Nancy, Douglas, and Jacques. You have really put your collective finger on it here. Think about it, reader. In social media, whether a message is cosmically or chaotically organized, if it's constructed from the perspective of one of the ideologies or commitments or presuppositions or values, then you're going to pay attention to it. Aren't you? For example, Mommy Bloggers are very famous and equally influential. How can you disrespect a Mommy Blogger? Well, at least publicly, that is. You can't because the frame of reference from which they write is about children, their betterment, and their protection. The Mommy Bloggers leverage that daily value of children, a societal commitment, an ideology necessary to the preservation of the human race. This type of approach is the same that was described in the book *Damage Control* when the authors quoted Ronald Reagan as saying, "Wrap every argument in a principle." [60] Corporate PR staffs have done this for decades.

Well, the skilled and smart ones have, anyway. Now individuals are "getting jiggy with the program" and they have the world's "ear" at their fingertips.

* * *

Let's just take a little time out here and pause on the discussion of the principles of propaganda. We'll come back to those momentito.

At this point in the book, I've gone through a lot of "heady" kind of stuff or you might be thinking a more technical term is applicable, a technical term like "gobblety gook." There is, of course, a reason for all this gobblety gook. I want you to understand my argument that insidious competition is a very real threat to business today, one like nothing business has experienced to this date. It is important that you as a businessperson understand the underpinnings of the threat, the nature of the threat, and what makes this threat tick. As I mentioned near the beginning of this chapter, and I reiterate here, by holding these understandings, you will be better equipped to deal with the threat, to combat it, and to overcome it.

What is at stake is not just a few percentage points on the bottom line of a corporate income statement. No. What's at stake here is a lot more important than that. Look past the numbers. What's at stake is what those "few points" on the bottom of the income statement represent. Those points represent things like the attainment of personal happiness enabled by employees who have secure jobs at a secure company, the balanced family life that is realized for children when the family breadwinner(s) has (have) those secure jobs, the maintenance of economic progress and the betterment of society via that progress which in turn supports human happiness, and other supporting sociological presuppositions.

I think you will agree that these objectives are important. Very important.

Okay. Now that I've wrapped my argument in several ideologies, commitments, presuppositions, and values, let's mush on.

* * *

6. Temporally Focused

Another principle of propaganda is that it tends to be overly focused on a specific time period. Jay Black captured this idea when he said that in propaganda there will be "an overemphasis or underemphasis on the past, present, or future as 'disconnected periods' rather than a demonstrated consciousness of time flow." [61] The danger in propaganda that I see him pointing out here is that a recipient would only be getting part of the story. Truth, and reality with it, evolve over a period of time, and to seek truths by relating a story, which may extend over many time periods, from within only one discrete time period, short-changes the audience's understanding of the story. In other words, it would be like telling a ten chapter story in one chapter. The receiver would only get a "partial truth."

So, in applying this principle of temporal focus, what would be the time period in which the propagandist, especially the propagandist in social media, would concentrate? Past, present, or future? I think Jacques has the answer to this one.

Jacques says that the propaganda message must be current, relating to something topical within the receivers' recent experiences.[62] So, using Jacques' theory, it would be the present which would be the time period of preference. Again, a perfect line up of a theoretical principle with the environment that exists within social media.

The issues discussed in social media are timely. Part of the caché of social media is that it's "cool" and if something is "cool," well then it usually doesn't include old news. It is this aspect of social media, its very coolness, that might be what saves a company from any one propaganda campaign that arises spontaneously.

From my experience, it appears to me that social media users are interested primarily in current topics, not in old news. Go to Digg.com to verify, if you like. I'd hazard any guess that you won't see too many, if any, "old" stories at the top of the Digg list. Somewhat of a saving grace to any company which is the victim of propaganda arising from insidious competition. The company can take small comfort, at least, in the fact that the assault will probably be short-lived. Of course, short-lived is a relative term and is not always the case. But even if the incident is short, whether that be hours, days, weeks, or months, an assaulted company should not take that as comfort. Remember that although the assault may be short, this stuff just lives out there "forever."

There could be a series of related events that the cosmic or chaotic propagandist(s) could exploit. By stringing enough slanted commentaries together, and by basing them within the societal presuppositions or values (i.e., the Societal Basics) and by tying them together with reference to a current event, the propagandist(s) keep(s) a negative message alive long enough for it to do harm to any company.

The accentuation of only present events and leaving out past events which may put a corporate incident in context, perhaps favorably for the corporation, is a definite manipulation in the solipsistic and epistemological process that we have discussed. The system of knowing gets tinkered with. And that, of course, will impact your company's corporate image.

7. Veracity

Propaganda is largely believed to be messages which are inaccurate or that vary wholly with reality. In other words, when we hear the word "propaganda" we think "lies." Now, of course as we have discussed, reality is a tricky thing. So let's take this idea to mean that propaganda is largely believed to be classified as messages stating a reality which may vary with our own individual versions of reality, whatever those versions may be.

This idea that propaganda is a pack of lies is often a gut reaction. That gut reaction is related to all that negative baggage which I asked you to leave in the baggage claim area as we embarked on this voyage of understanding just what propaganda is. So, can you leave those bags checked and proceed with the last leg of this journey? This final leg of the trip is important to your view of propaganda principles in social media.

If you are a successful propagandist you will know that one important element is the perceived veracity (i.e., the perceived lack of lies) which can be achieved when the message is seen as being sent by a credible source. Baruch Hazan emphasizes this element when he says that "trust and confidence in the propaganda source induce ready absorption." [63] When we consider this element of the overall principle of veracity, we can see that propaganda within social media might be very successful. Successful because, as we previously discussed in Chapter One, the Universal Mc Cann study said that we trust online "strangers" almost as much as we do persons in a face-to-face conversation. Thus, trust in social media messages would be very high. Given this finding, the "truthfulness" of propaganda in social media therefore isn't much of an issue. According to the Universal Mc Cann study, it would seem that social media is pretty much rampant with truth. It would seem that almost any message in social media could be taken for gospel. Good, I suppose, for the social media propagandist. Yet, given this condition, I would say that the social media propagandist would not want to stretch the "truth" too far. Jacques touches upon this point.

Jacques says that a critical principle in the success of propaganda is that it contains facts. He says that to put in lies, which could be disproved, would be counterproductive to the propagandist's purposes. Jacques says what pays off in propaganda is the pairing of facts with intentions and interpretations of the facts.[64] Is he talking about a one-sided argument? Yes. On this point, Douglas characterizes propaganda as a one-sided argument. Douglas says that "propaganda is a kind of advocacy dialogue that uses partisan argumentation to advocate one side of an issue." Douglas also says that "an essential part of all propaganda is the use of emotively charged words and phrases that make the advocated viewpoint take on a highly positive coloration." [65]

Emotively charged words? To portray veracity? Sure. As long as the source is considered credible and, per the Universal Mc Cann study, trusted, and as long as those emotively charged words aren't bold-faced lies, and as long as those emotively charged words deal with something that is difficult to verify, the emotional approach should work in the portrayal of "veracity." Jay touches on this same idea when he talks about a characteristic of propaganda as being "the utilization of unverified and perhaps unverifiable abstract nouns, adjectives, adverbs, and physical representations rather than empirical validation to establish truths, conclusions, or impressions." [66] Because empirical validation could be disproved, it would certainly seem that Jay is referring to the concept of those emotively charged words of Douglas'. And we shall see later on in the next chapter how emotively charged and abstract words can be used in the social media tools of the insidious competitor, applying the principles of propaganda to preclude debate and, by doing so, *re-package reality and change the meaning of your corporate image.*

Ah, yes. So, we have in the Veracity principle of propaganda the shading of the truth. But perhaps we should regard what Jacques, Douglas, and Jay are saying more in this fashion. We should regard their thoughts from the perspective that, as far as interpretations are concerned, no one can prove a one-sided interpretation true or false. It's an opinion. And when trying to disprove an opinion, well, all bets are off. Therein lies an opening for the propagandist, as *insidious competitor.* The interpretations to be made by the audience are dependent upon the effectiveness of the intentioned innuendo and the intended suggestions contained in the one-sided propaganda. That is what packs the punch. So, it is in the implicative language that the value of really good propaganda lies.

A simple example of this is the exhortation within a social media group that, "Company XYZ's customer service sucks. No one should ever buy from them again." Okay. We've heard people say this all of our lives, but now they can send it to a wider audience waiting with "bated eyeballs" to read it on the social web. Such an appeal contains no arguable lie, as it is paired with a fact (the exhorter received service from XYZ), and colored by an interpretation, the service "sucks." The emotive appeal is opinion, which cannot be disproved, but yet in its creation exists a simple derogatory message, one that will color the perception of Company XYZ's effectiveness to satisfy its customers. And let us not forget that with regard to what we have discussed previously concerning crowd behavior and an emotionally charged environment, emotive appeal from within propaganda should work very nicely, corrupting the system of knowing.

Politicians have been performing and perfecting this type of communicational behavior since Columbus discovered America, and even well before that. We, their constituents (and I use that term "constituents" loosely), who have picked up on this process and have learned this skill, perhaps implicitly, have learned to shade the facts with the best of them. And the product of our absorption of this process comes out in social media.

Propaganda Summarization

In this book so far, we've come through a lot of learning in a short period of time. We've discussed elements of sociology, philosophy, psychology, and communications theory. Now, so that we can move on toward the pragmatic parts of this book and so we can understand how the tools of the insidious competitor are applied, let's summarize just what propaganda is, combining that summarization with our definition of a crowd as established earlier.

Propaganda - From a source regarded as credible, a timely or topically, cleverly-worded, and emotively-based, one-sided message directed at receivers who are part of or under the influence of a group of anonymous people who feel powerful because of their anonymity, who have common interests, who may seem to lack formal organization, and who may experience behavioral contagion and perform instinctual behaviors as a result. The message must contain a theme grounded in basic social ideology or on societal values and that is also expressed in other media to which we will attend by our own choosing. The sender of the message can be an organization with a formal action agenda (cosmic organization) or an unorganized, informal, group which coalesces around an issue, "flash mob-style," and organically and instinctively develops a consensus toward action (chaotic organization).

Also by way of summary and for your convenience, I have included below Table 7-1, Seven Principles of Propaganda.

Table 7-1, Seven Principles of Propaganda

Principle	Explanation
1. Person & People	Address the individual and the masses simultaneously.
2. Totality	Receipt of one consistent message, which is often self-induced via "propaganda by choice."
3. Organizational Unit	Cosmic and chaotic forces flow to form and modify a propaganda message.
4. Goal Orientation	An orthopractic outcome is sought from propaganda.
5. Societal Basics	Fundamental beliefs supporting society; contains the four sociological presuppositions and four myths (values) supporting daily life.
6. Temporal Focus	A thematic concentration on current events attracts attention to the propaganda.
7. Veracity	Untruth within propaganda will undermine its effect; innuendo and conjecture do best.

We've now discussed the foundational basis for the success of the insidious competitors' tools. Whew! I'm glad that's done.

Let's now move on to the discussion of the four tools through which insidious competitors leverage the principles of propaganda.

Take-Aways from Chapter Seven – The Principles of Propaganda

1. The tools of the insidious competitor apply the principles of propaganda.
2. The Four Tools of the Insidious Competitor, supported by the principles of propaganda, are directed at the solipsistic and epistemological process (the system of knowing), that define the meaning of The Ephemeral Image.
3. The tools are Mutant Conversation, Social Engineering, Hip Chat, and Snark.
4. To combat insidious competition successfully we must understand not only the tools but also the principles that drive their success.
5. There are Seven Principles for Successful Propaganda which relate to social media. For success, all or some must be exploited by the tools of the insidious competitor.

Chapter Eight:
The Four Tools of the Insidious Competitor

As we discussed in the last chapter, the principles of propaganda are applied in social media via the insidious competitor's tools. It's those tools which we will examine in detail here in this chapter.

If you are starting this chapter without having read the preceding chapter about the principles of propaganda, I would suggest that you please read the preceding chapter first so you can get the most out of this present chapter. If you are starting this present chapter after having read the preceding chapter a while ago, it might be helpful to at least review the Propaganda Summarization which appears near the end of the preceding chapter. Because the Four Tools of the Insidious Competitor rely heavily on the principles of propaganda, having that definition of propaganda fresh in your mind will increase your enjoyment and understanding of what we're about to discuss.

The Four Tools of the Insidious Competitor, while not many in number, can achieve powerful effect when they are grounded in one or more of the Seven Principles for Successful Propaganda. As we learn about each tool, I'll point out how each tool uses one or more of the principles of propaganda. Remember the Four Tools of the Insidious Competitor – Mutant Conversations, Social Engineering, Hip Chat, and Snark? In the last chapter, we agreed that whether or not ***all*** insidious competitors are fully aware that these tools are grounded in the principles of propaganda or not, the fact remains that they are. And these tools, easily deployed within social media, are being used in the *insidiously competitive battle for the meaning of your company's corporate image.*

So, now in our effort to become better insidious competition warriors, let's go understand these tools.

Mutant Conversations

Okay. I want you to think back to high school. Think back to the conversations that took place during those tender years. Some you were a part of and others you weren't a part of. But of the ones you were privy to, you'd often find out that "reality" was usually "distorted" somewhere along the line of the conversation. So-and-so was or was not dating who else. This guy liked that girl and said such and so to her during whatever. No, that's not right. He's not dating her and he didn't say this he said that. Or did he say the other?

We all know this "telephone" game. When the truth starts out in a series of conversations to be one thing, and then at the end of conversational chain the truth turns out to be something else. Why does this happen? Solipsism and epistemology? Yes. But, right now I want to take you deeper into the system of knowing.

For right now I want you to keep your mind back in high school. But this time, I want you to think back to when you took biology class. Not the kind of biology class that is sometimes held under the bleachers in high school. Nope. I want you to think about the biology class that took place in an actual classroom; the biology class that was sanctioned by your local board of education. Think about what the teacher droned on and on about concerning DNA and adaptation. Why? Because, the same principle is at work within a conversation.

Conversational DNA and Mutations

Recall the quote from Margaret Wheatley that appeared earlier in this book. She was talking about how the forces of nature extend down through decreasingly smaller systems: "If nature uses certain principles to create her infinite diversity, it is highly probable that those principles apply to human organizations." [67] Systems of Mother Nature scale down and scale up. It's because of that whole fractal thing.[68] The larger forces of nature to which Margaret alluded scale down to apply to not only human organizations but also scale down further, all the way down to one of the processes that greases the wheels of human organizations, communication in the form of conversation.

The only certainty in life is that there will be change. Just as DNA evolves to transform living organisms, helping them adapt to their environment, so does conversation. And as we know from the conversational chain in high school, as well as from the biology class lessons that we took in high school so many years ago, that DNA adaptation affects other DNA and so on in a chain of events we call evolution. As organisms evolve, they form and/or modify the environment in which they live and that environment impacts other organisms around them. Likewise with conversation.

Conversations modify the overall environment which affects the conversations that follow those that modified the environment originally. It's a spherical and dynamic process. Remember that the only certainty is that there is change. Conversational content, or its makeup which I'll call "conversational DNA," evolves based upon the influences of its environment and the conversational DNA that preceded it. Just as biological DNA adapts so does conversational DNA. And as biological DNA evolves along a particular path, so does conversational DNA. But conversational DNA, as does biological DNA, sometimes changes or departs from the natural course it would have taken had there been no external influences. The reasons these external influences exist are many, and those reasons can be based in human intention or those reasons may be purely accidental, random, natural, and organic. When these external influences cause a gradual change, the effect is called a "variation," but when these influences cause an abrupt or sudden change, the effect is called a "mutation." Just as biological DNA can change abruptly, so can conversational DNA.

The conversations appearing now within social media, a virtual world, modify each other, just as conversations do in the physical world. The modifying, evolving, mutating forces of nature extend from the physical world right smack dab into the virtual. Yet, in the virtual world of social media the conversations are modified in a way that is different from that which takes place in the physical world. Why again? Because in social media there aren't the "checks and balances" that occur within normal conversation in the physical world. Checks and balances such as facial expressions, body language, or tone of voice augment what is being said, so that the receiver may use those cues to help put the verbal communication and its conversational DNA in context, identifying and verifying the sources, evaluating the sincerity of the source, or even the veracity of the information imparted. These visual cues mitigate the random effects on conversational evolution, helping to keep the mutations in check through the extra information that is included in the physical or vocal cues. In the real world, conversational DNA is fully configured. Well, at least as fully configured as it can be.

But this type of fully configured communication doesn't appear in social media. In social media, there are no physical cues, no kinesics, no body language, no tone of voice from which to interpret further the message laid down daily in social media. Because of this, within social media there are holes in the conversational DNA. What results, I believe, is an alternate process in the way that we as a society perceive the words, and even the pictures, used within social media. That alternate process, involving a difference in perception, is intended subconsciously to fill in for the lack of the extra information provided by the voice, hands, eyes, lips, and brow, when conversational DNA is fully configured. That difference in perception tries to fill in the holes of the conversational DNA. And that difference in perception causes a departure from the conversational path which would have been taken had that conversation been more fully configured and taken place within the physical realm. This perceptual difference takes place quickly. And this perceptual "quick change" creates mutations in the subsequent conversational DNA causing certain elements of the conversational DNA to be deleted or altered, thus *changing the meaning, or knowledge,* that was originally intended to be gained from the conversation. Remember. This is solipsism and epistemology, again. Experience. Perception. Knowledge. Errors quickly mutate within social media conversation, affecting the progress of the intended conversational DNA.

So, what I'm explaining here is damage to the integrity of the solipsistic and epistemological process, the system of knowing.

Mutants are difficult to understand. Even their existence challenges comprehension. Conversational mutations in social media can leave some participants behind, unable to comprehend adequately the meaning of the conversation in which they are participating. On the social web, where you would think "effective communication" would be vitally necessary, mutations lead to ineffective communication, the opposite of effective communication. Effective communication. What is that?

When I was an undergraduate majoring in communication, my professors told me that "there is no such thing as effective communication." Back then, I didn't really believe them. "How could this be?" I thought naively. Their very statement said that there was NEVER to be any effective communication. But hold on a minute. Isn't their statement in itself paradoxical in that if there is no such thing as effective communication, then how could they effectively tell me that there was no such thing as effective communication? Perhaps that is why I did not believe them at first. But as I've lived through several decades since that time, I now am perfectly aware of what they meant. The experience, perception, knowledge process is the best teacher.

Face it. There is no such thing as "effective" communication. Conversational mutations exist even in the physical world. Sometimes people will say things to us and our reaction will be that we look at them, as I mentioned before, "like they are from Mars." We just don't understand them sometimes. In the hope that my "conversation" with you is not currently mutating, what I'm saying here is that *conversational mutations exist to a far greater extent within the virtual, online world.* The conversational DNA of the virtual world is just not as fully configured as that in the physical world. The mutations that result within social media yield ineffective communication even more so than in the real world. You thought it was bad back in the halls of high school, in the physical world, where conversations were subject to the "telephone" game and to progressive and iterative interpretation? It can be even worse in the digital world. That handicapped iterative interpretation, based on holes in the social media conversational DNA, happens in a flash. Misunderstanding and inaccuracy flourish in social media. Because of the mutation probabilities that exist in the virtual world of social media, the solipsistic and epistemological process is more susceptible to disintegration than in the physical world.

And the danger to business presented by these "naturally-occurring" conversational mutations in social media, or worse yet, the "intentional" conversational mutations, is much, much greater than that you were susceptible to in those high school conversations. This is especially so when we consider all the ideas we have been learning about. Social media, remember, supports crowd behavior that can make individuals feel powerful. They can manufacture behavioral contagion, causing those powerful-feeling individuals to perform instinctual behaviors, which the individuals believe will be in support of group interests. And don't forget number five from our list of the

Five Factors of Insidious Competition – disdain. Consider all these things along with mutant conversation and what a meaning mess there indeed can be. "Reality" doesn't seem to stand much of a chance. Consider also the idea that social media enables individuals, who may think their voice doesn't count in the real world, to find their voice in the virtual world.

The Found Voice

We're all insecure to some degree. Many people think that they have "no voice" in the world. Imagine what happens when people who think they have no voice suddenly get one. And imagine what will happen to those people who suddenly get a voice when they encounter the mistakes, misunderstandings, and "half-truths" created by the mutated conversations that can occur in social media.

Having observed, and unfortunately participated in, the frailties and the imperfections of the human condition for several decades, I've *experienced* and *perceived*, and yes therefore have *knowledge*, that people "pile on" to a mistake, even a small one, once they have a voice. Piling on like football players on a fumble in a 2-point Super Bowl with less than a minute to go. Can you see how those who may have felt that they didn't have a voice, and suddenly find one through social media, might become "piler-oners" themselves? And they do this perhaps more easily than even they realize themselves.

Now, because of the "powerful feeling," given to them by the crowd in social media, they perform instinctual behaviors that they believe will be in support of the group. I hope you can see the inherent potential danger to the business world and to your company's *corporate image*. Consider that that potential danger is driven by, among other things we have discussed, the number of people who feel they are "without a voice" (of which there are many), social media, the Five Factors, and mutant conversation as a tool. Do you see how much of a threat this situation can be to a business? Mutant Conversation, as a tool, is set to *re-package reality* and *change meaning*, with all the potential negatives to the corporate image that may result. And all with a few easy keystrokes.

Doesn't your company work to define its own image? Isn't having and maintaining a meaningful, untarnished image of vital importance to your company's success and to the personal success of its employees? Does your company sit by and let its traditional competitors tarnish or redefine that image for the worse? Of course not.

So why would any company want to risk having its ephemeral image become the indiscriminate roadkill of casual, chaotic, piler-oners, influenced by the Five Factors of Insidious Competition? Worse yet, why would any company want to risk becoming the "hard target" of any cosmically organized, non-traditional and insidious competitor who recognizes and understands that the natural forces of Mutant Conversation are available to do their dirty work. Think it isn't happening right now in social media today? If you do, you are mistaken.

Employing the Principles of Propaganda via Mutant Conversation

Using the tool of Mutant Conversation is similar to the paper boy or paper girl deciding to use gravity as a tool when he or she chucks your daily edition onto your front step, driveway, or more likely into your bushes. Indeed today, this "bush delivery" probably happens less frequently. Not because the paper deliverer has gotten a better aim, but because, as we discussed earlier, subscribers to newspapers are a vanishing breed. By recognizing the availability of a force of nature that can be used as a tool, the paper deliverer reaches his or her goal. If it was not for the availability of the force of gravity, when the paper deliverer threw the paper, the paper would just continue in a straight trajectory into infinity, and probably through a window. The paper would not arc downward with gravity and land with a soft plop on the targeted, or woefully untargeted, destination.

In this same way, Mutant Conversation is a force of nature, human nature to be precise. And that force, like the Five Factors, is lying within social media, available and ready for use by the non-traditional, insidious competitor.

In other words, in using Mutant Conversation, this new type of competitor, the insidious competitor, like the paper deliverer, employs an existing force of nature as a tool and may guide and/or modify it for his or her own purposes. The paper deliverer doesn't necessarily think, "Hey. I'm going to go out and use gravity as the tool to accomplish my work today." Neither does the insidious competitor necessarily think they are going to go out and use Mutant Conversation on the social web. Both the deliverer and the insidious competitor know that the natural forces are there to be used to their advantage. The newspaper deliverer, wittingly or unwittingly, counts on the paper to be pulled toward the Earth. The insidious competitor, wittingly or unwittingly, counts on certain elements to be deleted from the conversational DNA, leaving only the elements that give a one-sided argument and that shade the truth, as we discussed in the Veracity section of the propaganda chapter previous.

The insidious competitor knows that the social media audience will be influenced by the principles of propaganda such as the Societal Basics and Temporal Focus. The insidious competitor knows that social media audiences will concentrate on the Societal Basics of youth, nation, work, and hero and includes those elements in their conversations. The insidious competitor knows that the social media audience will tend to concentrate on a Temporal Focus biased toward the present and slants their conversation toward that temporality. The insidious competitor knows that the social media audience will delete from the social media conversation the conversational DNA elements that don't correlate to these principles. How do they know these things? Solipsism and epistemology explain how. Just as the paper deliverer has experienced, perceived, and come to know that gravity will help him or her, so does the insidious competitor know the ways of Mutant Conversation. From experience, perception, and into knowledge.

Additionally, an insidious competitor will come to learn, wittingly or not, that using emotional language will benefit his work. That emotive language, as we discussed in the Veracity section of the propaganda chapter previous, can help put a "positive coloration" on the propaganda message. That emotive language can tend to be "dramatic." And from our previous discussion about drama in Chapter Six, we know that humans will attend to the drama. The social media audience will tend to concentrate on those emotional elements, the drama, deleting those conversational elements which are not emotional or dramatic.

So through Mutant Conversation, the insidious competitor, via mutated conversational DNA, modifies the social media environment with your *corporate image* as its subject. And, as I pointed out in the beginning of this section, just as physical DNA modifies its environment and that environment in return modifies the physical DNA, so does the social media environment modify the conversational DNA, back and forth, mutating the meaning of your *corporate image* in a dynamic and spherical process.

And in all of this, the solipsistic and epistemological process, that system of knowing, with particular attention to the perception step, on which we have come to rely for "truth," is detoured off of its natural course, allowing the truly insidious competitor to achieve his or her objective like the Sunday morning paper plopping on your doorstep.

Social Engineering

Just what is Social Engineering? You've probably heard the term before but never really paid attention to what it means. Is Social Engineering that process the federal government performs when it tries to redistribute money from the wealthy to the less-than-wealthy? Well, yes. That is one definition of social engineering. But in *Insidious Competition* we're not going to be discussing that type of social engineering which some believe does, in effect, *insidiously compete* with the growth of wealth and the economic progress of the nation. Let's save that discussion for a different book. In *Insidious Competition – The Battle for Meaning and the Corporate Image*, we're going to be discussing Social Engineering from within the context of how it has been traditionally used in the computer-based environment of "yesterday" and how it can be used in the Internet-based environment of social media "today" – and all of this with an eye on how social engineering can impact the *corporate image*.

In the book, *Secrets & Lies*, Bruce Schneier, a computer crypto-analyst and security expert, defines Social Engineering as "the hacker term for a con game; persuade the other person to do what you want . . . Social Engineering bypasses cryptography, computer security, network security, and everything else technological. It goes straight to the weakest link in any security system; the poor human trying to get his job done, and wanting to help out if he can."[69] In a nutshell, Social Engineering is about an attacker conning someone into letting them get into a computer system in which the attacker has no business being. And without breaking-in. In Social Engineering, the attacker goes in covertly via the attainment of the proper entry passwords, even though the attacker has no right to those passwords. In Social Engineering, the attacker has obtained the passwords by convincing people, helpful people, to reveal user names and passwords to computer accounts under the guise of "helping" the attacker. Seems weird? Let me explain a bit further.

Generally speaking, the way this is done is that the attacker poses, usually over the phone, as a fellow employee of the "attackee" or as a representative of a company with which the attackee or the attackee's employer does business.

Prior to the actual attempt to gain the necessary user names and passwords the attacker has done a great deal of research, some of it legal - some of it, well maybe not so much legal, to gain background information that will convince the attackee that the attacker is who he or she claims to be. That corroborating information also helps convince the attackee that the attacker actually needs the user name and password to complete a task defined to be important by the attacker. The social engineer preys on the weakest part of the computer system. The human desire to be helpful to a fellow employee or business associate.

You might think that this process of conning someone into revealing a user name and password sounds hard to believe and far-fetched. It isn't. To describe detailed incidents of Social Engineering is beyond the scope of this book. If you would like specific examples of this kind of Social Engineering, I refer you to the book *The Art of Deception* by Kevin Mitnick [70] which is filled with illustrations of how this can be done, should you be inclined to learn more.

Social Engineering has been around for a long time. It's not something that has popped up along with social media. The concept underlying Social Engineering for use as a tool by insidious competition was lying in wait, like a seventeen year locust in the ground, ready to jump at the chance to be applied to the freewheeling environment and fresh green crops of social media. The original intent of Social Engineering was to gain access to a computer system so that information could be obtained and retrieved wrongfully. The social engineer of yesterday wanted to gain those user names and passwords for a one time attack.

But the way Social Engineering has traditionally been applied in computer-based environments is not exactly how social engineering techniques are being applied in social media. Because in social media, it's not so much using Social Engineering to get into a social site, grab some info, and then leave without a trace. Although I suppose Social Engineering could be applied to social media in that traditional way. No. In Social Engineering's application to social media, it is much more about the "social" aspect. Social media Social Engineering is about gaining access to a targeted person's or persons' network(s) and creating conversations that can be used to change meanings. Social Engineering in social media exploits the human's desire to be social, our craving for interaction, as we've previously discussed. In social media, Social

Engineering is actually focused on the engineering of new social relationships from which *new expressions of meaning* may emerge. This is truly **social** engineering. Its application is so much more rich than the hit-and-run Social Engineering scenario of yesteryear.

The procedure of the social engineer within social media is to pretend to be someone else, someone who is known to or wants to be known by the target, in order for the engineer to gain access to the targeted person's social circle. Then over time: 1) the social engineer observes the online social behavior of the target; and then learning from that behavior, 2) the social engineer, with attention to the principles of propaganda, distributes information within the target's social network that *changes meanings* significant to the target or the members of that target's network. Or in terms of the system of knowledge, they change the perception step in the solipsistic and epistemological process.

The real objective of the social engineer is to further his or her (or his or her organization's) agenda. How he or she does this is by modifying the solipsistic and epistemological process, to get the target, or the network, to further his or her agenda. And with modification of the solipsistic and epistemological process (i.e., the system of knowing) comes modification to experience and perception and therefore *knowledge*. Here it is again, *repackaged reality* and *changed meaning*. Do you think that might include your *corporate image*? I do.

As you can see, using Social Engineering within social media is quite different than the way Social Engineering was previously applied. Social Engineering techniques can obviously thrive in an environment where social media users can be, and quite often are, less discriminating in accepting "friendships" than they are in real life. That looser, less discriminating, nature of accepting friendships is fostered by the "open and friendly" nature of social media itself, where individuals are supposed to help others and meet others, and accept at face value that all humans are good, one of the four sociological suppositions of a principle of propaganda, Societal Basics, which we explored earlier. This belief is reinforced by the masses within social media; it becomes expected that you'll accept friend requests, almost indiscriminately. Such is the psychological terrain of the social media environment, one that through Societal Basics can support propaganda and it is just waiting to be exploited by the social media social engineer.

Do you think you or your business doesn't need to worry about this?

Well, the European Union is worried. Perhaps you should be as well. The European Network and Information Security Agency (ENISA), an arm of the government of the European Union, published a report outlining many of the threats that present themselves in the use of social networks. Among many of the threats they discussed were the applications of Social Engineering within social networks, a part of the overall social web. And why do Social Engineering threats, not just those ENISA pointed to but social engineering threats in general, succeed? Not just because we assume that all humans are good, but simply because we are human.

As ENISA put it, "Sociologically, the natural human desire to connect with others, combined with the multiplying effects of Social Network technology, can make users less discriminating in accepting 'friend requests.' "[71] In other words, we like to be liked. We love to be liked. We've got to do what we must to stay out of "the chair." And one way to reinforce the fact that we are liked, either to others and/or to ourselves, is to increase the number of "friends" displayed within the various social network profile pages that seemingly define our online lives. Flaunting our likability will indeed probably make us more liked or desired by others. It's a self-fulfilling process that just keeps rolling on. Accumulating a significant amount of social network friends is more easily accomplished on the social web than in real life. Would-be friends are out there and waiting on the social web. The temptation to grab as many as possible is there, but succumbing to that temptation means being a bit less discriminating than we normally would be in real life. Less discrimination in friendships brings with it an increase in the number of threats to which we are exposed.

ENISA lists many threats that can be experienced within social networks and which would be attributable to the tool of Social Engineering, in particular. In its report, ENISA concentrates only on threats from and within social networks and not the social web in general. Specifically they list 15 threats within the following four categories: Privacy Related Threats, Variants of Traditional Network and Information Security Threats, Identity Related Threats, and Social Threats. Almost all of the many threats they discuss within the four categories are technical in nature or are related to more traditional network infrastructure and hardware security issues. What we are discussing here in *Insidious Competition,* however, is not threats that are of a technical nature, not those whose objective is to break into a network for the purpose of stealing information. No, in this book we are concerned with the more insidious threat of the type that can change meaning. And to put that in a business context, this book is concerned with the type of threat that *repackages reality* and *changes the meaning* of a conversation, and how that *changed conversation* can affect the *corporate image.* So for purposes of our discussion we will concentrate on the ENISA category which concerns those types of threats. That category is Identity Related Threats and as outlined by ENISA they refer to:

- Infiltration of Networks Leading to Information Leakage
- Profile Squatting and Reputation Slander via ID Theft

These are threats that may be implemented via the insidiously competitive tool of Social Engineering. Let's discuss these Social Engineering threats individually, placing them within the context of modern Social Engineering used as a tool by insidious competition and within the context of how the principles of propaganda can be applied through this tool.

Employing the Principles of Propaganda via Social Engineering

- Infiltration of Networks Leading to Information Leakage

To infiltrate a social network means that, as a first step, a friend request must be sent by the social media social engineer. Attention to propaganda principles must be paid here because the sending of the friend request can be considered a propaganda message in itself, and once the request is accepted the friendship can be used to send further propaganda messages. So it's critical that the friend request is built around some of the principles of propaganda.

As most readers may already know, information within a social network is only available to a member's friends, or followers, or a similarly named group of significant persons. If you've had experience within a social network you know this and, just as ENISA mentioned in their report, you know that it can be and is fairly easy to become someone's "friend" under false pretenses. Simply pick a name and an identity and create a profile. You'll get "friends." And let me emphasize that at least one of the reasons you'll get friends is founded on one of the four sociological presuppositions on which propaganda is based. Remember the principle of Societal Basics that I mentioned about six paragraphs ago? That principle highlights the belief that all humans are good. People don't generally think that a friend request is not from the person shown to be sending it. The social engineer knows this supporting principle of propaganda exists and uses it as a message foundation to gain friends under someone else's name. Demonstrating this theory, the ENISA report cites an experiment performed by an antivirus software company.[72]

The software company chose a social network and created a profile named "Freddi Staur," which is an anagram for "ID Fraudster." The profile page was built around this identity, which was in reality just a green plastic frog. The profile contained only a small amount of personal information. The software company then sent out 200 friend requests to test the response level of its request and more importantly what kind of information could be retrieved through the accepted responses. Here are the results of the friend requests:

- 87 of the 200 users who were contacted (43.5%) responded to Freddi, with 82 leaking personal information (41%)
- 72% of the respondents divulged one or more e-mail addresses
- 84% of the respondents listed their full date of birth (you may not think this to be so bad, but your birth date is one of your "personal identifiers" – so think again) [73]

ENISA commented in their report that they believed this approach was "not very effective." What do you think? I suppose a response rate of less than half would not be considered "**very** effective." But I do consider it "**effective**." To determine its efficacy, let's put it within the context of the purposes of social media Social Engineering.

For a modern social engineer who is targeting certain business people, this approach, if it can be used as representative, gives the attacker almost a 50% chance of gaining access to the target's social network and securing personal, professional, or business information which can be developed and leveraged into further and more sophisticated social engineering attacks. Not bad for what would be a minimal amount of time and effort. The personal information can then be combined with other "research" on the target and used by the social engineer to build a more sophisticated false identity through which to engage the target in more detail, or the target's network friends, and further secure more complex and significant information. With that more complex and significant information comes increased opportunities to infiltrate other targeted networks from which other propaganda messages may be launched.

Here in the Freddi Staur example, the social media social engineer built their friend request message on the propaganda principle of a Societal Basic that all humans are good. So the receivers thought that the request must actually be from Freddi Staur. Also, here the engineer leveraged the human weakness of, as ENISA put it, "the natural human desire to connect with others." And in doing so, Freddi Staur gained entrance to and infiltrated 87 personal social networks.

Once entrance is gained, then the real damage to meaning can be done.

To explore this idea, let's move on to ENISA's other Identity Related Threat which is:

- Profile Squatting and Reputation Slander through ID Theft

Once the social network of a targeted person is infiltrated, the social media social engineer can use their position to "squat" on an assumed identity[74] and thereby covertly gain more complex and significant information about the target, their business, their "legitimate" friends, and the businesses of those legitimate friends. This increased knowledge affords the engineer increased "credibility" within the networks infiltrated. As we discussed in the Veracity section of the propaganda chapter, the credibility of the source is vital to creating successful propaganda messages. From this enhanced position of credibility, the social media social engineer can easily attack the integrity of the solipsistic and epistemological process by sending messages throughout the social networks in which the engineer is squatting. Those messages would be built on the principles of propaganda. Messages from a "credible" source, based on principles of propaganda such as the Societal Basics and Temporal Focus and targeted at your company, can change the *meaning* of your company's *corporate image.*

More specifically, how can this "social media ID theft" affect a company? To answer this question, let's discuss two different types of companies and two different types of networks.

First, let's look at consumer companies and "consumer" social networks. Perhaps a marketing manager of a particular consumer products company would infiltrate a personal network such as might be on one of the many personal social networks that exist on the social web, one with millions of users. Under a false ID that manager could insidiously spread rumors about his/her traditional competitor's products, casting aspersions, making innuendoes, and one-sided arguments, leveraging the propaganda principle of Veracity as we discussed in the propaganda chapter previously. Working from the findings of the Universal Mc Cann study already cited in this book, in social media we tend to trust strangers' opinions over advertising, especially in "regulated" social network environments. It might take time, but such an insidiously engineered operation could eventually do damage to the targeted company's corporate image, not to mention their sales, especially as social media grows even greater in popularity.

Second, a similar situation could arise with business-to-business companies and social networks reserved for business contacts only. Again, the social engineer, the profile squatter, the attacker, the insidious competitor, whichever term you care to use, could assume the profile of a targeted businessperson, inviting other businesspeople of interest to become "friends" and engage in business-related conversations for the hidden purpose of securing business and personal information. And all that information, which was given so freely, is now available to this insidious competitor, to use to his competitive advantage against a company, either within the infiltrated network or outside of it, damaging that company's corporate image in the process.

Do you know if your social networks are infiltrated?

Could it be that your company is targeted?

Snark

What is snark and how is it used as a tool of the *insidious competitor*?

A snark was originally an imaginary animal created by Lewis Carroll for his poem "The Hunting of the Snark." That's the definition that I received when I consulted my print copy of Webster's Dictionary. But that volume is a bit out of date, especially when we consider that this word has more modern usages. Since we're discussing a modern environment like social media, most certainly a more modern definition is demanded.

So, from the online dictionaries which I consulted (especially UrbanDictionary.com), I'll define snark as a combination, a portmanteau, of the words "snide" and "remark" yielding "snark," meaning snide remarks, biting or cruel humor or wit which is used to attack someone or something. On UrbanDictionary.com, most of the "votes" were "up" on these definitions; so we'll go with them. Thanks to all the hipsters out there.

But to get at more of how Snark is used by insidious competitors to impact your company's corporate image and how those competitors co-opt that image for their own use, let's go to a definition written by someone who has written an entire book about snark. Titled quite simply *Snark*, the book written by David Denby gives us an interesting look into what today's snark is and how it's used. David defines snark as "the bad kind of invective - low, teasing, snide, condescending, knowing." [75] David goes on to say about snark that it is like a "rug-pulling form of insult that attempts to steal someone's mojo, erase her cool, annihilate her effectiveness, and it appeals to a knowing audience that shares the contempt of the snarker." [76]

Employing the Principles of Propaganda via Snark

Have I just described anything that seems familiar? If you have spent much time on the social web, and if you haven't you probably would not be reading this book, this definition of snark describes well the type of discourse that's in social media. Snark is all over the social web. Just read a blog post that has more than about a dozen comments and you'll see snark employed somewhere around the fourth or fifth comment, maybe even sooner. As you read those comments, you'll notice people trying to outsnark each other as the conversation goes along. Snark is infectious and it's all over our culture. You might be thinking that this is just the way our society speaks today, sort of like the words "ye" and "thee" that the Pilgrims are supposed to have uttered when they came to Planet America centuries ago. You think, "It's just a style." No. It's more than just a style. It's a tool of insidious competition.

David makes an important point about snark, one which we can apply directly to our discussion of how it is used as a tool of insidious competition. He says that like political correctness (PC), snark "refuses true political engagement, the job of getting at the truth of things." [77] Then if that's true, I suppose we could say that snark is less about its style and more about its message which is the obfuscation of facts. And if snark is about the obfuscation of facts, if it's about innuendo, then it's a direct application of the shading of the truth, an integral part of the Veracity principle of propaganda as we discussed in the propaganda chapter.

But Snark's being used as a tool to spread propaganda is veiled. Snark's function in the obfuscation of facts is disguised because of its perceived "coolness" as a method of communication. Indeed, David discusses Cicero's theory of invective and makes the point that when there is an opponent to be destroyed, the telling of truths is less important than making the audience scorn the opponent.[78] This is a scorn that perhaps can be achieved via innuendo. Seems like snark would be perfectly applied in that pursuit.

Snark is considered cool, hip. Just listen to any late night comedian. They use that style liberally and with great effect. Listen to college students speak among themselves and you'll hear the same sly, knowing, condescending invective used by them in attempts to: 1) separate themselves from the mainstream; and, 2) declare to each other that they are all part of the same contemporary group. (Would that be an epistemic group?)

The characteristic of message hipness employs and applies the Temporal Focus principle of propaganda. The currentness, the fashionability, the up-to-the-minute status, the contemporariness, of the Snark tool in social media attracts eyeballs like a magnet does iron filings. And through the attraction causes readers to pay less or no attention to conversations that aren't using Snark. That style, and stealthy tool, then spreads and permeates the Internet, and the social web in particular, in conversations about everything imaginable. The snarky style attracts and carves out its own social class and in doing so does nothing to support a conversation that gets at the truth. As David says, the Internet causes snark to become meme [79] and once the meme is created its truthfulness or falsity becomes irrelevant. Could your company's *corporate image* changed by snark be one of those memes? The invective grows and invites others who recognize it, acting as a "secret handshake," forming a sort of "club" dedicated to denigrating whatever the topic of conversation might be. Your company's *corporate image*, perhaps? The topics and the memes get quoted and mashed and rehashed, leaving few to know or even care where the truth is. What does it matter? Reading such snippy "narrative" is fun! And especially so about "evil" corporations. Remember from earlier in this book. Never let the truth get in the way of a good story.

When the topic of that snarky conversation becomes your company image, the solipsistic and epistemological process that yields the knowledge about your corporate image becomes infected with a hip, and "enticing" innuendo. The "hipness" alone attracts social media users to *experience* the joys of snark. That attraction causes those social media users to have more disproportionate *experiences* with the solipsistic and epistemological process of the snarker's choice. Then, the resulting *knowledge through perception* is influenced by the slyness and invective of the snarky tone.

When your good corporate image meme gets mangled via Snark, even just a little bit, it doesn't bode well for your company or, by extension, you. That corporate image will be condescendingly, knowingly, slyly, snidely, teasingly lowered in effectiveness by a pervasive "style" of writing and speaking that can do nothing else but. And don't forget. As I mentioned previously, this is all done within the anonymous and free-wheeling atmosphere of social media where there is little to no connection to responsibility or to fear of liability.

Hip Chat

Once you understand Snark, it's easy to understand Hip Chat.

No, Hip Chat isn't the title of a TV talk show on which people discuss the pros and cons of hip replacement surgery. Although, that wouldn't be a bad title for such a program.

Hip Chat is on the obverse side of the coin on which Snark lives. Whereas Snark endeavors to carve out a social clique through the usage of cynical communication, Hip Chat endeavors to carve out a social clique through the use of idealistic or optimistic communication. Snark denigrates a target. Hip Chat extols a competing target.

Employing the Principles of Propaganda via Hip Chat

Hip Chat is much the same as Snark when it comes to the obfuscation of facts and innuendo. Hip Chat, like its cousin Snark, applies the Veracity principle of propaganda and makes innuendo or shades the truth via implication. But whereas Snark would directly denigrate your company's corporate image, Hip Chat extols other corporate images, and not the image of your corporation. So, if your company's corporate image is not praised by a hip chatter, if a hip chatter praises your company's direct, traditional competitor, then by *implication* the *meaning* of your company's *corporate image* is changed from what you would like it to be.

Hip Chat also positions the "chatter" himself (or herself), as positive. By not saying anything negative, the chatter appears to be of good personality, friendly, and approachable; a person that we would like to get to know.

Like Snark, Hip Chat is, well, hip. And its contemporary flair attracts eyeballs. Similar to Snark, in this way Hip Chat gets the reader to identify with a group, an epistemic group. The group experience that Hip Chat attracts then applies in conversation the daily values or the sociological presuppositions (i.e., Societal Basics) relevant to that group, a principle of successful propaganda. This attraction of this epistemic group is a control of the system of knowing, which creates through attraction more *experiences* than social media not containing Hip Chat, which changes perceptions, and then alters the meaning of the corporate image that was "ignored."

For example, users of Hip Chat attempt to attract supporters by saying how sophisticated and progressive they themselves are by drawing special attention to things that they do which illustrate that they are "with it." (This is that element of positive self-positioning mentioned above.) In using Hip Chat in reference to a targeted corporate image, the insidious competitor says little about the targeted corporate image (e.g., the corporate image of your company) and implies that other companies, perhaps your company's traditional competitors, are hip. We might see a situation where the insidious competitor, via Hip Chat, praises a direct competitor of yours for their corporate social responsibility efforts in sustainability, or labor reform, or climate change. This then leaves the reader to discern, by implication, that your company is "not doing those things" and is therefore "not with it" or is "uncool." The *meaning* of the *corporate image* of *your* company is then changed, by implication or by innuendo, from that which you would prefer, with little or nothing being said directly about it.

Snark attacks directly; Hip Chat attacks indirectly.

Take-Aways from Chapter Eight – The Four Tools of the Insidious Competitor

For the insidious competitor in social media, there are four tools with which the principles of propaganda are applied to the solipsistic and epistemological process of company image.

1. Mutant Conversation depends upon the intentional or natural changes in conversational DNA.
   a. Conversational DNA in social media is not as fully configured as it is in the physical world.
   b. Less fully configured conversational DNA in social media makes the solipsistic and epistemological process more susceptible to mutation than in the physical world.

2. Social Engineering is a tool used to create fraudulent social relationships within social media.
   a. The objective of Social Engineering within social media is to use false relationships to affect knowledge of a targeted company's image and change its meaning.

3. Snark is a portmanteau of the words "snide" and "remark." Snark is a low and teasing invective, seeking to insult someone or something.
   a. As a tool of the social media insidious competitor, the objective of Snark is to change the perception of the solipsistic and epistemological company image process.
   b. Snark achieves this objective by using the propaganda principle of Veracity, slipping innuendo and aspersion into the knowledge process; thereby distorting meaning.

4. Hip Chat is the opposite of Snark.
   a. Hip Chat implies that the target of the image change **is not** "cool" by saying, for example, that the target's direct and traditional competitor **is** "cool." Hip Chat does denigrate a target directly.

Section Three:
Attack Classes and Types of Insidious Competitors

Chapter Nine: Dangerous Days Are Trending Nearer
Chapter Ten: Classifications of Competitive Attacks
Chapter Eleven: The Reality Benders
Chapter Twelve: The Nasties
Chapter Thirteen: The Friendlies
Chapter Fourteen: The Digital Pirates

Chapter Nine:
Dangerous Days Are Trending Nearer

Now that we have discussed, from Chapter Six, the Nine Elements of Social Media Danger to the Corporate Image, and from Chapter Eight, the Tools of the Insidious Competitor through which they apply the principles of propaganda, we come here, to Chapter Nine, to start our discussion on the Attack Classes and Types of Insidious Competitors that are out there waiting to mangle the meaning of your company's corporate image.

Just as I said we needed an understanding of the Nine Elements so that we may better deal with insidious competitors, and just as we need an understanding of how they apply their tools, having knowledge of their methods and types of attack will greatly assist your ability to subdue, or even prevent, their offensive.

Before we go on to discuss the Attack Classes and the Types of Insidious Competitors, I would like to discuss quickly just one more thing that I see as aiding the insidious competitor.

Early in Chapter Seven, I quoted The Mackenzie Institute as saying, "As the Internet continues to grow and expand, it may be the ultimate antidote to propaganda. Let's make sure the whole world becomes plugged in." Relative to that quote I said that I understood what they meant, that it sounded all warm and fuzzy, but that I couldn't disagree more, and that I would return to this point later.

I have returned.

The idea of an entirely plugged-in social world mitigating or eliminating propaganda, as proposed by The Mackenzie Institute and many others, presents great opportunity. Through the "democratization" of information that the Internet enables, doesn't it seem reasonable to assume that the "truth" will naturally surface? Maybe. However, as in the Chapter Four quote from Michael Strangelove who pointed out that the Internet weakens the "hegemonic construction of reality," an entirely plugged-in world can be susceptible to the insidious spread of *meaning change against truth* rather than in the *support of truth.* How are we to believe that, just because every individual on the planet is "now plugged in," somehow all conversations will be for the good? And just what does "good" mean anyway? Isn't "good" subjective and dependent on your experience, perception, and knowledge process? Can't there be more than one version of "good?" Of course, there can. That is what our whole discussion on the repackaging of reality centered on.

It is the opportunity for *meaning change against "truth,"* on a global scale, the weakening of the "hegemonic construction of reality," that presents unprecedented dangers to companies everywhere, from Singapore to Seattle and from London to Lima and back again. And unfortunately for companies, preserving their corporate image, which is vital to their bottom line, gets harder, much harder in the entirely "transparent" world of the Internet where *repackaged reality* and *meaning change* can occur and endure, continuously.

From what we have discussed so far in *Insidious Competition*, you can see that having a worldwide forum presents opportunities to sway not only political opinion but commercial opinion as well. Face it. When you come down to the essence of what makes each tick, there isn't much difference between business and politics; one receives ballots while the other receives "economic votes." With a global forum literally at our fingertips, individuals will be able to broadly and globally influence others. And they can do so either overtly, or covertly, with their own agenda (or their organization's agenda) in mind. There is a basic concept at the root of marketing. That basic concept is that there should be a connection between a business and the minds of its customers. This is the true principle of marketing. This concept is what all those social media in business books espouse; that individuals should be "heard" by the companies that serve them, so that consumer needs and wants may be more accurately fulfilled. Using social media presents a perfect marketing opportunity for companies. Social media give companies the opportunity to listen and speak with customers on a more "personal" level and in a two-way conversation. But with opportunities also come threats; they are two sides of the same coin. *Insidious Competition* is not about the opportunities. There are plenty of books that discuss the marketing opportunities within social media, without giving much or any attention to the threats lying therein. *Insidious Competition* is about the threats.

While having an entirely plugged-in world, as suggested by The Mackenzie Institute, magnifies opportunities, we're here to discuss the opportunity for magnified business threats, read that as *meaning change* and *corporate image redefinition*, either through cosmically or chaotically organized efforts making full use of the Seven Principles for Successful Propaganda in the ways outlined in this book.

Remember that in Chapter Seven I asked you to think differently about propaganda? I asked you not to think of propaganda as either a negative or a positive – just simply as a set of principles which influence the solipsistic and epistemological process. While I still want you to think of propaganda in that way, as a means to an end, as we get ready to enter the next chapter I want you to think now about something that is core to the survival of every business – *competition*. I want you to remember that, in the game of business, competition exists. In the game of business, your job is to "win." And to win, you have to prepare for, defend against, react to, and out-strategize your competition.

You probably know a lot about your current "traditional" competitors. But how much do you know about competitors of a different class – the type who are just waiting to take your company down. Some of them don't even realize it yet. Some of them have an agenda (the "cosmics") while others do not (the "chaotics"). Some of the chaotics crowd are simply waiting for an agenda that tickles their fancy to come along so they can have some fun. (AEFAP, pronounced A - FAP, Any Excuse For A Party) Those with the agenda are only too happy to pick up those agenda-less, would-be supporters and roll them into their agendized effort to mess with your company's corporate image.

Why do they want to do it? The list of reasons could be as long as all of the arms in the world put together. Honest belief in a cause. A tilted sense of reality. Improper potty training. A perceived cheat or snub by a company. Personal insecurity. Legitimate gripes about products or services. Dissatisfaction with personal finances. Religious fanaticism. A lack of personal responsibility. Ad infinitum. The point here is that now all of them have a platform, a worldwide platform, from which to speak and organize.

So now, let's continue our understanding of the insidious competitor so that we may deal with them more effectively. Toward that goal, we are going to look at the various attack classes of insidious competitors. After that, we'll delve into the several types of insidious competitors.

Take-Aways from Chapter Nine – Dangerous Days Are Trending Nearer

Just one.

We're headed for an entirely "plugged-in" world. And your company's corporate image is at the mercy of the *repackaged reality* and *meaning change* – on a global scale - that come from such a world.

Chapter Ten:
Classifications of Competitive Attacks

Here in Chapter Ten, I will classify the different types of competitive attacks on your company that can take place from within social media. In this chapter, we'll see the terms of "competitor" and "attacker" used interchangeably. Knowledge of these classifications and an ability to classify the different types of attacks which your company might experience, can help you later identify the countermeasures or preventive measures that can be applied against the attack. I apply these "type classifications" to both the "type of attack" and the "type of attacker."

Cosmic Attacks & Chaotic Attacks

Back in Chapter Seven, in discussing the Organizational Unit principle of propaganda, I introduced the concepts of cosmos and chaos into our discussion of insidious competition. I said that insidious competitors could be organized formally (cosmic) or that insidious competitors could be organized informally, created by emotional reactions to human instincts (chaotic). Understanding the nature of the insidious competitor's organization can contribute greatly to your strategy creation on how they may be countered.

The next pair of classifications describes the objective of either the cosmic or chaotic attackers' attack.

Semantic Attacks & Cognitive Attacks

There has been a lot of discussion, in both the academic computer science literature and the popular computer science literature, about semantic attacks and cognitive attacks. From a review of sources from both of these types of literature, essentially, I see cognitive attacks as a subset of semantic attacks. Let me explain with interpretations from the academic literature which I believe sum up many of the theories I've seen scattered across all of the literature I've reviewed for this book.

Semantic attacks have as their objective the *changing of meaning* and can be subjective in their definition, whereas cognitive attacks are more functional in nature and can be objectively defined. Cognitive attacks are aimed at individual gatherers of knowledge, who for purposes of this book and for the sake of simplicity we will call "computer users." Cognitive attacks have a specific objective, the changing of a computer user's resulting behaviors based on a change in the knowledge acquired.[80] Very interesting. Remember that here in *Insidious Competition*, no good thought goes stale. So, then let's think about this a bit more.

The above definitions for semantic and cognitive attacks, which are from the team of Cybenko/Giani/Heckman/Thompson of Dartmouth College, touch on some of the concepts which we have already explored in this book. But first, before we go back to those concepts, for an enhanced understanding let's quickly return to the dictionary. (You knew I was going to do that, didn't you?) Semantic and cognitive.

semantic - adj. - *of or pertaining to meaning, esp. meaning in language*
cognitive - adj. - *relating to the result of the process of knowing*

That process of knowing, which we saw earlier is:

Experience >>> Perception >>> Knowledge

The semantic element in this process pertains to what "knowledge" or "meaning" comes out to be, the end product of the effects of the experiences and perceptions, the solipsistic and epistemological process we've been discussing for some time now. The semantic attack would only be concerned with affecting knowledge or meaning and, in order to do so, would concentrate only on changing or impacting experiences and perceptions. The cognitive attack is orthopractic, a major element in the Goal Orientation principle of propaganda as we saw back in Chapter Seven. The cognitive attack is concerned with what behavioral changes occur after the knowledge or meaning has been "adjusted." So whereas a semantic attack may have a non-specific objective, not aimed at any particular type of behavioral change, and would concentrate solely on changing experiences and perceptions without attention to what degree those changes would affect knowledge or meaning, a cognitive attack is very specific. The cognitive attack wants behavioral change; it wants an orthopraxy for a perceived "wrong" and a furthering of the attacker's agenda. The cognitive attack needs to attend very carefully to the changing of the *experiences* and *perceptions* so that the desired *change in knowledge or meaning* will create the targeted, orthopractic change in behavior. In other words, for purposes of comparison only and not description, we could say that a semantic attack is "play" whereas a cognitive attack is "work."

According to Cybenko/Giani/Thompson, we can break down this classification even further. Concentrating only on cognitive attacks, there are two types of cognitive attacks, or cognitive hacking as it is also called. Those two types are overt and covert. An **overt** cognitive attack consists of hacking, or breaking, into a web or social site and intentionally defacing information. The defacement is often intended to be a spoof of the original information and there is no attempt to disguise the attack. Such work is often done by persons known as "hacktivists," which is a portmanteau of the words "hacker" and "activist," and its reason is often related to a social or political cause.[81] I believe this is one way to define an overt cognitive attack, but for insidious competition I don't feel that a break-in or a defacement is actually a necessary condition to define this classification. I think an overt cognitive attack could include a break-in but, for our purposes in this book, should also be applied to any identifiable act taking place within social media where there is an obvious effort to *change the meaning* of an ephemeral corporate image and, by doing so, change the behaviors of people (an orthopraxy) who *experience* and *perceive* this "changed image." Does this sound far-fetched to you? Activists and non-governmental organizations (NGOs) do this daily. Successful cognitive attacks employ some or depend on all of the Seven Principles for Successful Propaganda which we discussed back there in Chapter Seven.

Again according to Cybenko/Giani/Thompson, **covert** cognitive attacks may consist of a break-in followed by the subtle manipulation of information in order to influence perception differently than that of the original information's intent. In a covert attack, a key to its success is disguise.[82] I believe that this is one way to define the covert cognitive attack, but not the only way to define this classification. For our purposes here, I feel that break-ins may or may not be present within this classification. What really defines this classification is that there is an *unidentifiable* effort to *change the behaviors of people* by *changing the meanings* of the information they access.

Indeed, the type of covert cognitive attack in which we would be most interested for the study of insidious competition would be those with no break-in, raising the importance of the criterion of "subtlety" in the definition of the word *insidious*. This subtlety would go to support source credibility, an element of the Veracity principle of propaganda. An example of a covert cognitive attack with no break-in would occur through the use of various social media tools [83] requiring no unauthorized access perpetrated either through an actual or anonymous screen name. Very much like the type of "average" conversations we see going on every day within the social web. In this type of attack, the watchword for the insidious competitor would be "subtlety," rather than "stealth."

Now, for ease of understanding on how insidious competitors can impact the ephemeral image, let's look at Table 10-1, Classes of Attack or Attackers, which I have included below to summarize the definitions for each of the classifications we've just discussed.

Table 10-1, Classes of Attack or Attackers

	Cosmic	**Chaotic**
Semantic	An organized effort to change meaning.	An unorganized effort to change meaning.
Cognitive Covert	An organized and unidentifiable effort to change behavior by changing meaning.	An unorganized and unidentifiable effort to change behavior by changing meaning.
Cognitive Overt	An organized and identifiable effort to change behavior by changing meaning.	An unorganized and identifiable effort to change behavior by changing meaning.

To define your insidious competitor, so that you know how to deal with him or her, it is imperative to know the classification into which they fall. We will later explore various strategies that may be useful in dealing with different classifications of attacks and attackers. We will also discuss how selecting the best strategy is influenced by both the "type" of competitor and by which of the tools that competitor is using to apply any of the principles of propaganda. The applications, the tools, we've already discussed. The "types" of insidious competitors we'll start discussing in the very next chapter.

Where we might run into some problems in classifying an insidious competitor is when we think the definitions of covert and overt blur. This blurring can occur when the subtlety, or the perceived validity, or the believability of a covert message comes into question. For example, an attack intended to be covert may leave information that is not highly believable, converting its status from covert to overt.[84] This would apply whether or not there is a break-in. Based upon the audience's background knowledge, with believability varying by audience, some will see a "covert" cognitive attack as just that, "covert," while other more knowledgeable individuals may see the cognitive attack as "overt."

Based on the title of this book, *Insidious Competition*, you may think that the only type of cognitive attack with which we should concern ourselves is the *covert* variety. After all, you say, if the attacker is *overt*, wouldn't that be contrary to the definition of insidious? Nope. Insidious doesn't mean secret. That's a common misconception. So, it's back to Webster's again and as we saw in the Introduction insidious means "proceeding in a gradual or subtle way, but with harmful effects," which also means "more dangerous than seems evident," another definition that I retrieved from a different edition of Webster's dictionary. Certainly the covert type would qualify here. But so would the overt type, if the overt type is not taken seriously. And that is exactly what is happening now. At this writing, many companies are not taking the conversations in social media seriously. Although it is the "covert cognitive" attack that requires the most finesse, using several of the principles of propaganda to be successful and with "veracity" being the most critical, the "overt cognitive" attack can be just as devastating.

Devastating, indeed. The general public has believed for decades that they have been exposed to what they characterize as "corporate propaganda." Now that social media is available, it gives the average person a worldwide platform from which to "return fire" and propagandize back. Turnabout is fair play and "payback is always a bitch." Now ordinary people have the equipment, and relatively inexpensive equipment, to "stick it to the man."

From 1996 to the time of this writing, I have spent much time on the Internet, for business pursuits, for pleasure, and especially for the research of this book. In that time, and especially during the last few years, I've come to learn that there are several different categories of what I am calling *insidious competitors* - who companies need to start caring about. Those categories are: Reality Benders, The Nasties, The Friendlies, and The Digital Pirates. The Reality Benders, The Friendlies, and the Digital Pirates can be a product of that "return fire" mindset. The other group? Well, they're a bit different.

In the following chapters, we'll discuss each of these categories and, within those categories, several types of insidious competitors. So, let's get started.

Take-Aways from Chapter Ten – Classifications of Competitive Attacks

1. There are two classes of insidious competitor attack organization: cosmic and chaotic. Cosmic is formally organized. Chaotic is informally organized.
2. There are two classes of attack objective: semantic and cognitive. A semantic attack's objective is the changing of meaning. A cognitive attack's objective is a behavioral change.
3. Cognitive attacks may be further subdivided into either covert or overt.

Chapter Eleven:
The Reality Benders

In my 14 years of Internet travels leading up to this book, I have found that there is a lot of trash-talking going on out there. Of course, in real life there always is, but as I started to organize the basis of the Five Factors of Insidious Competition in my mind, it occurred to me that because of the characteristics of the social media environment, that trash-talk was a lot more dangerous in social media than it was in real life. From these initial thoughts came my first classification of insidious competitor, the Reality Benders.

When the concept of the Reality Benders first started to coalesce in my mind, I thought of them as "net gandists," a portmanteau for "net propagandists." At that point I had not yet immersed myself into the finer points of propaganda which were presented earlier in this book. Well, actually let me clarify that. I did have some familiarity with the finer points of propaganda, although they were a little fuzzy because I hadn't dealt with them for quite some time. I mentioned earlier in this book that I have had the book *Propaganda* in my library since I was a sophomore in college. The finer points of propaganda were a bit vague in my mind and needed some sharpening before I could have the discussion of propaganda that you and I have had in this book. I got *Propaganda* out from the back of my bookshelf and pushed the cobwebs out of the "understanding of propaganda section" of my mind. It was then that I understood that the type of insidious competitor that I was thinking of in the category that I coined, Reality Benders, was somewhat like a propagandist. They were "changers" of reality, or more accurately "benders," and were using some of the principles of propaganda to do so.

Reality Benders are disseminators of misleading or one-sided information. Reality Benders are just out there banging away, insulting the "truth;" some perhaps not even realizing that they are, in effect, "competing" with the companies about which they write within the social web. Let's talk about three types of Reality Benders which are, in fact, insidious competition to businesses today. Two types are fairly unsophisticated, while one type is relatively sophisticated.

Reality Benders can be anonymous or they can be identifiable. And they can be classified as either cosmically organized or chaotically organized. Their attacks can be semantic or cognitive. Let's take a look at the three specific types of Reality Benders. They are: Tagging Terrorists, Mommy Bloggers, and NGOs/Activists.

Tagging Terrorists

Are these people, the Tagging Terrorists, actually terrorists in the conventional sense of the word? Well, no, of course not. I don't mean to imply that Tagging Terrorists are out there doing physical damage, blowing things up, etc. What I do mean to do by referring to them with this label is to get your attention. I want that attention because these people can do a lot of damage to the general consensus of "meaning," as it exists on the Internet, on the social web in particular, and as it exists in society in general.

The Terror of the Tag Defined

My concept of the Tagging Terrorist came together after reading this sentence in the social media book *Groundswell*. "Tagging seems innocuous, but of course, you have no control over how people classify you or your products." [85]

The tool of a Tagging Terrorist is "Snark" ("the low kind of invective, condescending, knowing" [86]) and Snark is employed through a social bookmarking site. Tagging Terrorists are a business threat. They use humor or satire, their "snarky tag," as a way to make a statement about a corporate image. The employment of humor or satire disarms the social media user, causing them to think that the humorous tag is just entertainment. But the "tag," and the meaning it attaches to *your corporate image,* is more than humor. It's an attempt at *changing the meaning of the corporate image*. I'm running ahead of my outline again. Let's back up a bit and bring in some explanations for those not quite familiar with the social bookmarking terrain.

What's tagging? What is a social bookmarking site? Is it a place where people go to trade and/or talk about bookmarks? Well, actually my smart aleck response to my own question is not very far off target.

A prime example of a social bookmarking site is del.icio.us or as it's now more easily known, delicious.com. The function of a social bookmarking site is to allow members (membership is usually free) to "bookmark," or "tag," Web sites which they have found and consider to be significant, helpful, cool, interesting, educational, etc. So instead of, or in addition to, bookmarking Web sites on your bookmark list in your web browser (also known as "favorites"), you may use a social bookmarking site to publicly share a list of Web sites you like or even dislike. Social bookmarking site members classify their lists of sites by using "tags," also known as keywords, by which other members may search and receive a list of common Web site bookmarks. The sites that are bookmarked by members are ranked in popularity, based upon how many other members have also bookmarked the same sites. The ranking of the sites is intended to help other members to determine which sites, within the member's topics of interest, or "their tags," are worth visiting. Good sites as well as bad sites are bookmarked and ranked. Sites are tagged with keywords that are factual or based upon opinion, and can be associated with any "tag," or keyword, of anyone's choosing.

The "key" issue there in that keyword discussion is "of anyone's choosing." I think by now, in your journey to becoming an insidious competition fighter, you can see where this is heading.

The Tool of the Tagging Terrorist

I say that the Tagging Terrorist uses Snark as their tool. Their tool is Snark because, by attaching a Web site to a perhaps less-than-flattering tag, the Tagging Terrorist is making a snide remark, a low, knowing, condescending attempt at invective, in only one or just a few keywords. To be effective, the keywords, or tags, that are selected are grounded in the principles of propaganda. Easy. Selecting a word or two that makes sure their message contains elements of truth (the Veracity principle of propaganda) or relating their message through the selection of a keyword that conveys a connection to societal values (the Societal Basics principle of propaganda) such as the protection of children, or the preservation of the nation, or the attainment of happiness in all its vast definitions, shouldn't be too difficult. Just a word or two or three. Snark doesn't need sentences to be an effective tool of propaganda.

When this is done, the snarky Tagging Terrorist is often doing so in a sarcastic manner. For instance, the Tagging Terrorist might attach a tag of "healthy eating for kids" to the websites of companies that produce greasy hamburgers, heavily caffeinated soft drinks, or sugary breakfast cereals. The message is clear. The Veracity principle comes into play because the tag is about eating, a clear truth, but the element of innuendo is introduced with the word "healthy," sarcastically implying that the food is unhealthy. Well, the food may not be healthy if consumed in large quantities over a long period of time, but it is not unhealthy if consumed only occasionally. On this issue, the tag shades the truth.

The Societal Basics principle of propaganda would also come into play here because it deals with the protection of children. Who doesn't want to protect a kid? When the tag "healthy eating for kids" is clicked on by other social bookmarking site members who want to protect their kid from bad food and may want to find "healthy" menu items for their own finicky-eating rug rat, the discovery of the aforementioned Web sites attached to the tag may create or reinforce an image that these food corporations don't care about "protecting children."

The use of the tool in this manner can create a threat.

Why They Are a Threat

So, following the illustration just given, I think you can now understand where I've been heading with this.

The threat from Tagging Terrorists lies in the fact that an effort can be mounted by an individual, or an organization, for the express purpose of *mangling the meaning* of a selected target company. It's pretty easy to create numerous, hundreds, or thousands of member accounts on a social bookmarking site for the purpose of "tagging" a specific company's Web sites to less-than-flattering keywords. I'll explain further.

The way it works in social bookmarking sites is that the more "tags" that are attached to Web sites about Company X, then the higher in popularity ranking, on the social bookmarking site, will be those Web sites about Company X. This means that, the higher the popularity level of Company

X sites, the more likely it will be that the average social bookmarking site member, searching for some information on Company X, will find the Company X sites with the highest popularity.

And what would those sites be? With a busy Tagging Terrorist, the average member of the social bookmarking site wouldn't find a "balanced view" of Company X, but would find the information about the woefully targeted Company X that the Tagging Terrorist wanted the average user to find. An example of a cosmic attack? Yes.

The amount of "terror" that this sort of "tagging vandalism" would generate in the mind of the corporate communications or brand professional would be almost palpable. And the amount of damage that such a process would inflict upon the *meaning of the corporate image* in the mind of the average person could be incalculable.

The attack type from the Tagging Terrorist can be classified as "semantic" because the tagging of a site related to corporate image can be seen as directed at *changing the meaning of the image* in the mind of the average user. ("Hey! Wait a second. This food isn't healthy!") In my experience in analyzing this type of threat, I can say that I haven't seen much, if anything, in the way of cognitive attacks (i.e., where the tag would be seeking an orthopractic action).

And what about a chaotic attack? Can it also occur? An example of this would be where individuals would "just be fooling around," tagging corporate sites in a humorous or satirical manner. Doing so might seem harmless or amusing to them, yet the consequences of these individual, chaotic actions could collectively amount to so much more damage than this chaotic tagger could imagine. Today, it is the chaotic form of organization which appears to be most prevalent. Even though an attack may be chaotic, if that chaotic attack occurs in significant numbers, well, you can see what kind of damage can be done. Do you see where this "terror tagging" could lead?

Even if this terror tagging is done by a relatively small number of individuals, either cosmically or chaotically, it is the "effects" of which we must be aware. "Casual" viewers of these "tagged" relationships can get an unfavorable view of the company image, true or not, slanted or not. Our average user, or casual viewer, has unwittingly become a victim of *meaning change.*

Now, it's time for an example.

An Example

On Friday, August 7, 2009, which is the day that I wrote this section, I went to delicious.com and entered the search term "KFC." I picked this keyword because I knew from experience within the social web that there are many people who associate positive opinions with this keyword as well as negative opinions. I looked at the raw, unranked results just as an average person would. I say that because in order to look at delicious.com results ranked according to some criterion, say popularity, a user needs to have the Firefox browser with Greasemonkey installed and a special, free plug-in which is available at UserScripts.org. Now I have Firefox, and I also have that free plug-in which will rank the results. But, I don't consider myself the average Internet user. In my experience, it seems that the "average" web surfer would not know about the Firefox browser and the popularity ranking plug-in. So, to duplicate that "average" experience, I used the Safari browser which did not rank the search results. The Safari browser simply gave me the raw, unsorted, default results that delicious.com serves up automatically. I believe that, using this approach, I saw what the average user would have seen when searching on the "KFC" tag. So, what did those raw, unsorted, default results reveal?

The default results showed 25 Web site links, many of which were unflattering to KFC. Here is a synopsis of what was found. And please remember that these results were unranked. In order of appearance:

- The fourth search result shown was a link to the "Kentucky Fried Cruelty" Web site, an NGO/activist culture jam. (We'll learn more about culture jamming later on.)
- The fifth result referred to an Ad Age article about a marketing program mistake.
- The seventh result identified an article about the KFC recipe possibly being revealed online.
- The ninth result linked to a site titled "Unthink what you thought about KFC."
- The tenth result showed an article titled "Make Reverse Engineered KFC at Home."
- The eleventh result showed a link to "KFC Hunger Strike." The link went to BigDaddyBoxMeal.co.uk, but that link was dead when I tried it. Nevertheless, the title of the link and its

accompanying description as shown in the delicious.com search result isn't flattering.

- The twelfth result was another reference to the secret KFC recipe being online.
- The fourteenth result was an article titled "27 Observations About the Goddamn KFC Line I'm In." Very cute, very snarky.
- The fifteenth result shown was another reference to the KFC recipe possibly being in the wind. Actually, it was same as the seventh result, but with a slightly different URL.

You see where I am heading.

At least 8, as shown above, out of the 25 total results, which would greet the "average" viewer upon searching "KFC" in delicious.com, weren't the type about which you'd like to write home to Mom if you were a KFC marketer. If you disliked KFC, well then these are the kind of results that you probably could not wait to e-mail to Mom. These results weren't devastating to the corporate image, but neither were they flattering. Were there any that could counteract the unflattering sentiment of those eight? Not really. In my opinion, the rest were either neutral or just links to company sites. There were no search results "singing the praises" of KFC.

This example clearly demonstrates semantic attacks. There is no attempt to change behaviors here, only meaning. And the attacks appear to be quite chaotic. I saw no indication that this was an intentional effort by a formally organized group.

Now, as I mentioned above, because I did not use that popularity ranking plug-in, I did not see these Web sites listed in order of their popularity (i.e., the number of times delicious.com members tagged each of these sites). But, please note that when looking at an unranked site list like this, you will still see the popularity score for each site. In this particular example, as far as the unranked popularity score for each of the eight negative search results goes, they were all less than one hundred, meaning that less than one hundred delicious.com members had bookmarked, tagged, or in other words "voted" for, any of these links. There might have been other KFC search results that had higher popularity scores, but because I did not employ the popularity ranking plug-in, I did not see them. I, acting as the "average" viewer, did not see them. So, you're thinking, "Hey, only 100 people or so ranked these sites with a less than 'positive' connection to KFC. Where's the problem?"

Parenthetically, that "Where's the problem?" type of thinking is what is making today's corporation's susceptible to insidious competition. The competitive danger is not being regarded as the serious threat which I am demonstrating in this book that it is.

Where's the problem? The problem is, as I said in the "Why They Are a Threat" section above, even if a small number of persons "terror tag," cosmically or chaotically in a semantic attack, those tags are there for the casual viewer to come upon. A popularity rank of 100 or 100,000 doesn't matter. The tags are still there, waiting to be viewed. Meaning, and what the corporate image really is, is then susceptible to a portrayal different from that which the KFC brand marketers might prefer.

In our example, are any of these tags taking advantage of the principles of propaganda? Yes, they are, but I would say indirectly so. As I stated above, with the exception of the link to the Web site "Kentucky Friend Cruelty," I don't find any of the tag relationships here as being overly negative. There just weren't any "singing the praises" of KFC. Excepting the "Cruelty" site link, there were no tagged relationships denying any of the sociological presuppositions or daily life values. Also, I noticed that there was no support of nation, or work, or the notion of a hero, or that humans are good, etc. By not finding any connection of KFC supporting any of those positive values or presuppositions, yes, the *meaning of the corporate image can suffer.* Suffer because the image is designed to support those values and presuppositions. When that positive support is not reinforced, through the eye of the average social bookmarking site user, the meaning of the corporate image can indeed suffer a loss.

Mommy Bloggers

Mommies are nice. But, Mommies are a business threat. How could that be? After all, they're mommies. Everyone loves a mommy, if only just their own. Go ahead. Think the word "mommy" and you get a nice, warm fuzzy feeling inside. (That is, of course, unless your mother was something more like a "Mommy Dearest" character.) Therein lies a seemingly counter-intuitive reason for you to include Mommies on your list of insidious competitors.

Why They Are a Threat

This "niceness" is one characteristic of two that makes Mommies a business threat. Mommies' presumed niceness seemingly precludes them from being a "non-traditional competitor." Their niceness is disarming. You don't expect them to be a business threat. But they are. After reading this section you'll understand why.

The second characteristic that makes them a business threat is that Mommy Bloggers are all over the social web. They're hard to avoid. Their ubiquity across the social web fits in generally with the Totality principle of propaganda. In social media, Mommies are everywhere, 24/7/365, so when you make that "freedom of choice" selection on the social web, as we discussed in the Totality section of the propaganda chapter, you are fairly likely to get the viewpoint of a Mommy Blogger. Why are you likely to run into a Mommy Blogger? Because Mommies are quite eclectic in the subject matter they take on within their spread across the social web. So when searching for any subject, you are likely to land on a mommy blog. Unlike tech blogs, sports blogs, music blogs, celebrity blogs, auto blogs or any blog that specializes in a particular subject, per Michelle Mitchell from Problogger.net, mommy blogs are more widely targeting, covering subjects ranging from parenting, to protecting the environment, to politics, to crafts, to food, to homeschooling, to gardening, to household products, to design, to travel or to simply the creation of funny stories.[87] The influence of mommy blogs is felt far and wide across not only the social web, but in the wider Internet in general.

What tool does the Mommy Blogger use? No, it's not a blog. Remember that we said the blog was not a tool, but rather the blog is a venue in which the tool is applied. From the list of the Four Tools of Insidious Competition, we can see Mutant Conversation and Snark at work in the social media conversations of the Mommy Blogger. Shortly, we will consider their usage of these tools in more detail as we go through our discussion of how Mommy Bloggers can knowingly or unknowingly become insidious competitors to business. For right now, let's pause briefly for my definition of what is meant by the term "Mommy Blogger."

Mommy Blogger Defined

A "Mommy Blogger" is "a mother who is . . . therefore she blogs," to paraphrase Descartes, and she blogs about a wide variety of subjects, as pointed out by Michelle Mitchell per above. Mommy Bloggers are women, with children, who may work full-time outside the home or who may work full-time inside the home or who may work full-time outside and inside the home. Mommy Bloggers are women who, using blogs as their platform, get deeply involved in their roles as communicators, who see themselves as experts or develop their knowledge into expertise on subjects of their own interest and choosing, and who may become "celebrities" in their own right with a significant online readership and following.

Per the above, Mommy Bloggers cover a lot of subject territory in the blogosphere specifically, while also using other social media as added support for their blog message. Mini-blogging, such as in the venue of Twitter, or social networking efforts, such as in the venue of Facebook, augment and amplify Mommy Bloggers' main work in their blogs, extending their reach and influence into other venues of social media, which in turn draws additional participants into the Mommy Bloggers' domain. Because of this reach and influence, Mommy Bloggers are well known throughout popular culture.

Mommy Bloggers – They're nice, they're everywhere and they converse with other mommies far and wide, 24/7/365 on a broad range of topics. So how can that be a bad thing, or pose a threat to business? Let's discuss how their use of Mutant Conversation and Snark influences "reality" and can impact the corporate image.

The Tools and Strategy of Mommy Bloggers

Well-known as a group they may be. They have a lot to say about many different topics. But should we believe them? Or even pay attention to them? One reason we, as a society, pay attention to Mommy Bloggers, and often believe them, is that they write with passion. As Michelle Mitchell said, posts in mommy blogs are "usually written with an emotion and personality which connects with readers in ways that other niches often can't and they speak about subjects that naturally carry strong emotions: home, family, marriage, children, the environment - all of which encourage dedicated readers." [88] We have already discussed how emotionally charged language supports the

Veracity principle of propaganda. So, the passion displayed by Mommy Bloggers helps their message to be regarded as "true."

Another reason that we pay attention to Mommy Bloggers, and believe them, is because their message themes are well-grounded in the Societal Basics principle of propaganda. In other words, they communicate about things that are important to humans and to society at large. They write in defense of, or advocate for, home, family, marriage, a clean environment, and especially children. Emotion brings in Veracity and both are wrapped around the basic supporting concepts of society. How can we as responsible members of society detract from any of these subjects? How can we as responsible members of society even begin to argue against their advocacy? Therein lies the key to the Mommy Bloggers' success. Because they are Mommies, we see them as protectors, as protectors of social mores. Essentially, when viewed as such, they are "morally unassailable."

From this position of strength, they use the emotion to bundle together subjects like child rearing, the value of work, dedication to nation, or the pursuit of happiness. And when they do so readers will start to "cherry pick" what's most important to them. Then, those readers will pass on only those "good" parts. When that occurs, what happens to the conversation? It gets taken out of context. Their posts "drift," digitally. Pieces of the conversational DNA drop out. And what's that called? Say it with me. Mutant Conversation. Then, when the Mommy Bloggers throw a dash of Snark into their blog posts to attract that "knowing audience," perhaps the audience with the same disdain for the company about which they are writing (your company?), when they say snarky things that will preclude honest debate over issues related to your company, and when they snark away to communicate hipness, connecting to the Temporal Focus principle of propaganda, well then, the Mommy Bloggers have nailed it. They become *insidious competitors.*

Wow!

And it works. This choice and configuration of tools works because, as you can probably see by this point in this book, the application of the tools is founded beautifully in those principles of propaganda.

Now, imagine when they turn those tools to work against *your* company's *corporate image.* Talk about competition. It's hard to compete either with what Mommy Bloggers knowingly and directly "say" about your company, or with what their readership "infers" and then passes along in a mutated mess of your corporate image.

By employing this approach, whether intentionally or unintentionally, whether cosmic or chaotic, the strategy is brilliant, even if serendipitously or unconsciously applied by many a Mommy Blogger. The brilliance of the strategy lies in the fact that for any person attempting to argue against any Mommy Blogger position, even if that argument is unrelated to the Societal Basics, it becomes incumbent upon that person to dissolve the "moral shield" which is wrapped around the Mommy Blogger. The moral shield that, like Snark, because of its very presence can preclude honest debate. Why?

Because she's a Mommy. No one wants to argue with a Mommy. Why?

Because Mommies are nice.

It's time for an example.

An Example

In the blogosphere where reading a blog is a quick affair, it would seem that dissenting mommy blog readers would not want to take the time to analyze the argument and the situation at hand and wouldn't realize that there is a "moral shield" at work there. If one isn't aware of the moral shield, then arguing against any Mommy Blogger position can make one look, at best, insensitive or, at worst, like a jerk. Indeed, from the mommy blogs that I have read, that is often the way mommy blog "dissenters" are reacted to, handled, and portrayed on mommy blogs. They are called jerks. So much for honest debate.

Not too long ago I read an article that likened Mommy Bloggers to The Borg, that inexorable force of Star Trek fame. This comparison was suggested in an article titled, "The Borg: Mommy Bloggers Assimilate Johnson & Johnson." [89] This article, written by Robert French, referenced the then recent "Motrin flap" that engaged Johnson & Johnson in a *battle for meaning* with Mommy Bloggers. What was the "Motrin flap?" Good question, and before we can discuss Robert's Borg comparison in a meaningful way, we'll need to put that comparison in context with some background on that "Motrin flap." Let's learn about, what I have referred to previously in this book as, The Motrin Incident.

In November 2008, The Motrin Incident was a "dust up" that began on the social web. The makers of Motrin, J&J's Mc Neil Pharmaceuticals, had placed a video on their Web site, the subject of which was to advocate how their analgesic could help alleviate back pain suffered by mothers who carried their children in slings, or "schwings" as they were referred to in the video, which hung from the mothers' shoulders. Mommy Bloggers noticed the video, and started a discussion on the social web about how they believed that the video was insulting to children. It was the contention of angered Mommy Bloggers that the video was disrespectful to children's paramount place in society. The angered Mommy Bloggers, among other issues, primarily maintained that the video positioned benefits to the mother, specifically achieved through the mother's own pain relief via the analgesic, above any presumed bonding benefits to the children that could be obtained by carrying the child in such an intimate manner. So, you can imagine that the social web discussion of this video was quite robust. More robust, I think, than most other incidents of this sort to that time.

The first Mommy Blogger objections to this video occurred on a weekend and caught fire very quickly. By the time Motrin marketers arrived at their desks on Monday morning, the incident was a raging inferno. Corporate disdain ran rampant. Within the social web, there were many calls for the makers of Motrin to remove the video from the company's Web site, which Motrin management did. The removal of the video was also accompanied by a company apology for any misunderstanding.

The mainstream press caught word of the incident and ran stories about it. Some stories in that press, and in the general blogosphere, characterized the group calling for the video removal as a "vocal minority," wondering if J&J had "caved" too quickly.

Whether J&J caved too *quickly* is not at issue here in *Insidious Competition.* What is important to our discussion here is that they caved *at all.* And that decision to cave is directly related to the ideas that Robert French brought up in the previously mentioned article. Let's go now to The Borg comparison.

In that article, Robert makes a comparison between Mommy Bloggers and The Borg and he includes a significant quote from The Borg mind itself, likely familiar to fans of Star Trek: The Next Generation.

> *Strength is irrelevant, resistance is futile. We wish to improve ourselves. We will add your biological and technological distinctiveness to our own.* ***Your culture will adapt to service ours.***

Let's take this mission statement apart. Yes. That is a mission statement. Their objective is: "We wish to improve ourselves." How will the objective be achieved? By adding your distinctiveness to our own which means your culture will adapt to service our culture. That's how we will improve ourselves.

The bold shown in the above quote was in Robert's article, but had he not added it I would have bolded it because it is an important point.

Your culture will adapt to service ours.

I'll take it that in his article Robert implies that the "we," in the Borg mission statement, are the Mommy Bloggers, while the "you" (implied) are companies from whom the Mommy Bloggers buy. (This analogy is somewhat ironic because, in pop culture, it is often the "evil corporation" that is being compared to The Borg.)

By using this analogy of Mommy Bloggers to Borg and "you" to companies, I can see that in a way the Mommy Bloggers have it right. Your culture (the company's culture and the way it operates its business) will adapt to service our society, or at least Mommy Bloggers' interpretation of what they think society is, or should be, with particular attention to the Mommy segment of that society. This doesn't seem too unreasonable, does it?

Business is supposed to serve the consumer. Businesses exist to fill a need or a want. Businesses exist to solve someone's problem. Isn't that the way it was set-up in the first place? Isn't that the point of commerce? Long ago when the first entrepreneurial Cro-Magnon emerged from a cave somewhere in the south of what is today France, holding in his overly huge head an idea about an offer that no other Cro-Magnon could refuse, an offer that didn't involve a bash on the head with a club even more huge than that Cro-Magnon head, an idea that instead was intended to serve the betterment of his tribe, (or was it his "crowd?"), wasn't that the beginning of business? Yes. Business was set up that way in the beginning, but somewhere between that huge-headed cave dweller and here today smack dab in the middle of the land of faceless multinational corporations, the idea must have gotten misplaced. I say that only because of one of the first lessons I learned in business school, "The purpose of the corporation is to enrich its stockholders." I thought then in amazement, "You mean the purpose of the corporation isn't to solve its customers' problems?" Apparently not. It shows. Just look around.

I'm sure I don't have to quote stacks of studies about how people think modern corporations are unresponsive to the needs of the average consumer. That's common knowledge. Going back to our discussion of disdain for institutional power, as seen in the Five Factors of Insidious Competition in Chapter Three, I think we can all agree with the idea that there is little respect given by consumers to many of the companies from which they buy their products or services. If this wasn't true, would corporations today be falling all over themselves to use social media in an effort to get "closer to their customer?" Disdain, however it is manifested or perceived even if the perception is subjective, breeds disdain. You get what you give. It's this kind of sentiment that breeds events like The Motrin Incident.

In The Motrin Incident, disdain reigned. The Mommy Bloggers called upon that deeply engrained disdain, that desire to "dis the man" who they felt was "dissing" them and they summoned their passion, loaded with Snark and with emotionally charged words, defending Societal Basics, and demanding, like The Borg, that you, Mr. and/or Ms. Corporation, will adapt your cultural and social thinking to ours and in doing so serve us better. They did so chaotically organized and "shielded" by a morally unassailable theme, children. Children. Remember that they are one of the daily values.

The pleas, the attacks of the Mommy Bloggers, were both semantic and cognitive in nature. Some being simple disparagement, semantic, allowing their future readers to choose a course of action. While other of their pleas were more cognitive in focus, exhorting the makers of Motrin to remove the video from their Web site. All through the progress of these pleas, the tools of Mutant Conversation were knowingly or unknowingly being deployed, with elements of the conversational DNA being deleted, rearranged, or just chewed up and spit back into the mix. The Snark "called" others into the group, helping to preclude rational debate, while telling others that these Mommies were contemporary and hip, but yet still serious mothers. All of this helped to cast out the corporation and frame it as a target of disdain, with all the damage to the corporate image that goes with such actions.

Yet, in The Motrin Incident there was no real service issue at stake. There was no problem with the product. The only problem perceived by the Mommy Bloggers was in the way that the Mommy Bloggers perceived the company to have perceived **them,** *as above children.* So the Mommy Bloggers responded, like The Borg, en masse and without mercy. A solipsistic or epistemological mistake? Caused by mutations?

Now, if you'd like to e-mail me or engage me on my blog in honest debate on this particular subject, I'm all for that. But if you are, instead, considering sending me letters or e-mail or blogging or tweeting about what an insensitive jerk I must be to equate Mommy Bloggers with The Borg, (as did Robert French in the aforementioned article, so let Robert share the credit with me) think about what you are doing. Think about the "moral shield." Would you in your criticism of my theory be able to dissolve that shield? Are you precluding honest debate because of the niceness of a mommy, and her status as "protector?"

Understand that I'm not saying that the Mommy Bloggers are mindless automatons like The Borg. Indeed, they are certainly much more than that. But do they, *as a group*, actually have different thought processes from The Borg? Or are their objectives the same? To answer those questions, let's think about how each group is organized.

When The Borg were (was?) first introduced into the Star Trek story we were led to believe that they were mindless automatons, carrying out orders decided by a "hive" mind. The Star Trek fans reading this section will probably be thinking this. But we came to find out later in the Star Trek saga that The Borg orders were actually issued by a Queen, a central authority. Let's put that discovery aside. I put the Queen discovery aside because, commonly, when we think of The Borg or use them as a pop culture reference, we think about a large, unstoppable, inexorable, relentless, overwhelming force, chaotically organized without a central authority, moving toward its goal which is "to improve ourselves." So, please no letters or emails from Star Trek fans about The Borg management theory departure that I am taking here.

Their Goal

We can think of Mommy Bloggers, and indeed this is what I believe the comparison in the Robert French article is pointing out, as also being chaotically organized and moving toward a common goal, in a crowd-like fashion. Both The Borg and the Mommy Bloggers are numerous; a large, unstoppable, inexorable, relentless, overwhelming force, a crowd, that is moving toward a goal; a goal which we can parallel and compare to the stated Borg objective which is "to improve ourselves." Go back to Chapter

Three and think about the Mommy Bloggers in relation to the Five Factors of Insidious Competition:

Factor #4 - Yielding to instinct to support the collective crowd interest.

That Mommy Blogger goal, that collective crowd interest, is not the biological and technical improvement sought by The Borg. The Mommy Blogger goal is a different type of improvement, and action toward that goal is energized by the "hive" mind of the mommy blogosphere collective. The "hive" mind generates a form of "collective intelligence," which is an actual term used on the social web to describe knowledge generated within social media and held commonly by its participants. The social media "hive" is influenced by, or operates according to, what is known by the collective. So what is the improvement goal of the Mommy Bloggers? Preservation or elevation of ego. This is plainly seen in The Motrin Incident.

Don't take this view as derogatory. That's not my intent. Take it as a logically derived proposition because maintenance of ego is a natural human response. And, so that we may better understand them, regard this view as an analysis that is being made into the motivations of an insidious competitor.

Many "tuning" into The Motrin Incident would perceive it as an example of Mommy Bloggers "rightly" responding to what they perceived as a diminishment of a mother's bond with her child, or in sociological terms, a diminishment of the "value" of children. It would be hard to think otherwise. Remember the "moral shield?" Mommy Bloggers, and their audiences, felt that that video put the comfort of mom above that of her child. So believing this, it is reasonable to think that any responsible mother would disagree strongly with the video and "support the collective crowd interest" and to seek "change" (orthopractic, in this case).

But let's think about the incident more deeply. Wouldn't any mother not defending the status of "child" as "superior" to the status of "mother" be herself deemed a "bad mother?" So can we really say that Mommy Bloggers worked toward the sociological "protection of children" – or were they, in fact, working toward ensuring that they themselves were being seen to be "good mothers?" Defense of ego and improvement or maintenance of self-image. Perhaps. To quote a line from a popular *Seinfeld* episode, "Not that there's anything wrong with that."

That Motrin Incident / Mommy Blogger response would probably be the same for most moms, with or without blog access. But what makes Moms who have blog access more dangerous and more insidiously competitive than Moms who don't have blog access? Simply the number of people they can influence. You can "talk" to more people, more quickly, 24/7/365 with global reach by using a blog, than you can without one. Perhaps Michelle Mitchell, whom I quoted earlier in this section, hit the nail on the head when she said:

Women want – no we crave and demand – social interaction . . . [90]

Then if that is true, Mommies will use whatever technology is available to them to get that interaction, to avoid "the chair," and to spread their messages. Michelle goes on to say how for those women, whose "office is their home," the Internet opens on a world of new friendships, interaction, debate, and learning. And I'll add that the Internet also opens up a world of social movements, cosmically or chaotically organized, in which women can participate.

With the venue of social media, Mommy Bloggers can now satisfy that craving more easily than ever before. With the wide reach afforded by social media, their influence can, by design or by default, leave your *corporate image* by the wayside as collateral damage in *the battle for meaning.*

As illustrated in the example, the attack class of the Mommy Blogger can be either semantic or cognitive, depending on the nature of the Mommy Blogger post. Sometimes they just trash a corporate image, a semantic attack, while other times they call for an orthopractic action, a cognitive attack. If the Mommies are acting individually, they are a chaotically organized force. But if organized with an intended purpose, as are some Mommy Bloggers who write for various online publications, then they are clearly cosmically organized. Alternatively, groups of Mommy Bloggers banding together under a common cause and forming a social movement against a targeted company are, by definition, cosmically organized and are capable of either covert or overt cognitive attacks, although I suggest that Mommy Bloggers would be fools to conduct any attack covertly. The strength of their attack lies in their identification as Mommies. For this insidious competitor, the identification of the attacker is one of the strengths behind the attack. Thus, all their cognitive attacks would be overt.

Speaking of a social movement, let's move on now to the third type of insidious competitor within the category of Reality Benders. Let's move on to NGOs and Activists.

NGOs and Activists

Before we get too deeply into a discussion of NGOs and Activists as insidious competition, let me explain what NGOs and Activists are and why they pose a business threat from within social media.

NGOs & Activists Defined

NGO. The letters stand for "non-governmental organization." Simply put, these organizations attempt to perform governmental functions without actually being a government. NGOs are almost always non-profit corporations, devoted to issues in the "public interest." Examples of NGOs are: the Friends of the Earth (FOE), Greenpeace, Rainforest Action Network (RAN), and thousands of others. What a NGO attempts to do is forward a social, cultural, or political agenda that they have deemed significant. These agendas can run the gamut from health care insurance to pollution or from public transportation to consumer protection. Name your favorite issue and there is probably a NGO that addresses itself to that problem.

Ostensibly, the agenda of the NGO is set by those who are the "dues-paying" members of the NGO and/or its donors and supporters. But in practicality the NGO's agenda is effectively set by its board of directors or executive staff. Even in situations where an NGO's agenda could be set democratically by its membership at-large, because that membership represents such an infinitesimally small proportion of the overall population that the NGO claims to be "defending," that agenda is still not going to be representative of the public that the NGO claims to serve. In either case, whether or not the NGO agenda is set by the membership or by the board of directors, the fact remains that the public *did not* elect the NGO to act for it as a "governmental organization" in its, or in anyone's, interest. Yet, this lack of wide representation (i.e., "public" representation) does not deter NGOs from acting in areas traditionally reserved for governmental policy makers, who were either directly elected, or who were appointed by those who were directly elected. Nor does this lack of wide representation deter NGOs in their attempts to influence those very policy makers in directions that are consistent with the self-selected NGO agendas and their missions.

In my discussions with people about the effects that Activists and NGOs have on businesses, both from within or from outside social media, many people make a distinction between Activists and NGOs. Generally, I don't make these distinctions. I see Activists and NGOs as the same type of animal. Their goals are similar, to affect social change, where much of that change will be at the expense of business. In actuality, however, much of that social change comes ultimately at the expense of the customers served by the businesses at which NGOs and Activists point their agendas. And those customers *are* "the public" in whose interest the NGOs and Activists claim to act. Ironic, isn't it?

The main difference I see between these two types of animals is their organizational structures. NGOs are large or medium sized organizations, often structured on models similar to those used in organizing multinational corporations. Again. Ironic, isn't it? Activists are generally smaller, grassroots organizations with fewer resources.

Most NGOs, in addition to having administrative, public relations, and finance personnel on their staffs, will have "campaigners" on their staffs with different modifying adjectives appearing before that "campaigner" title. For example, "Genetically modified food campaigner." Well, that would be termed more accurately: "Anti-genetically modified food campaigner." I don't know of too many NGO campaigners in favor of genetically modifying food. They're generally against it. People who are in favor of that practice would more likely belong to trade or scientific associations. Other NGO campaigner titles would be in the area of the environment (quite a broad area of coverage), such as, nuclear power, pollution, climate, etc. These campaigners can be compared to marketing personnel in a major corporation in that they are, like the brand managers, tasked to the growth of a certain area of the organization's activity. The ultimate goal of the product brand manager is to achieve specific revenue or market share targets. Such it is with the campaigner. But instead of the campaigner reaching revenue or market share targets (although the production of revenue, i.e., donations, resulting from the success of the campaigner's efforts is vital to the organization), the campaigner is tasked with the responsibility of identifying specific problems within their area of responsibility and then devising strategies, with accompanying tactics, designed to resolve those problems in a manner deemed desirable by the NGO. That's their goal and, please remember, the resolution of that problem, the goal, is in the "public interest." To achieve the goals, the NGO campaigner has at his or her disposal the organization's resources and the legal and liability protection, as an employee, of the corporate NGO entity.

NGOs often use volunteer staff to accomplish their goals, and often the NGOs will refer to these volunteers as "activists." In other words, Activists can be defined as not only small grassroots organizations with relatively fewer resources, but also as "freelancers" acting in concert with a larger corporate entity, the NGO. But the goals of the two, NGOs or Activists, often remain the same (i.e., to further their own agendas). NGOs, with their volunteer "activists," are cosmically organized, as are the smaller grassroots organizations.

There are, of course, situations where chaotically organized groups of individual Activists may coalesce around a problem or an issue, and social media may facilitate their transition from the chaotic to cosmic organization.

If you're feeling a bit edgy now, I understand. I know people are touchy when it comes to criticizing Activists and NGOs. It's because of that whole moral shield thing I mentioned before. Yes, I have been somewhat critical of NGOs and Activists so far. That's because they are insidious competition. And as such, I am about to criticize them even more, so "hold on to your hat."

The moral shield. The reason there is such controversy when Activists and NGOs are criticized is due to the type of agendas set by the Activists and NGOs. They act in the "public interest," right? They claim to endeavor to achieve goals which will have great benefits for society in general, right? So they will rebuff any critics by categorizing those critics as "mean spirited" or even *immoral.* They will categorize critics as being in opposition to the Four Myths or Values Supporting Daily Life, or the Four Sociological Presuppositions which we discussed earlier. But perhaps all that those critics are doing, as I am doing here, is objecting to the lack of a democratic process for any actions claimed to be in the public interest. Certainly such a democratic process, if created, would be in support of those values and presuppositions we have discussed in so much detail.

Perhaps my criticism of NGOs and Activists would not arise if their efforts were indeed always in the public interest and, regarding the specific concerns of this book, if their social media actions toward that public interest were not so one-sided. However, because the "public" has many different interests, determining what is really in the "public interest" is nearly impossible. The term "public interest" is subjective; it is not an absolute. Short of a general public election to determine NGO and activist agendas, these groups can never actually represent the public interest.

Why They Are a Threat

Why are these groups a business threat from within social media? Well, the nature of their threat to business is that they, like Mommy Bloggers, are wrapped within a "moral shield." NGOs and Activists "act in the public interest" against pollution, human rights violations, etc. Again. Tough to argue against that. Tough, but not impossible.

By taking their "morally shielded" cases to social media, they are able to quickly leverage the Five Factors of Insidious Competition - anonymity, power, contagion, instinct, disdain – for the greater advancement of their agendas. And in doing so, they can, and often do, distort their position, bringing social media users along for the ride. Easy to do. That's the nature of their threat within social media. Falsehoods, wrapped in moral protection, spread through the ready, waiting, and uninformed social web, with those Five Factors ready to fan the flames.

How and Why NGOs and Activists Use Their Social Media Tools

Now, let's look at how and why NGOs and Activists pull companies into their politicized process, how social media dovetails into this action, and understand why NGOs and Activists use the tools of the insidious competitor: Mutant Conversation, Snark, and Hip Chat.

"Anti-corporate campaigners have discovered that the best way to promote their issues is to associate them with a well-known brand." This quote is from the book *Damage Control*, a work about corporate public relations efforts in corporate crises and written by PR experts and corporate crisis meisters Eric Dezenhall and John Weber.[91] Anti-corporate campaigners. I'm pretty sure that Eric and John are referring here to NGOs and Activists, people with an axe to grind, or with motivations ranging from altruism to personal gratification and self-validation.

In the *Damage Control* chapter, from which the above quote comes, Eric and John say that NGOs and Activists don't have a significant effect on sales and/or company share price over the long run. They believe that the more noticeable effects from the anti-corporate actions of NGOs and Activists are in the areas of:

- Decreased customer relations and employee morale,
- The corporation's decreased ability to recruit young, "liberal-minded" college graduates; and,
- Higher costs of corporate efforts to deal with the communications actions of NGOs and Activists.[92]

Well, as corporate PR specialists, I suppose that Eric and John would know about the costs of corporate efforts to deal with the communications actions of NGOs and Activists. And, although Eric and John legitimately point out that the actions on the part of NGOs and Activists do lead to the effects listed above, I think these two fellows may be short-sighted. I *do* believe that the actions of NGOs and Activists can indeed have an effect on sales or on the company share price over the long-run, a negative effect. (Share price is an important consideration here because, remember as I said previously, the purpose of the corporation is to enrich the stockholders, regardless of what you or I think of that objective.)

De-motivated employees, customer relations that are not optimal, constantly or even periodically having to hire PR consultants or devoting unexpected resources to corporate PR efforts, can all impact the bottom line for sure, at least on a short-term basis. I'm not so sure about the effect of not being readily able to hire "liberal-minded" college graduates as being a problem. I suppose the corporate value to that, to paraphrase former President Bill Clinton (a liberal himself), depends on what the meaning of "liberal" is. But even if the effects of NGOs and Activists are short-term on the bottom line, all short-term events have an impact in the long-term. Nothing happens without affecting the future. Let's keep this idea of short-term events having long-term consequences from going stale and develop it a little more.

"Protesters naturally turn to the net to organize, distribute propaganda and communicate . . . it makes you wonder how they managed when they only had phone, mail and smoke-filled rooms," said David Bowen in a British newspaper article entitled "Corporate Nice Guise." [93] David continued in this article to say that the use of the Internet by protestors puts "small, flexible groups on a par, and often above, their giant enemies." He goes on to cite as one of the "enemies" Shell Corporation, which was challenged by Greenpeace in a famous dispute over a deep sea oil drilling platform. In the article he details some of the Internet actions that both parties used during the dispute. As David put it, "The web is such a powerful tool in such slanging matches because you can do things on a Web site you can't in other media. You can lay out complex arguments and update them whenever you want." [94] Indeed, because of its flexibility, usage of the web can be especially effective in a dispute that is fluid.

The article by David was written in 2003 when the type of web engagements to which David refers involved Web 1.0, a relatively static type of web publishing, where "one" was talking to "many." In today's Web 2.0 social media environment, which is relatively dynamic and more interactive than Web 1.0 could ever hope to be, where "many" talk to "many," using the web, as David said, "to organize, distribute propaganda and communicate" makes protest movement against a corporation many times more effective in a "slanging match." And because Web 2.0 is "many to many," communication and distribution of the protester's message can be interactively effective.

In this more dynamic, more interactive, more effective Web 2.0 world, imagine that a corporate crisis is conjured up by a NGO (or activist group.) Imagine that the NGO states its case within the social web, starting and entering into conversations to communicate its position, or its argument, on a particular issue. Imagine that the NGO does not present all the relevant parts of the argument, or that part of the argument is cutely positioned by the tool of Snark, or that part of the argument has elements of truth, using the Veracity principle of propaganda, but is painfully slanted with perhaps inaccurate or questionable science. Imagine that within this informational configuration, the social media conversations spread far and wide and even become increasingly susceptible to the effects of the ever present tool of Mutant Conversation. Social media readers digest what they want and pass along only the conversational DNA relevant to them, already from a one-sided argument. And as a result, this process causes a 1% drop in the targeted company's sales for six months. Okay. That drop is a short-term event, such as was suggested by Dezenhall and Weber above.

Now for all of you analyst-types out there, I acknowledge that correlating that drop in sales to the NGO or Activist social media campaign just mentioned is going to be statistically difficult to determine. Correlating that decrease in sales would be difficult because of all the other factors in the business environment which are always changing, which are impossible to hold constant, and which could also have an effect upon the sales that we are trying to measure. But let's just suppose. Let's suppose that we *could* correlate that social media action to the drop in sales. Some folks out there might think, "Hey. One percent in six months? Half a percent over a year. No big deal. Who's going to notice?" Please continue to imagine. Imagine from the perspective of short-term events having long-term consequences.

What if that company, the target of the NGO's or the Activist's attention on the social web, had annual sales of $500 million? Do the arithmetic. That amounts to $2.5 million lost in the fiscal year. $2.5 million dollars lost. $2.5 million that couldn't go to employee raises. Not executive bonuses, mind you. I mean rank and file employee raises.

$2.5 million that couldn't be applied to create better manufacturing facilities and processes, perhaps to make a "greener" company.

$2.5 million that couldn't be donated to charity in the company's "good neighbor" program.

$2.5 million that couldn't be channeled toward employee 401K contributions.

$2.5 million that couldn't be used to improve the company's corporate social responsibility program.

In the United States, at a 33.3% federal income tax rate, $833,332 that doesn't go to the federal government to waste. (Oh. Wait a second . . . perhaps that's a good thing.)

$2.5 million that couldn't be used to help pay employee health insurance premiums, forcing employees to reach further into their own pockets.

$2.5 million.

Gone.

No, one-half of one percent isn't a big deal. Until you start to think about it. Until you imagine what could be done with that money. Until you start to think about the impact that the $2.5 million could have had but now is suddenly not there. And for no good reason other than because a group, not elected by the public, was acting in "the public interest" and was using social media to present a propagandistically-based, polemic argument. An argument that was mutated in conversation by social media users who chose to read the message because of the "freedom" of "propaganda by choice," as discussed in the Totality principle of propaganda in Chapter Seven, and that drew strength and effectiveness from the Five Factors of Insidious Competition.

Still think that NGO and Activist social media actions aren't any big deal? Keep reading.

Your Image Really Isn't the Target

A few pages ago we saw Eric Dezenhall and John Weber say that the best way for an anti-corporate campaigner to promote their issues was to link those issues to a well-known brand. From our discussion so far, you and I can see that essentially what Eric and John meant was that NGOs and Activists will associate their issue with a corporate image, one built by a brand image.

NGOs and Activists recognize a "free" ride when they see one. Well, free at least to them. Certainly not free to your company. NGOs and Activists are going to hitch that axe they have to grind to your corporate image, built by your brand(s). They are not necessarily doing this because they think that your corporation or its image is something evil. They may or may not think that your company is evil. Your corporate image is not necessarily their issue. Their issue is their issue. Your image is just a **vehicle** taking their issue along for a ride. Your company has spent years, decades, or perhaps a century in building that image to mean a certain something. That corporate image is well-known; it has a built-in audience. That audience cost millions, tens of millions, or hundreds of millions of dollars to build. NGOs and Activists don't have that kind of money, nor do they have that kind of time. They can't afford millions. Well, actually some can. Not many, but some. But even if they have that kind of money, they don't need to spend it because your corporate image is available to further their issue, their agenda. So they hop on it. And like a parasite they'll suck on your life force. They'll put Mutant Conversation techniques to work and toss in a little Snark for cuteness. Using both tools they will apply some principles of propaganda like Temporal Focus to keep it timely, like Societal Basics to call upon those daily values and the sociological presuppositions, and like Veracity to keep that message within the context of similar messages found in other media, and in doing all this they'll use your image and your millions of delneros for their own purposes.

Their issue receives its notoriety, parasitically, on the backs of the "hosting" brand and *corporate image.* And how does this help them achieve their goals? How does this action help complete their agenda? To answer those questions, let me draw some parallels. Let's discuss in general some advantages that groups can gain from media coverage of their actions. Here are a couple of quotes, and I'll edit them a bit, explaining why after the quotes.

Advantages that [groups] gain from media coverage of [their actions]:

> *generating public interest in the [groups'] activities and enhancing their influence; attributing a positive spin to the . . . acts of the . . . organizations and shaping their image; [and] portraying [groups] as the weak side in the conflict and promoting support for their motives.*

Let's continue.

> *The media coverage is supposed to intimidate the public, and in this way influence the political perspectives and attitudes of the citizens. The anxiety felt by the nation's citizens will be translated into public pressure on decision makers to accede to [the groups'] demands and make decisions that coincide with the interests of the [groups].*

Note: Brackets mine. The source for these quotes will be given five paragraphs from here.

To me, these quotes summarize the grand communications strategy of NGOs and Activists. NGOs and Activists mount actions (calls for boycotts, generally negative publicity, product accusations, etc.) which gain attention from the public. These actions, and their transmitted stories, are positioned within a public interest theme and are portrayed from behind the "moral shield." Specific to our discussion of social media, as the NGO and Activist initiatives gain momentum and their stories are spread throughout the social web, and if the themes of the stories are positioned properly relative to any of the elements of the Societal Basics, then the mainstream media pick up their stories and run with them. I say "stories" because "stories" are what the mainstream media likes.

The mainstream media, businesses like any other and big businesses at that, want a narrative, with the elements of story, a drama, to which audiences will attend and watch or read over a series of days. Good stories contain several elements, among them: theme, characters, conflict, climax, and resolution. The theme, a goal protected by the "moral shield" and grounded in the Societal Basics, is already set by the time the mainstream media picks it up from within the social web. The characters are David and Goliath, the "underdog public" and the "corporate giant." The underdog, representing the "greater good," is the Hero in this conflict. And who wouldn't want to be a Hero for the "greater good?" The mainstream media, loving a good "underdog public" vs. "corporate giant" story, picks it up from the social web, giving the NGO's (or the Activist's) issue the momentum it needs to reach a climax and a resolution. The perfect conflict, launched within social media, developed into a story by the mainstream media, where the Hero wins and with your company perhaps taking it unfairly "on the chin."

So are the NGOs and Activists to go brand by brand, or image by image, company by company, in their struggles to further their agendas? Will they reach their goal via the *changed actions* of corporations and the effects that those changed corporations can have upon society? Well, if they must, I suppose they will. But that is both a time consuming and inefficient process. There are simply too many companies and corporate images. Attacking each one would require too many resources and too much time. No, these people want more bang for their buck. They want more efficiency. What they're really after is the accomplishment of their goals via political influence. Your image really isn't their target. *Your corporate image is just their vehicle.* Your image is just their way of achieving their agenda with greater efficiency.

NGOs and Activists are politicians, known today as "private politicians."[95] Their primary goal, altruism or personal satisfaction notwithstanding, is to achieve their goals by first achieving political influence. And the avenue to political influence runs right through your company, its brands, and the corporate image that those brands generate. Your corporate image becomes their "soapbox," not their target. They will pummel your image using media strategies like those quoted above (italicized) until they get the political decision makers to decide the way that they, the NGOs and Activists acting in the "public interest," want them to decide. To get this attention and the political influence that they seek, NGOs and Activists need only to "ride" on one or two corporate images, not all of them. Very efficient.

Now, let's go back to those italicized quotes above. Why did I edit those italicized quotes and from where do those quotes come?

First, their source: "Dilemmas Concerning Media Coverage of Terrorist Attacks," *Terrorism and Counterterrorism, Understanding the New Security Environment - Readings and Interpretations.*[96] Second, my edits substituted the words referring to "terrorist organizations" with the neutral word "groups." The brackets, as I noted, were mine. I made those edits because I wanted you to think about the subject of the quotes. I wanted you to pay attention to the general media strategy described with regard to the goal of political influence, rather than have you be shocked by the "T" word. I feared that if I had left in the "T" word, you might have thought me a radical, possibly chucking this book into your pile of "Books I Never Finished Reading."

Am I equating NGOs and Activists with terrorists? Not exactly. Yes, the overarching goal of both parties is political influence. Yes, both want change via a political process. However, the means to their ends are, of course, entirely different. While it is true that some Activists have engaged in violent acts, when the means of Activists cross the line into violence, then they become terrorists, regardless of what they may call themselves. And that extreme level of activism is in an entirely different category – and clearly not the subject of this book. No, I am not *equating* NGOs and Activists with terrorists, but I am *comparing* general NGO and activist communications strategies with the general communications strategies of terrorists. Much has been written about the latter and we can use that research to learn more about the former.

Their Tools

So. What does all of this have to do with social media? Much.

Per the example drawn above, social media is now a prime environment through which NGOs and Activists can achieve the political influence they seek and thus achieve their overarching goals. Within social media there is a ready and waiting audience. Much of that audience is young and socially liberal. These characteristics represent the "target market" of most NGO and Activist organizations. This target market has a high potential for being enlisted into the NGO or Activist cause, aided by the Five Factors of Insidious Competition which are always actively at work. And those Five Factors, anonymity, power, contagion, instinct, and disdain, perform even better in social media when they are teamed with an issue that is wrapped in a moral shield. Perfect.

By jumping into this social media environment, the NGO or Activist can gain political influence from the social media population. They can gain and control positive spin in a "slanging match" of their own choosing and making. The NGO or Activist can generate public interest, shape an image, control the solipsistic and epistemological process, and finally entreat citizens to engage their governmental representatives toward the NGO's or Activist's own favor, thereby achieving the influence and resulting action toward the change that they seek.

Doing all these things within social media, rather than relying exclusively on traditional media, is so much more easily accomplished. Access to social media is inexpensive and, as such, social media are fiscally well-positioned for the presumably not-very-well-heeled NGO or Activist. Access to social media is uncontrolled; no need to have vast resources to curry favor with editors of newspapers, magazines, or television stations. It would be hard not to agree that social media are perfect for this dramatic "underdog." Also consider that social media are pervasive. The audience is vast and becoming more and more vast daily. More and more people use social media to "speak" every day and even more are "listening" to what is said on the social web. Pursuing their agenda within social media also gives the NGO or Activist access, often free access, to the mainstream media. Why? Because, as I alluded to before, social media are the birth place of many stories that make their way into the mainstream media which, as the accepted "agents of common knowledge" and keepers of our reality, provide just that much more credibility, and exposure, to the NGO or Activist message, adding strength to the propaganda principles of Veracity and Totality.

By understanding and exploiting the tool of Mutant Conversation, and how it can change conversations because of its lack of the visual and vocal cues that fill-out real world conversations, NGOs and Activists practice the art of half-truth or a "truth of convenience," one arranged for their own purposes. By inserting their versions of truth about your corporate image into social media conversations, the new found voice of social media participants, through the tool of Mutant Conversation, leads to a generation of half-truths, provoking further propagation of the NGO or Activist message with mutation occurring at each iteration. The Five Factors are on the side of these insidious competitors and these competitors gladly allow their messages to be influenced by those factors, particularly the factor of institutional disdain.

NGOs and Activists also employ the tool of Snark. Their opponents, the companies whose images they "ride," are the targets of Snark, snide remarks and low invective which makes those companies appear "uncool" and someone with whom "cool" or "right-thinking" persons should not want to associate. Snark, which alienates readers from the corporate image and precludes honest debate, is particularly effective when grounded in the Five Factors.

The tools, Mutant Conversation and Snark, are designed to ride on your corporate image's notoriety like an attention parasite, to generate public interest and positive spin for the NGO or Activist cause, to intimidate and influence the public's political opinion on some related issue, and to encourage the public to push for political action. Yes, NGOs and Activists are that new type of competition we have been discussing, non-traditional. And your company needs to recognize them as the insidious competition that they are.

Hip Chat is used by these non-traditional competitors, too. Where Mutant Conversation and Snark may aim directly at your company's corporate image with the intent of damaging that image, the tool of Hip Chat generally will not. Remember, Hip Chat's intent is to directly identify those who are fashionable or trendy, to leverage that Temporal Focus principle of propaganda to the maximum. In its use by NGOs or Activists, Hip Chat's intent is to rally the followers, to attract them with something trendy, while promoting the image of the NGO or Activist directly. And then after assembling the troops with Hip Chat, it's time for the deployment of Snark and Mutant Conversation to inflict further causalities on the *corporate image* of the targeted company.

An Example

The following is an example of Hip Chat which would be used by NGO and Activists to create business change and, in the long run, political influence.

Carrotmob.org calls itself "a method of activism that leverages consumer power to make the most socially-responsible business practices also the most profitable choices." The way Carrotmob.org works is that they encourage their members to patronize businesses who have agreed to make operational or marketing improvements that are deemed important by the operators of Carrotmob.org. As stated on their site, examples of socially-responsible changes are energy efficiency improvements to the physical plant of a business or the cessation of the sale of environmentally harmful products.[97] The definition of "environmentally harmful" is apparently determined by Carrotmob.org. Here's how Carrotmob.org works toward their goals.

Their site asks people to sign up with Carrotmob.org and wait for an "event" to occur. An event is defined as when a business agrees to make energy efficiency improvements or when a business agrees to change its product offering to something Carrotmob.org prefers. When an agreement between the business and Carrotmob.org is reached, Carrotmob.org members are notified (presumably by e-mail, text message, tweets, or other social media venues, etc.) The site gives as an event example a hardware store that is to go "green." Carrotmob.org members in the area of that hardware store were notified and they were encouraged to go buy something in that store. A photo of a long line of customers (most of whom appear to be in the young adult demographic), presumably outside said hardware store, is shown on the Carrotmob.org site.

The Carrotmob.org site implies that power for change occurs when many individuals, for example, show up at a store and buy something (i.e., the "mob" in Carrotmob). They say going to the selected store is easy and "when a whole mob of people do this easy thing, the mob becomes extremely powerful, and we can compel the hardware store to put solar panels on the roof, stop selling 5,000 year-old endangered rainforest lumber, or whatever we want!"[98] This all sounds like what we discussed back in Chapter Two, with crowd behavior trying to rule the rulers. Well, didn't we discuss that social media is a crowd?

Not an NGO, but Activists they are. In fact Carrotmob.org declares on their About page, "Carrotmob was created by an activist who was frustrated by the ineffectiveness of traditional methods of activism." [99] Explaining further, Carrotmob states that they do not campaign *against* companies who do not wish to work with them (which Carrotmob characterizes as the "stick" method), but they campaign *for* companies who do wish to work with them (which Carrotmob characterizes as the "carrot" method). Yes, this is a good example of a situation where Hip Chat would apply. It's a positive approach to raising the value of its own organizational image as well as the image of only the companies that cooperate with them.

Through their Web site statements, the organization is implying that they, as well as the hardware store that they co-opted, are hip, fashionable, in-the-know, trendy, and "right-thinking." Doesn't this sound like the Temporal Focus principle of propaganda at play? In using Hip Chat in this way, Carrotmob.org automatically excludes any non-co-opted businesses and indirectly and negatively affects their reputations. And it is interesting to note that these types of effects could be unwarranted. Perhaps the other businesses have better products than those of the business that Carrotmob is promoting. This is possible.

With Carrotmob.org playing the role of arbiter in these commercial transactions, a role that is demonstrated by the phrase "whatever we want!"

(and the usage of the exclamation point underlines their role as arbiter), they usurp the "democracy" of the free-market system, which has been separating the good from the bad products on its own for millennia. Such arbitration, performed by one organization, can encourage inferior products into the marketplace. But that danger may not be perceived by the audience, which is attracted and blinded by the Hip Chat. Indeed, attraction to the activist's agenda may bolster the audience's general attitude toward activist issues, well-grounded in economics or not, and compel the audience to contact its governmental representatives for the purpose of promoting any of the agenda items listed by Carrotmob.org, or other activists in general.

Carrotmob says on their site, "We're playing by business rules. The game is business. The values are business." [100] In my opinion, these statements are not true. The game being played by Carrotmob.org is politics. Their method is not that of a pure commercial transaction, the basis of true business. Their method is rather the corruption of the economic process, supplanted by the political process. This is the mark of a truly insidious competitor.

Based on our preceding discussion of NGOs and Activists, and especially from the brief example of Carrotmob.org, we can see that the attack from the NGO or Activist would be classified as cognitive and sub-classified as overt. Overt, because NGOs and Activists, like the Mommy Bloggers, benefit from the "moral shield," and thus there is value for them in being identified. As previously explored in our discussion and especially in the brief example above, we can most certainly see that the NGO and Activist are cosmically organized. Cosmic they may be, but please note that they would not turn down a little chaotic organizational benefit as they co-opt people along the way of their campaigns. The cosmic NGO or Activist would spread its message in a cosmically organized manner within social media and, as individuals pick-up that message, those individuals would in a chaotically organized fashion exponentially spread that message through social media.

Cosmic and cognitive. NGOs and Activists are definitely people with an agenda.

We now leave the Reality Bender class of insidious competitor and turn to a new class of insidious competitor who are also cosmic and cognitive. They are The Nasties.

Take-Aways from Chapter Eleven - The Reality Benders

1. Reality Benders are insulters of truth. They exploit the psychological terrain, craft messages with truth interwoven, and theme their messages within the Societal Basics.
2. There are three types of Reality Benders:
    a. Tagging Terrorists
        i. Tools: Snark
        ii. Attack: Semantic
        iii. Organization: Cosmic or Chaotic
    b. Mommy Bloggers
        i. Tools: Mutant Conversation and Snark
        ii. Attack: Semantic or Cognitive Overt
        iii. Organization: Primarily Chaotic
    c. NGOs/Activists
        i. Tools: Mutant Conversation, Snark, and Hip Chat
        ii. Attack: Cognitive Overt
        iii. Organization: Cosmic

Following is Figure 11-1, Reality Benders, a graphic representation of this insidious competitor.

Figure 11-1, Reality Benders

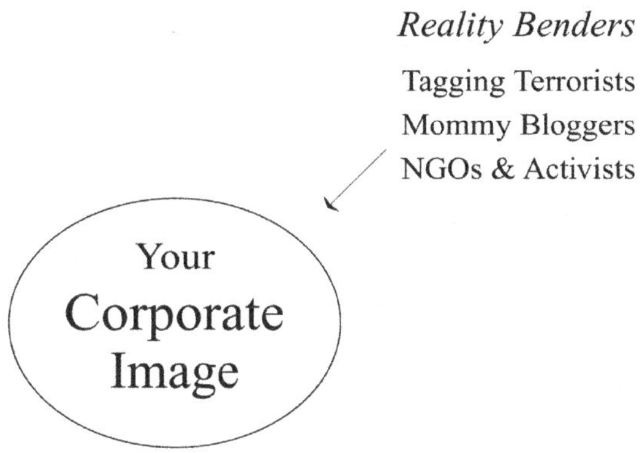

Reality Benders

Tagging Terrorists

Mommy Bloggers

NGOs & Activists

Your

Corporate

Image

Chapter Twelve:
The Nasties

Different from the Reality Benders, who disseminate misleading or one-sided information, The Nasties are a group of individuals who intentionally disseminate false information from anonymous or false sources. Reality Benders bend reality, meaning that there is some truth intermingled in what they are saying. Not so with The Nasties. The Nasties are liars. That's why I call them Nasties.

The Nasties come in one organizational flavor, cosmic. Their actions are formally organized. These people know what they are doing. There is absolutely no chaotic organization to what they do, although their work can subsequently have chaotic organizing influences on other groups within the social web such as the Tagging Terrorists, the Mommy Bloggers, the NGOs and Activists, as well as other types of insidious competitors which we'll explore in later pages.

Finding instances of these cosmically organized groups is difficult; it's difficult because they are "slippery," and they are slippery intentionally. I offer up the concept of The Nasties as theoretical, and I do so for two reasons.

The first reason is because of a fateful pivot in history. Prior to September 11, 2001, the mission of airline hijackers was thought to be either: a) to hijack a plane, hold hostages, and demand a ransom; or, b) to hijack a plane and then have it flown to an extraordinary destination, such as Cuba. But, on the morning of that fateful day, we learned to think differently about the hijacking threat and about so many other threats in general. I raise the idea of

The Nasties now in order for it to function as a wake-up call to an insidious, yet perhaps unrealized, threat. At this stage of my research into insidious competition and the business effects of the social web, in my mind The Nasties are an incipient danger; I can see the conditions and forces which will enable their effectiveness beginning to form. But just because this insidious competitor is, perhaps, only in its infancy, that doesn't mean that they aren't a threat. They are a danger, an insidious danger, which can, and probably does, exist to a greater degree than even I realize. But, unfortunately, singling one out is not easy. Why? Because by their very nature they want to operate "under the radar" and, in the freewheeling, anonymous environment of social media, they can find that perfect opportunity. Social media is the environment for which The Nasties have been waiting.

The second reason that I offer up the idea of The Nasties is because of a forecasted increase in cyber warfare. Cyber warfare, or information warfare, is usually defined as the hacking into, and disruption or destruction of, computer systems which control vital functions of society such as financial systems, utility systems, telecommunications, etc. The possibility of such war is real. Per i-Policy.org in an article entitled, "Threat of Next World War May Be in Cyberspace:"

> *The next world war could take place in cyberspace, the UN telecommunications agency chief warned Tuesday (October 6, 2009) as experts called for action to stamp out cyber attacks.*[101]

You and I touched upon this idea of cyber warfare in Chapter Ten of this book when we discussed hacking and classes of attacks. Cyber warfare, information warfare, and hacking are all directed at damaging the hardware and software of computer systems. The above quote impresses upon us that Internet warfare, in general, is a very real thing, a danger with which we must now live. But in this book, we are leaving aside the technical aspect of Internet warfare. Earlier, we discussed the distinction between hacking and insidious competition saying that, for this book, insidious competition was oriented toward *changing or damaging meaning*, not destroying computers or their software. Revisit this passage from Chapter Eight, the "Tools" chapter:

> *What we are discussing here in Insidious Competition . . . is not threats that are of a technical nature, not those whose objective is to break into a network for the purpose of stealing information. No, in this book we are concerned*

with the more insidious threat of the type that can change meaning. And to put that in a business context, this book is concerned with the type of threat that repackages reality and changes the meaning of a conversation, and how that changed conversation can affect the corporate image.

Internet warfare is about damaging the enemy without leaving home, without investing billions in national treasure for materiel, and without risking lives. Cyber warfare fits this profile. But even cyber warfare carries risks, one of the foremost being the risk of discovery which, regardless of how well the cyber warrior covers its tracks, invites retaliation. Now, with insidious competition's tools and strategies, warfare via the Internet can be made without leaving home, without materiel, without risking lives, *and* with less risk of the aggressor being identified due to the anonymous nature of the social media environment. There is little chance, perhaps even less than in a traditional cyber attack, that in an anonymous (covert) insidious competitor attack the attacker will be identified. For provocateurs wanting to deploy an alternative, or an addition, to full-out "technical cyber warfare," this less risky version of Internet warfare can do significant damage over a period of time. Such stealthy and continuous, and insidious, damage is very difficult to trace, but in the long run it can be no less, and maybe more, damaging than the hit-and-run scenario of traditional cyber warfare.

Who would be these provocateurs and how would they inflict their gradual damage?

Would agents of foreign governments fit this model? Absolutely. Agents of foreign governments would especially fit this model if those agents would have as their objective the destruction of the economic status of their foe. After all, if you can cripple your adversary's economy, you can cripple their nation. And, if you can do this insidiously, so much the better. How could such agents, within our understanding of insidious competition, be successful? One way would surely be to direct propaganda, from within the social media environment, against multinational corporations which are based in the targeted nation and which form a significant foundation of the targeted nation's economic prosperity

Why would I think this? Why would I even dream up such a possible threat to business? Why would I worry you about an attack on *your* company's *corporate image* from a foreign government on the opposite side of the globe?

Because of the way my thinking changed after the dust settled on September 12. And because certainly there is precedent for it.

Foreign Governments & Their Agents

There is precedent for this type of thinking, this thought that governments can and would direct their efforts toward business disinformation activities within the social web. Some governments have had much experience that is similar.

How They Are Organized

Would such attacks be organized cosmically? No doubt about it. They are governments. And they aren't fooling around with semantic diddling on the chance that people might get a "bad impression" of their target. No. These would be serious people, with serious experience in a related field, and with serious objectives. Additionally, wouldn't it stand to reason that their attacks would be cognitive and covert? Let's explore more.

On a United States Department of Energy Web site appears a paper entitled, "A Case Study in French Espionage." [102] On the first page of the paper appears this quote:

> *This espionage activity is an essential way for France to keep abreast of international commerce and technology. Of course, it was directed against the United States as well as others. You must remember that while we are allies in defense matters, we are also economic competitors in the world.*
>
> *- Retired Director of the DGSE, Pierre Marion*

What is the DGSE and what do they do? Let's have another quote, this one from the bottom of page one of that same paper, which is dated October 3, 2000:

> *deGaulle initially authorized the aggressive collection of economic and technological intelligence information in order to assist French companies and industries become [sic] more competitive in the international marketplace. The assignment, initially given to the Service de Documentation Extérieure et de Contre-Espionnage (or SDECE), was eventually taken over in 1968 by Service 7 of the Direction Générale de la Securité Extériure (DGSE - the successor to the SDECE) at the instigation of President Francois Mitterand. Since that time, Service 7 has collected intelligence information from a*

variety of target countries, industries and companies using a wide variety of techniques, means and people. Its acknowledged mission is the gathering of secrets, technologies and marketing plans of private companies, and the French government has publicly acknowledged its operations on behalf of Compagnie des Bull against IBM and Texas Instruments, among others.

Years ago, when I ran my competitive intelligence consultancy, this situation was common knowledge among my peers. In fact, we would advise business people traveling to France not to take sensitive information with them or if that could not be avoided, then we would counsel them not to leave the information in their hotel rooms, or even to place it in the hotel safe.

When you watched the movie "Casablanca" were you shocked that "there is gambling at Rick's?"

Certain governments have experience in corporate intelligence and business targeting. Making the switch to become insidious competitors within social media, if they haven't done so already, would be easier than child's play.

While we're discussing France (and ironically they did speak French in Casablanca), let's have another example of precedent which influences my thinking about this type of insidious competitor.

According to a New York Times article, the French government in July 2009 was, indirectly at least through its 85% ownership of the company Électricité de France (EDF), involved in a case of cyber hacking and corporate intelligence. Even though, according to reports, there was no evidence directly linking the French government to the hacking and, at the time of this writing, the case was still being investigated and adjudicated oddly enough by French government authorities, the case is still intriguing from within the context of our current discussion.

The legal issue in this case revolved around EDF's alleged acquisition of information concerning the activist group Greenpeace. The acquisition of the information was alleged to have occurred through hacking activities performed by "consultants" hired by EDF.[103]

The New York Times article goes on to say that corporate intelligence people maintain that information in the public domain is "considered fair game." Having had some experience in this field, I can attest to that statement. If it's "out there" and accessible by the "average person," then that information is fair game. Those same corporate intelligence folks said that theft of information (i.e., that which is not in the open public sphere and like what was being described in the EDF/Greenpeace case) was going too far. I agree because 80% of the information you need about your opponent is in the open. Ironically I think that it was Napoleon who first stated that 80% rule. So theft really isn't required to get a lot of great competitive information, provided the collectors and analysts are astute enough to make sense of that which has been gathered. This accent on what is in "the open" is critical to our discussion here, because the landscape of competitive information is changing, and much of that change is being driven by social media. The Times article pointed out that because of the "automated targeting of the 'cloud' of information that people and organizations generate through their online activities" subterfuge may no longer be required as technology advances.[104] Part of that "cloud" of information is what's being deposited in social media. In other words, much of the same information retrieved via high risk activity (e.g., the type of activity that was described in the EDF/Greenpeace case which led to the identification of an alleged perpetrator) may now be obtained via lower risk activities, activities in the "cloud" that can be more completely anonymous. Mining that cloud is both an art and a science, as is interacting with, responding to, manipulating, and analyzing it for commercial purposes.

The precedent exists that governments have been involved, at least to some degree, with corporate intelligence and with countering economic competition. And although these examples of precedent may represent "higher risk" cases, if agents of foreign governments are willing to pursue "higher risk" competitive intelligence activities, then would they not also pursue the "lower risk" activities? Why would they not analyze that cloud? Wouldn't they not only analyze that cloud, but also participate, covertly, in that social media cloud that is getting larger every day?

Why They Are a Threat

Should government intelligence agents choose to concentrate on the cloud, that lower risk path, that wealth of public information floating in the social media sphere, would there be a tendency or a temptation for them to do more than just mine it? Would there be a temptation to interact with it in a way that changes its meaning? Read on.

Going back to the Cold War, Soviet propagandists were touted as experts in the process of disinformation. These agents were reported as "planting specious stories in obscure corners of the media claiming, for example, that the CIA invented AIDS." [105] Does this accusation sound familiar to you? Or perhaps a variant of this idea? I know that I've heard this in passing conversations or in snippets of news stories. This accusation just keeps floating around.

The accusation continues to float around because it's a meme, pronounced "meeeem." I've mentioned memes in earlier points in this book. Now that we're going to discuss them in more detail, let's have a definition. No, sorry. Not a dictionary definition this time. Instead, I'll give you a definition from my own learning about this subject.

The word meme refers to a self-replicating idea, one that keeps perpetuating itself, as does a virus. The concept or idea represented by a meme spreads through a population of people like a virus. (No pun intended here relative to the reference to AIDS.) You've probably heard about or read about this meme regarding "the CIA's creation of AIDS." Memes can be as inconsequential as the latest slang phrase or something as serious as that used to discredit or defame a person, an organization, or a nation.

The Communists were using memes effectively long before the age of the Internet.[106] I suppose we could call them the "meme meisters." They, and their successor nations, are not likely to stop now, especially since a meme now is more easily spread than it was during the height of the Cold War.

What's all this meme stuff got to do with insidious competition from The Nasties? Well, at this point in the book, I hope *you* would be able to tell *me*. Just consider this question: Simply because the Cold War is over, why should these meme meisters resist the temptation to manipulate the meaning of what is in the cloud of social media?

The Communists got much practice at meme meistering during the Cold War. They have an institutional skill in this area. If they haven't already started, they must be itching to continue their perfection of this skill, but this time for rubles. Things for the Communists have changed geopolitically. The Soviets aren't Soviet any longer. The Chinese are still communist, technically speaking. But they're not really communist, are they? They're sort of "Communist Lite." Back in the day, much, if not all, of the communist disinformation meme practice was oriented toward political goals. Political goals are still important to the communists. Politics is important to any government. Yet, for the Communists and ex-Communists in the East today, political goals are not the be all and end all any longer. Rather than them "telling" us how superior communism is over capitalism and using political propaganda and memes to do so, and rather than beating their shoes on their desks at the United Nations General Assembly and telling us that they will "bury us" (excuse me for showing my age), they've now gotten "jiggy" with the quotidian flow of life - making a living, capitalist and not collectivist style.

They have realized that all that meme propaganda stuff about communism being superior to capitalism wasn't putting much borscht or rice on the plates of their people. Yes, nice parades and snappy uniforms on their soldiers, and great graphic designs on those signs in Red Square and Tiananmen Square. (For examples of what I mean by great graphics, see the International Institute of Social History, http://www.iisg.nl/exhibitions/chairman/) But where's the food, Boris? For them now, and since the collapse of the Iron Curtain, making a living is right up at the top of their list along with the rest of us schlubs. So, why would they stop the meme stuff now?

Their companies have to compete on a global scale with the companies of free-market Western societies, companies who have collective free-market experience adding up to at least several millennia. Meme mangling against those well-heeled and highly experienced Western competitors could help improve the global competitive position of these newly-minted Eastern companies clawing their way onto the world stage of commerce.

More Evidence in Support of the Threat

Let's look a little bit into the Russian psyche.

In the book *Sway*, the authors, Ori Brahman and Rom Brahman, write about psychological influences that impact human decision making. They give examples of how these influences vary from culture to culture. One of the cultures they examined was the Russian culture, and as an example of influences on behavior they discuss the Russian version of the television show "Who Wants to Be a Millionaire?" Particularly the authors discuss the impact of the audience lifeline option on the contestant's success.

The authors report that in the American version of the show, the audience lifeline response provides the correct answer over 90 percent of the time. But not so in the Russian version of the show. Unlike in the French version of the show, where the authors demonstrated how the audience intentionally misled contestants that the audience deemed to be too dumb to win, the

Russian audience lifeline was found to mislead both smart and less-than-smart contestants. What's behind this deceptive behavior?

For the answer to that question, the authors consulted an expert in Russian history, Professor Geoffrey Hosking, a faculty member at University College in London. In Geoffrey's view, isolating the cause of the deceiving behavior was a matter of comprehending and interpreting the Russian view of fairness. The authors of Sway quoted Geoffrey as saying that he thought Russians had the belief that "people who departed from the norm could be dangerous to the whole community" and that Russians would "seek the center" and "resent people who were misfits." From this insight, and some others, Ori and Rom concluded that the audience in the Russian television studio viewed the contestants as "trying to get rich on the backs of the audience members - and why should they (the audience) contribute to such unfair behavior?" Indeed. The authors said that the misleading behavior exhibited in the lifeline segment occurred so often that the contestants of the Russian version of the show learned to "be wary" of the audience lifeline response.[107]

So, can it be said that subterfuge, at least an element of it, is a way of Russian life shown toward those regarded as misfits by Russian culture? And if so, would not that way of life revolve around issues of perceived fairness? This is very much unlike the West. In *Sway*, Geoffrey was quoted as saying, "Americans regard it as justified if someone becomes rich." But for Russians, Geoffrey is quoted as saying, "I think they (the Russians) resent the very fact that these people (the rich) have become so much richer than everyone else." [108] It's that resentment of the departure from the norm and the feelings of exploitation that can power the type of insidious competitor that I'm discussing in this chapter, agents of foreign governments.

For the Russians it may be very natural for them to take these opinions about fairness, combine them with their experience in cyber warfare, Cold War propaganda, and general meme mangling skills, and advance comfortably into the social media sphere as their next national and economic battlefield; one that is in support of their own national corporations. For them it would just be a way of "doing business," except now that phrase really connotes business and it's not just a euphemism for international political intrigue. Disinformation and meaning change, toward American and Western companies, would be a way for any government new to the capitalist system to attempt to level the playing field in the game of international business. Watch for it within social media.

Their Tools

The West and the East are no longer adversaries, per se. More accurately, in this world of globalization, they can be described as rivals, competitors. But for the East, the former or dwindling communists, the old routines of competition are still part of the game. They would never consider those old methods not to be a part of the new game. And if they can use their disinformation skills at discrediting American or Western companies, in the hope that business will be redirected toward their own national companies (many of which sell in the United States and other Western nations), then why wouldn't they do so? For us in Western cultures, that kind of play is generally out of bounds. But for them, the tools of disinformation, because they were part of their culture, are very naturally in fair territory.

The changing of meaning through meme propagation and distortion is so clean, so untraceable. And what would meme distortion be without the tool of Mutant Conversation. It's there; it's a naturally occurring instrument. To this type of insidious competitor Mutant Conversation is just begging to be used, especially since the Five Factors of Insidious Competition make its use all that much more attractive. The tools of partially configured conversational DNA are perfectly applied in the game of mangling a meme to give your competitor on the other side of the globe a figurative black eye. Via Mutant Conversation, the bastardization of the solipsistic and epistemological process could start those foreign cash registers ringing.

Mutant Conversation is hard to trace and can be very effective in moving commerce away from one company and toward another, via the trashing of a corporate image. Just imagine how difficult it would be to trace or identify such perpetrators of this kind of disinformation competition. This is just what the doctor of those former spies would order.

Understand that I am not saying that this is actually happening or is being done by any specific government. There are no specific accusations here, and the preceding serves only as a theoretical example. I am only saying that it is possible based on previous history and national culture and a little imagination. But given all that I have presented, it is difficult to believe that it is not happening now, or won't happen in the very near future.

Last night you saw in your favorite social network a conversation trashing an American sportswear maker. You saw that conversation mutate, be misunderstood, become augmented with some Snark to gather some piling on, or perhaps supplemented with some Hip Chat favoring a non-American sportswear marketer. You then saw that conversation propagate further across the network. How do you know that that conversation was not started by a former member of the DGSE, or the KGB, or some other governmental agency? How would you know?

The experiential audacity of these insidious competitors would not preclude the use of Social Engineering. Playing this game of subterfuge and deception would be right up their alley. Imagine what business information highly experienced government intelligence agents could glean from this practice. Are you sure that all of your connections in your professional social network are who they claim to be? What have you let loose in that environment about your job? Your company? Your co-workers?

Still think this theory of The Nasties is far-fetched or unlikely? Then just sit back and remember how up until September 11 you thought that no one would ever intentionally fly a commercial airliner into a building.

All right. Now it's time to move away from The Nasties and on to something a little more pleasant. The Friendlies are the subject of the next chapter. But don't get too comfortable with the title. The Friendlies are not as friendly as you may think.

Take-Aways from Chapter Twelve – The Nasties

1. The Nasties are just that. Nasty. This class of insidious competitor intentionally disseminates false information.
2. There is one primary type of Nasty:
   a. Foreign Governments & their Agents
      i. Tools: Mutant Conversation, Social Engineering, Snark, and Hip Chat
      ii. Attack: Cognitive Covert
      iii. Organization: Cosmic

Following is Figure 12-1, Reality Benders & Nasties, a graphic representation of the insidious competitors that we have discussed so far.

Figure 12-1, Reality Benders, & Nasties

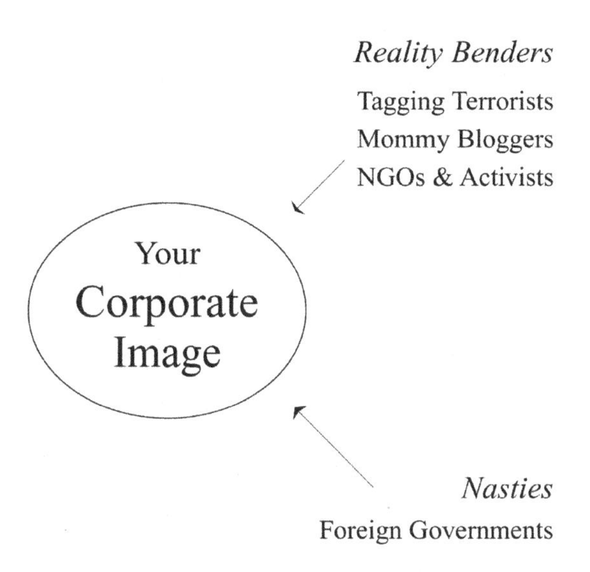

Chapter Thirteen:
The Friendlies

We've discussed, so far, two classes of insidious competitors: The Reality Benders and The Nasties. Either would seem nefarious, to some degree; neither would seem particularly friendly. You wouldn't have a good feeling when you first think of either of them. But now we move on to something different. We move on to an interesting class of insidious competitor. They are interesting in a different way, though.

What's interesting about them is that thinking about this new class of competitors as "friendly" is somewhat deceptive. The title of this class, "The Friendlies," is a bit of a misnomer. They are: Customers/Clients/Consumers, Employees, Activist Stockholders, and Labor Unions. If The Friendlies are insidious competition, then why am I referring to them as friendly? Shouldn't all competitors be considered as unfriendly? Not exactly. Many adjectives are relatively applied, as is this one. These types of insidious competitors aren't necessarily friendly in the objective sense of the word, but they are relatively and subjectively more friendly to your company than are the other types of insidious competitors described in this book. Generally when their names are mentioned we would think, "Oh. These guys don't pose any threat to your company. They are 'part' of your company. Why would they want to hurt its image?"

Yes, these people are "part" of your company, but their objectives are not necessarily the same as those of the company. They are not always moving in the same directions as is your company. Think of these people as "stakeholders," the fashionable term bandied about within corporate social responsibility circles. These are people whose lives are affected by your company and partially on whom *your corporate image* depends for its maintenance and elevation. As I said, the objectives of The Friendlies are not necessarily the same as those of your company, but they do share at least some overlapping goals, one of which would be that your company continues to exist. Whereas The Reality Benders and The Nasties often share no commonality in goals with the companies with which they compete, The Friendlies do. Some Reality Benders and Nasties would be quite happy if their actions put their target companies out of business. Not so with The Friendlies. The Friendlies derive some of their daily "problem solutions" from the companies they target. Putting these companies out of business would only create more problems for The Friendlies than their actions would solve. No. The Friendlies do not wish to "terminate" the companies they target. The Friendlies only wish to *influence* targeted companies to get them to do something which The Friendlies believe will be to the benefit of The Friendlies.

Who are these people exactly? What makes them insidious competition? What makes them a threat to *your corporate image*? Let's take a closer look.

Customers/Clients/Consumers

Different businesses have different names for the people who buy their goods and/or services. Call them what you will, customers and clients and consumers often have a love/hate relationship with the companies from which they buy. The dance between the two major elements in the commercial equation, the seller and the buyers, is eternal and its tension is what is at the root of the free market. Companies try to fulfill needs and wants; Customers/Clients/Consumers look for the goods and/or services which will best meet those needs at a price that those buyers believe offers the best value for their money. Customers and clients and consumers look to companies to offer goods and services that are "problem solutions." People don't buy products or services; they buy solutions. Customers/Clients/Consumers, as insidious competitors, target companies just enough to attempt to convince those companies to produce "better" solutions. Customers/Clients/Consumers, as insidious competitors, don't target companies enough to drive them from the marketplace. If they did, then these buyers would further complicate their lives by having fewer problem solutions from which to select.

Why They Are a Threat

When buyers feel that their purchase has been on either end of the extreme (i.e., they have gotten a deal that was very high in value and solved their problem efficiently or, conversely, a deal that was very low in value and solved their problem inefficiently or not at all), it is then that buyers are likely to "sound off." With social media at the fingertips of most of the developed world, sounding off is easy and inexpensive. Whether it's good or bad, people are going to "talk" within the social media sphere about your company. You can't stop them. The positive comments, the accolades, are not insidious competition against your corporate image. Certainly not. You want to encourage those accolades and take steps to do so. But it's those negative comments that come up and bite you from behind. Those are the ones you've got to watch out for, to understand and minimize. It's those negative comments that are the insidious competition to your company. Are the negative comments really significant? Is there enough negativity out there to actually make a difference? Let's go back to the previously cited Universal Mc Cann study to tackle this question.

That study found that within social media people are more likely to share a positive opinion of a product or service than a negative opinion. Answering the question, "What motivated me to share my opinion?" on a scale of 1 to 5 (where 5 equaled "very motivating" and 1 equaled "not motivating at all") the responses were as follows:

"Good personal experience" achieved a rating of 4.1

"Someone you trust having a good personal experience" achieved a rating of 3.7

Interesting ratings, but do these findings mean that no one complains? Well, no, of course not. Customers and clients and consumers are always complaining, although not always directly to the company. Not all commercial transactions are perfect. With commercial transactions in general, there are almost always grounds for someone to "bitch" about something. Nothing ever goes perfectly all the time. And the execution of those complaints is often dependent upon the perceived level of fairness. We saw how important "perceived fairness" can be when we discussed the different cultural versions of "Who Wants to Be a Millionaire." Perceived fairness by buyers is a very important factor in commercial transactions. Although its degree is culturally dependent, when unfairness is perceived in a commercial transaction and there is no or little chance for satisfaction, look out. The complaints within social media will happen. Those complaints and comments will cut *your* company's *corporate image* up like a Russian studio audience with an audience lifeline as their tool. Let's continue with more of the findings of the Universal Mc Cann study and now look at the complaints.

In the Universal Mc Cann study, it was found that within social media, negative comments were made less than were positive comments. Answering the question, "What motivated me to share my opinion?" on a scale of 1 to 5 (where 5 equaled "very motivating" and 1 equaled "not motivating at all") the responses were as follows:

"Bad personal experience" achieved a rating of 3.3

"Someone you trust having a bad personal experience" achieved a rating of 3.2

Ouch. Those motivations for negative responses aren't significantly different from the reasons for the positive responses. Now, lest you think that the study was subject to demographic or cultural bias, please know that the sample was 17,000 active Internet users from 29 countries, with each market sample representative of sex and age in the 16 to 54 bracket. Skewed? Probably not.[109] Okay. So more folks in social media are being positive about your company image than aren't. But can we put a proportion on that relationship? Can we set it into an order of magnitude to try to determine its importance? Yes.

eMarketer published some survey results relating to this question. According to eMarketer, an Anderson Analytics survey said that social network users by a two to one margin said something good about a brand or company as opposed to saying something bad. In that study, from a sample size of 1,000, 46% "said something good about a brand/company" as compared to 23% who "said something bad about a brand/company." [110] Now, although this study did not have as large of a sample as the Universal Mc Cann study, and although this sample was limited to the United States, the results from this study are consistent with those from the Universal Mc Cann study. There are simply more people saying good things about your company than bad things. But, if I was you, after reading this I wouldn't be running off to the bank while laughing giddily just yet. Within the Anderson study we see that two to one margin. Think about that for a moment: a two to one margin. This margin means that for every two persons singing your praises in the social media sphere, there's is one complainer out there trashing you. As I said, no giddy laughing and bank running yet. This margin is not exactly an overwhelming position in your favor. In social media, according to the Anderson study one-third of the comments about your company are negative. What a horror, like the "Dell Sucks" example we'll see shortly.

Perhaps your company has even experienced these horrors first hand. Incidents of dissatisfied buyers freaking out within social media have been documented ad infinitum, and yes ad nauseum, and to do so again is beyond the scope of this book. You may Google a well-known brand name of your choosing, perhaps your company's brand name, along with the word "sucks" after the brand name, and see what you get. It's gospel within social media business circles that doing so will yield at least some results. Some brand names more than others have this particular problem. This is the nature of the threat from The Friendlies. You are no longer in total control.

The book *The Cluetrain Manifesto* was written about a decade ago and dealt with the switch in power between buyers and sellers, asserting that that switch (or the cliché, "paradigm shift," as business authors often like to characterize it) was created by the advent of the commercial Internet. The balance of control changed. Written before social media, per se, became a powerful force on the Internet, *The Cluetrain Manifesto* was prescient in this regard, and saw that competition for *your* company's *corporate image*, among the very people who buy products and services, had the potential to become, what now is indeed, insidious. In my opinion, the authors of *The Cluetrain Manifesto*, using other words, identified The Friendlies as insidious competitors long before *Insidious Competition – The Battle for Meaning and the Corporate Image* defined the concept of the non-traditional competitor and put names to the various classes of these insidious competitors and identified their characteristics.

Have you already forgotten that one-third of social network participants commenting on a company or brand are doing so in a negative way? Don't forget this. Doing so, and ignoring that fact, makes The Friendlies all the more insidious.

How They Are Organized

The actions of The Friendlies are largely chaotically organized. Customer/Clients/Consumers don't get together and conspire against your company image. If they did, or actually I should say when they do, we would call them something else, a different type of competitor. If Customers/Clients/Consumers were cosmically organized with intention, they would be categorized as one of the other types of insidious competitor that we explore in this book. No, this type of competitor competes chaotically. When a Customer/Client/Consumer feels that they, or people who they value, haven't been treated "fairly," then they, who comment about products or services within social networks, do so. One-third of them. They make the "friendly" threat.

Now, let's not let this idea go stale by taking this idea a step further, but within the first concepts that you and I discussed in this book. Let's go back to Chapter Two, where I talked about the users of social media being influenced by crowd behavior, and let's go back to Chapter Three, where I talked about the Five Factors of Insidious Competition. Those factors you will recall are anonymity, instinct, power, contagion, and disdain for institutions. Also let's revisit the idea of the activist co-opting the public, as presented in the NGOs and Activists section of Chapter Eleven where I said that the cosmically organized activist, in applying his or her tools, will pick-up support from the social media public who will extend the activist's message, chaotically, throughout the social media sphere. Let's think of all of these ideas from within the key scene of the 1976 movie *Network*.

If you don't understand my cultural reference, or if you haven't seen this movie, you may view the key scene via the miracle of YouTube.com. If you aren't familiar with this movie, or the scene specifically, before you proceed with reading further, to get the most value from what I am going to say, please go to YouTube.com. In the search box type in "Howard Beale." Then select the "I'm As Mad As Hell . . ." video. There are several. Just about any one will do.

In the key scene, when Howard Beale, a network news anchor, goes on the air "to make his witness" to his audience of millions, he does so while wearing a rumpled raincoat, with hair matted wet from the rain in which he just walked sans umbrella. At this point in the movie, he's quite daft, driven over the edge by dual problems of the state of the 1970s economy and of 1970s society. But, even so, the network "powers that be" allow him to go on the network air. It's then that he makes his famous ranting proclamation that he is "mad as hell" and he "isn't going to take it anymore." In his rant, Howard asks everyone watching him to whip open their windows and repeat his words at the top of their lungs. And they did.

"Are they shouting in Baton Rouge?," the network brass queries. Network peons answer in the affirmative.

Howard walked into the studio with a mission. Near the beginning of the scene, as the guard lets Howard into the studio, Howard tells that guard that he is going to "make his witness," as I mentioned above. Howard is a cosmically organized force. He has intent. He had intent before he walked through the studio door, announcing that intent to the guard. But Howard's audience does not have intent, yet they influence each other. The people listening to Howard just let it rip, across the network, across the country.

The audience members listened to a cosmically organized force and responded to it, in crowd fashion, and as a group of people shouting from windows and therefore largely unknown to each other, feeling the force of anonymity. A group of people shouting from windows feeling also the power, the contagion, responding to instinct, with disdain for the institutions they felt to be behind their misery. They may appear to be unorganized, but organized they were, in what I'm characterizing in this book as a chaotic fashion. Yes, mostly chaotic. They merely needed a spark to get them started. Howard was that spark to get them to leave the "negative comments" within the "network" to which they were attending at that moment. They then let the instinct kick in. Beale was an activist in this situation, or an agent provocateur, or a catalyst. He incited the "crowd" and entreated them to act. In 1976, the year of the movie *Network*, the average Customer/Client/Consumer had few, if any, media avenues to express their opinion. But for the people represented by the audience, the crowd, in this movie, Howard presented them with their opportunity. Fictitious, yes. Yet, this classic moment in American film represented an actual, unfulfilled urge. And the movie showed how this urge could be met, chaotically, without further organization or planning. Think of the shouting out the window as a crude, and limited coverage, social network of the 1970s genre.

Why do I present this illustration here? Why do I think you should be interested in learning about this scene? What does this have to do with insidious competition and *your corporate image*?

I present this illustration because it represents the forces of timeless human nature that can be released, at any time in history, when sparked by one person with a network at their fingertips. Think about that as your consider the importance of *your corporate image* to your company's viability and success. Think about that as you consider the connection between *your* company's *corporate image* and *your personal success.* Think about this scene as your consider what we discussed above, that one-third of social media users expressing an opinion are expressing a negative one. Then think about how many of those negative expressions might be about your company, and then think about how those people are the Howard Beales, lighting a cosmic fire to your company's corporate image that can spread uncontrollably and chaotically within social media. Think about all this and then think about how Customers/Clients/Consumers are insidious competitors.

In a Forbes article, it was stated that since 1990 the web has created more than 100,000 citizen social and political groups. "Customers are joining with activist non-governmental organizations (NGOs) and advocacy groups, using blogs, wikis, social networking sites like Facebook, and video sharing sites like Google's YouTube to proliferate their messages, create communities of activists and even for counter-branding purposes." The article goes on to say that, no surprise, under such conditions companies are losing control of their reputations because the world is filled with so many communications channels.[111] Yikes! Did this new reality sneak up on you and your company? These more than 100,000 citizen social and political groups, some of which are the "chaotically" organized Customer/Client/Consumer type I alluded to in the previous paragraph, are just ready to "flame-on" at the spark of the cosmically organized "Howard Beale" activist.

Thus, the organization of the Customer/Client/Consumer is chaotic, but it can be ignited by a cosmic force, like Howard, or another chaotic force, like another random buyer doing no more than ranting about an "unfair" commercial transaction.

The attack type of the Customer/Client/Consumer can be either semantic or cognitive, depending of course upon their intent and the ferocity of their attack. Customer/Client/Consumer attacks are likely to stem from any perceived unfairness that they think they've experienced. A simple trashing of the brand name, product or service, without specifics would be classified as a semantic attack. A "call to action," like a call to the company for satisfaction or a call to other Customers/Clients/Consumers to stop patronizing the company, would be classified as a cognitive attack, with a change in behavior as its goal. When this insidious competitor makes a simple call for others to stop buying from a company, then it is likely to be covert, as there is no need or value to identification and, in fact, the protection of personal identity would be preferred. When the Customer/Client/Consumer calls for satisfaction, as in the case of a dissatisfied customer, then identity is necessary and therefore overt. We'll see examples of cognitive overt attacks very shortly.

Their Tools

Chaotically organized, this insidious competitor makes good use of the tools of Mutant Conversation, Snark, and Hip Chat. Following are two examples.

Example #1

Writer and media executive Jeff Jarvis is famous in his own right, but he is especially famous for starting one of the first consumer revolutions online and for taking some credit in affecting the brand name of a computer maker.

According to his book, *What Would Google Do*, in 2005 Jarvis purchased a Dell laptop, paying extra for the at-home service option. Per his story, upon first booting the laptop it had problems. He, like most of us would, attempted to resolve those problems by calling customer service, but found no satisfaction in the process. Not being able to obtain the at-home service, for which he had paid, he sent the laptop in to Dell service several times "only to find something new wrong every time" after it was returned to him.

In not being able to achieve satisfaction and to vent his frustration, Jeff went to his blog and wrote a post entitled, "Dell Sucks." The post chronicled, very colorfully with some swear words sprinkled in, his experience with the Dell laptop and his experience with Dell customer service. His post garnered support. Remember Howard Beale?

Jeff writes that people started to get behind him. He said that it started with hundreds then evolved to thousands of people. Per Jeff, people left comments on his blog post and wrote similar articles elsewhere and linked to his Dell Sucks story. A result of this linking was that his original post started to climb higher and higher on Google search result pages and he stated that eventually his post was only a few slots away from the Dell home page link in the Google search results. Jeff claims, in his book, that his "blog post was beginning to damage Dell's brand." He backs this claim up by saying that, about the time this was happening, Dell's customer service ratings were falling and the company share price was about 50% of what it was at the time he began his Dell Sucks quest. Whether or not Jeff was the cause of an effect on Dell's "ephemeral image" and whether he affected the slide in the stock's value is debatable. There can be many causes for such a slide. Even Jeff concedes this point in his book. But, certainly we can see that his actions were potentially, at least, a peripheral cause to such changes. And his status as a media executive and a relatively well-known blogger, at a time that blogging was just becoming popular, likely didn't hurt his case against Dell. Indeed, having his story picked up by Business Week two months after the saga began, probably contributed to the power of this insidious competition to the Dell image.[112]

So here a chaotic force, with no obvious intent other than "to vent," gathered momentum and created a reaction that some analysts say made Dell a better company today than it was in 2005. Jeff's venting, though, was not what I would classify as semantic. I don't think that he just wanted to trash Dell's brand image. He wanted more. In the long run, he wanted his machine fixed. He wanted the satisfaction for which he paid, a cognitive action. His attack was chaotic cognitive and overt. He made no attempt to hide his identify. Did he get satisfaction?

His machine was not repaired, but, according to his book, Jeff did receive a refund.[113] His attack benefited from the Five Factors when people left comments on his blog post and when other bloggers started to write similar stories on other blogs, linking to his original story. Jeff's followers were similar to Howard Beale's and their actions were supported by the Five Factors. How about the principles of propaganda? Were they at work in this example?

Yes. Jeff's story leveraged the principles of propaganda in that the story used the Temporal Focus principle, because others were writing about similar problems, and addressed two of the Societal Basics in that "humans are naturally good" (he implied Dell wasn't) and that the "overarching aim in human life is happiness," a happiness that he led readers to believe he could not achieve. Jeff's story played on the opposite of those Societal Basics, entreating others to act from within the Five Factors, figuratively screaming, "I'm as mad as hell, and I'm not going to take it anymore."

The Dell Sucks story is a classic example of the insidious competition structure that we have discussed in this book. The cognitive attack, the principles of propaganda, and the Five Factors are all present in this example. And although the Customer/Client/Consumer may not specifically have, as a primary target, your company's image in their cross-hairs, once these people get done seeking their satisfaction, the gradual and subtle effect of their actions can be the same as if they did.

The Dell Sucks story is an example from 2005. Are examples of this type likely to continue? Will companies allow this type of customer or client or consumer dissatisfaction to turn into insidious competition?

Using web monitoring software, Dell is now "listening" to social media, as are many other companies, in an effort to "nip in the bud" any insidious competition against "The Ephemeral Image" and, perhaps, in an effort to serve their customers better. An example of such action follows.

Example #2

Early in 2009, one of the PCs in my office had been having some problems. This agony had been going on for quite a while, so I decided to bite the bullet and call for help. I called Geek Squad because I thought they knew what they were doing. I was surprised, but not pleasantly.

When Geek Squad showed up at my office, I explained the PC's recent behavior to the agent. After several minutes of trying to explain the problems, I wasn't feeling hopeful. I still had a few more things to explain, but at that point he seemed "checked-out" and wanting to sit at the machine to do that "voodoo." So I let him.

After about an hour and a half of diagnosis, he couldn't find "anything wrong with it." Curious. If nothing was wrong with it, why would I call Geek Squad in the first place and why was I getting the following errors from the PC well-before I called the Geeks?

- Security package not updating correctly.
- Firefox crashing about, oh, eight times per day.
- Irregular recognition of external hard drives.
- OSA.exe error notices.
- PC crashing periodically upon Outlook booting.
- Generic host process for Win32 services on start-up, periodically.

- Periodic notices at start-up that Windows had recovered from a serious error. (Yes. No kidding. I think the most serious error was to buy a Windows machine in the first place.)
- Periodic file checking notices in Outlook due to a file not closing last time Outlook was in use.

Interesting that with all those problems he couldn't find "anything wrong." So, instead of the $300 I was quoted when I called in for the appointment, the agent charged only $139 for their "Quick Fix Service." He went happily on his way.

But I didn't go happily on my way.

For days after the visit, the machine kept making the same errors, and new ones were added to its dastardly repertoire.

- Upon shut-down, blue screen errors occurred saying there was a memory management problem.
- Windows would not update automatically.
- Software installation was disabled.
- Outlook archive folders were missing-in-action.

I looked at my copy of the Geek Squad Service Agreement for information about their warranty and here's what it said:

Item 4 - Labor Warranty: Geek Squad guarantees services provided to you at your home or business for 30 days; however, for repairs necessitated by a virus or spyware, the 30-day warranty is valid only if the antivirus and antispyware protection for your product is installed or updated during repair or before you access the internet again. If there is a problem with the service provided to you at the Geek Squad store and if you notify us at 1800 GeekSquad (1-800-433-5778) within the 30-day time period, Geek Squad will work to remedy your original problem quickly and at no cost.

After reading the warranty, I saw nothing there that would disqualify me from trying to get a further remedy. So I called them. Two service reps told me that the "Quick Fix Service" was exempt from their warranty. (Yes, two. The first rep and then her supervisor.)

Huh? Where does it say that in the warranty?

The original problems were not caused by a virus or spyware. That much the agent determined during the visit, so they couldn't pull that clause out on me. After debating the *meaning* of the warranty statement with two service reps who just kept repeating over and over again the same company policy that the warranty doesn't cover Quick Fix service, I told them that this incident would take one of two courses of action.

One: They could honor their warranty and return an agent to my office to fix not only the original problems, but the problems that started to occur after their visit, which a reasonable presumption would say that they had caused, and after such visit everyone could go away happy, or,

Two: Because I believed they were violating federal law by refusing to honor a stated guarantee, which was in writing, (like the Sonny Crockett reference earlier in this book) I would clear my desk of all my other work and make their life a living "heck" (yes . . . I said "heck" because I didn't want to swear on a call I knew was being recorded). I said unless they got me someone quickly I would complain to the Federal Trade Commission, my state consumer protection division, my county consumer protection agency, my municipal attorney, their municipal attorney, their county consumer protection board, their state consumer protection agency, my state's attorney general, their state's attorney general, and anyone else I could think of who might be interested in listening and who would bury Best Buy and the Geek Squad in paperwork inquiries and depositions from now until the next ice age.

The Geek Squad service reps told me there was nothing they could do (i.e., they chose the second alternative).

After I hung up with their reps, I reasoned that taking course number two would cost me more time than the whole incident was worth. I reasoned that it would, after all, be more cost-effective to chuck that piece-of-crap PC running Windows XP in the trash and buy a Mac, just as Jeff Jarvis did after his Dell Sucks experience. But I thought I'd try one more thing first. I thought I'd pull a page from the Jeff Jarvis playbook. I started to tweet. What a powerful tool.

I tweeted for almost an hour, sending the same tweet over and over and over and over and over, about how Geek Squad didn't fix my problem, made it worse, and violated my warranty. I had previously read that Best Buy (Geek's

Squad parent) monitored Twitter. I knew they were "listening," but I wasn't sure if they'd respond.

They did respond, and in a short period of time. An agent from the Best Buy Online Community called me and said he wanted to make things right. Too bad I had to tweet for almost an hour to get them to do something they should have done when I first made a simple request for them to honor their warranty.

I told the Online Community agent that I wanted them to fix the original problems, plus remedy the ones they apparently caused, and with a different agent since the first one didn't find "anything wrong" and didn't really give me the feeling like he knew what he was doing. The Online Community agent did make an extraordinary effort to get another agent out to my office and relatively quickly. I was impressed, but still disappointed that I had to make such an effort to get them to do something they should have done in the first place.

The outcome of the story is that the second agent did not fix the problems in my PC. In fact, that machine was stable for a while after this second visit, but then more problems appeared and those problems grew worse. I can only conclude that, as the second agent suggested during his visit, Windows will never run perfectly. Like the old joke, if Microsoft made cars, the highways would be littered with crashes. No matter what these Geek Squad guys do, that PC will never operate as it should, and that really is the fault of Microsoft more than that of the Geek Squad. And after all, the Geek Squad warranty does say "Geek Squad will work to remedy your original problem." Their warranty does not guarantee satisfaction. The warranty does not say that they will actually fix the problem. But, how could they say that really? A Windows PC is such a mish-mosh of code, it's about as susceptible to catching a bug as a preschooler in a classroom filled with drippy-nosed toddlers.[114]

So I, in this incident a chaotically organized insidious competitor like Jeff Jarvis, created a cognitive attack, and an overt one, at that. I wanted satisfaction, as did Jeff. I wanted what I paid for and was legally entitled to. My attack incorporated the principles of successful propaganda. I used Veracity. I used, like Jarvis, the Societal Basics with an allusion to two of the four sociological principles: that humans are naturally good and that I could not achieve happiness (satisfaction) because the Geek Squad was not being "good" by not honoring their warranty. And I depended upon the presence of the Five Factors, which are alive and well in social media, to achieve my goal.

Even though my tweets did not spread far and wide, and even though I didn't gather a large number of followers saying figuratively, "I'm as mad as hell, and I'm not going to take it anymore," the Five Factors came to my aid. How? The Best Buy Online Community agent knew those Five Factors existed. He knew that those factors could fuel a social media reaction and generate insidious competition. He knew that.

And he took the steps to prevent or mitigate the damage.

Companies are more aware of customer or client or consumer generated insidious competition than they were in 2005. But only some companies. And for those who are unaware, which as of this writing appears to be most companies, the future holds runaway insidious competition from customers or clients or consumers in a potential "Dell Sucks" incident of their very own.

Employees

This type of competitor is "friendly." Sort of. If you are an employee of a company, you'll understand what I mean.

Employees are definitely stakeholders of a company. They are seen as part of the company. Employees and their company have a "symbiotic" relationship. It would be difficult to have a company without employees. Without the company, employees have no job. With no job, those individuals have no solution to their problem, the problem of how to put food on the table every day. So, if employees need the company to help them put food on their daily tables, how can Employees be insidious competitors to the company? Perhaps your company? Let me answer a question with a question: Would you rather do something else than have to report to work five days per week? Most people just don't like to work, especially for someone else. Yes, there was gambling at Rick's.

It's because of this necessity to work and put food on the table; it's because of the fact that most people don't like to go to work; it's because Employees are usually viewed by senior company management and outsiders as part of the company and who would be expected to have the same agenda and goals as the company (even if they don't), that this type of insidious competitor can be very damaging to the image of a company, the very same company for which the Employee works. Curious situation. Let's not let this idea go stale, either.

In what unrelated work activity do workers like to engage? Sorry, I don't have any statistics to back this one up, but my statement here is based on thirty years of being exposed to the work environment on a daily basis. People at work like to complain about work and about things directly connected to work.

And, in today's work environment there exists a new wrinkle to make work even more "bitchable."

No longer do you have to wander around the office looking for a sympathetic ear so you can pour into that ear thousands upon thousands of words about how you hate your job and think that the boss is a moron and the way that things are done around the office is dumb and that the woman with blonde hair didn't really get that promotion because she was so skilled and her hair isn't really blonde anyway and why don't they serve Starbucks in the coffee room and why doesn't someone clean out the fridge in that break room and the air conditioning duct over your desk dumps too much cold air on the back of your neck except in December when it toasts the top of your head and that guy in the next cubicle makes too much noise when he drinks his soda through a straw and anyway he should trim his nose hairs and meetings make no sense because they only waste time that could be applied to more bitching and on and on and on and on and on.

Oh, man.

You can pour only so many words into a sympathetic, or semi-sympathetic, ear or an ear that seems to be sympathetic for only so long until your pouring privileges are rescinded and that ear just wants to turn you off and shut down. But now there are millions of "ears" out there who can "listen" to your work-related troubles and maybe even engage with you about what a stupid place you work in. Now you actually have an audience, a real audience, for your kvetching. This is an audience that is actually seeking out the subjects of your complaints. This is a ready, willing, and able audience. They are going to be so much more listenable then those poor schmucks that are held captive in your office for eight hours per day just like you are. Social media.

Why They Are a Threat

In social media, though, you'll probably want to do this complaining, anonymously. I can't imagine that you would actually want to attach your name to it. Again. Social media is perfect for anonymity, isn't it? You can be anyone you want to be; just pick a screen name. Pick a screen name that portrays a persona which you would like to assume. For obvious reasons, I find it difficult to imagine that in social media anyone would actually want to complain about their job and/or their company by using their real name. Or maybe using your real name *is* the perfect dodge? If anyone calls you on it, you can always act shocked and deny it. After all, you say to them, who would be stupid enough to use their real name in social media? I'm not recommending this, of course. I'm just saying, somewhat humorously, that it is possible.

There is one social site, in particular, that allows you to get the kvetching therapy that you desire without bothering anyone in your office. By remaining anonymous, you don't need to run the risk of being labeled an "office gossip," as you might be when you're away from your desk, scouting "cube-land," searching out those sympathetic ears. You may go to JobVent.com, a very popular site (at least as of January 2010 when I wrote this paragraph), and write as much or as little as you like about your current job and/or employer. Or you may look up different jobs and employers on the home page list of "loved" and "hated" jobs and employers. Your company may or may not already be listed there, but no worries. You can just go ahead and start a conversation thread. Just as you would complain about your coworkers and your company during company time in the real world, while your company is actually paying you to do company work, you can use this site, or others like it, also during company time. Again, I'm not recommending any of this, of course. I'm just saying, somewhat sarcastically, that it is possible.

So, how can this type of behavior be considered insidious competition? People have been complaining about their companies for years, for decades, for centuries. I'll bet if that entrepreneurial Cro-Magnon that we discussed back in the Mommy Bloggers section of Chapter Eleven had employees, they grunted and groaned about working for that big-headed, ugly guy who literally looked a lot like an ape. This is all nothing new, perhaps you are thinking. Yes. But the venue is new. Previously your trash talk was kept, for the most part, on the inside, the inside of the company about which you were complaining. Now, welcome to the 21st century. That trash has gone public. Very public. Globally public. Painfully public.

For example, on each conversation thread on JobVent.com, the site very conveniently provides link buttons so that you may send a JobVent.com post of your fancy into your Facebook, Digg, or MySpace account, or simply make a comment, as on a standard blog. They make it insanely easy to spread your favorite workplace ranting.

But remember what I said above about not using your own name in social media to comment about your employer? Well, the pass along to Facebook, Digg, or MySpace could be less anonymous, depending upon how your Facebook, Digg, or MySpace account is set up. But remember, if your Facebook, Digg, or MySpace account is set up in your real name, you could claim to just be sharing the post which you would be passing along. You could note that you didn't actually create the original snarky, castigating, inciting, malcontent, snide remark that you are sharing with your social media friends on Facebook, Digg, or MySpace. You could note that you were just passing it along so all could have a "good laugh," or a "good cry." And here are two drivers of this whole process of Employees publicly trashing their companies, thereby causing a problem for the *corporate image* of the company that employs *you* and provides *you* with a solution to your problem of your "daily bread." One driver is that "laugh." The other driver is that "cry."

Again, I'm not recommending you do any of this. I'm simply drawing a picture of what is very possible so that you will realize that your company is highly susceptible to insidious competition from its own employees.

People like to laugh about where they work. They also cry about it, too. The reasons they love to laugh about work are numerous. Those reasons are at the foundation of the success of comic strips such as Dilbert, and are outside the scope of this book. The reasons people cry about work are as numerous, possibly even more numerous, possibly even awaiting examination by a shrink of their choice and therefore are also outside the scope of this book.

What is inside the scope of this book, however, is the effect of the effort that was put into eliciting that laugh or that cry via social media. It is online conversation that draws out these emotions as the writers anonymously purge their feelings in a public forum. No longer discussions over cubicle walls, or over the break room table, these social media discussions are public. The trash is public. The unwashed, dirty laundry is hanging in the backyard, without having gone through the washing machine, for the whole neighborhood to see. Employee conversations about the work environment may or may not be valid. Those discussions certainly aren't objective; they aren't vetted. Those discussions are opinions, subjective, critical, adverse, damaging, harmful, and slanted information which can tip a reader's *perception* of the company toward the less-than-positive. And much of this online griping, takes the form of a story, a drama, with all the elements of that art form as loved by humans. So that Employee gripe about his employer spreads. Remember. We crave a good story.

Comments about employers spread very quickly. They spread from sites like JobVent.com if only just by readers passing it along to their Facebook, Digg, or MySpace accounts. They spread even further outside the primary venue, the job bitching site, and the secondary venues, such as Facebook, Digg, and MySpace, because that trash talk gets indexed by search engines. While writing this section that you are reading, I ran a check of the source code on JobVent.com (i.e, the HTML code that runs the site).[115] (Yes, I can do that. So can you. Actually, anyone can. It's public information.) My check on their HTML code revealed that they do not block search engine robots or spiders, meaning that any search engine can index any of the company comments that are on their pages. Just to be sure that this is the case, I cross-checked by Googling a couple of the specific rants about different companies as they appeared on JobVent.com pages. Sure enough. Those rants appeared in the Google search results.

Now you can see why Employees are insidious competition.

They mess with the *perception* step of the system of knowing and therefore the *meaning* of the company, and they can now do so right out in *public.*

In terms of insidious competition, this means that any web surfer seeking information about a particular company may also pick up, for example, the JobVent.com comments about that company, in their search results. Any reader viewing those comments, even if just for amusement, can't help but be influenced by them, at least to some degree.

Your Employees compete with your company's efforts to improve and maintain its image. Insidiously. You pay to improve your company image. And you pay your employees. Could it be that you are working at cross purposes?

How They Are Organized and Their Tools

Employees, as insidious competition, may be either cosmically or chaotically organized. From my experience it seems that the chaotically organized group kvetching about one particular company is the more common type of organizational form. But that may not be the only form that exists. Let's discuss what I see as the most common scenario, chaotic, and then let's discuss the cosmic form this type of action may take.

On a social media site, in the chaotic form, we would see that one employee of Company XYZ complains about this and that as well as the other. Then another employee of Company XYZ happens to see the post and adds their opinion, and so on, until it becomes one big pile-on. This chaotic type of activity is fueled by the Five Factors of Insidious Competition, all very informal, and uses the tools of Mutant Conversation, Snark, and maybe there is some Hip Chat thrown in, too. All very informal, yes. In the chaotic organizational form, it's most likely that their attacks will be classified only as semantic, and not cognitive. I haven't seen any of these venting rants that are really oriented toward influencing the behavior of others against the company in question. And if there are some, chances are high that those calls to action would not be taken seriously. Why wouldn't those calls to action be taken seriously? Because, those calls are in a "bitch session." Everyone reading the rants would know that. Mutant Conversation's effectiveness might not kick in completely because the conversational DNA is more fully configured when each reader identifies it as a "rant." Social media conversation participants realize the motivations behind a bitch session, so no, I think this type of attack will remain largely semantic in nature and directed only at *changing meaning.* Even though most readers recognize a bitch session when they see one, a bitch session can still have a *meaning* effect on all who witness it. And, in addition to other employees, this would include non-employees, and perhaps customers, of the targeted company who happened to stumble on the bitch session during a web search. Indeed I had an experience similar to the one I describe.

An Example

In preparation for a client meeting with a pharmaceutical company, and in preferring to have at least a little *knowledge* about the people I am about to meet for business, I ran a very basic web search on the director of the department that I was to visit. From that web search I received some of the usual search results such as links to this person's LinkedIn profile, Facebook account, Twitter profile and other social networking accounts. But I perceived some surprising search results under a site called CafePharma.com, "the Web site for pharmaceutical sales professionals." After reviewing the expected results on the director's LinkedIn and Twitter pages, I indulged my curiosity, now piqued from having CafePharma.com appear in my search results. So, I clicked.

In general, CafePharma.com is a site that contains news about the pharmaceutical industry. But CafePharma.com also features social areas such as chat forums. These are social areas that are used by those involved in the pharmaceutical industry, like employees of the different pharmaceutical manufacturers. The search results I found on the director with whom I was to meet referred me to the forum section of the site. Here's where it got really interesting. The conversations on that forum excoriated, mercilessly, the person with whom I was going to meet. Well, I just had to *perceive* these discussions in more detail. Hey. I'm only human, just like you. Never let the truth get in the way of a good story.

The forum participants, who all had, not surprisingly, the same screen name which was, again not surprisingly, "Anonymous," denigrated this person's management abilities and personal appearance. Additionally, the forum participants severely criticized this person's work at a prior company and designated that work, in the opinion of the excoriators, as the cause of poor sales at that company. The participants in this conversation also described this director by liberally and repeatedly using derogatory terms throughout the discussion thread. Most of those terms were of the four-letter variety.

In my work I travel the social web far and wide. I see a lot of this type of thing and worse. When I view these sorts of conversations, it is usually in a detached manner because I don't *know* the people who are getting trashed in the conversation. But, this conversation was different. I didn't *know* this person yet, but I was about to *know* this person. So I must be honest here. I have to say that the conversations on CafePharma.com did influence my *perception* of the person even before I arrived at the meeting. These conversations affected my *perception* of that person and subsequently my accumulated *knowledge* of that person. So, the conversation had a *meaning* effect on me. The conversation played a part in my reality construction of this person.

Then, I went to the meeting.

Although in person I did not find this personality on the surface to be the way it was portrayed in that forum, during my presentation I kept thinking, "When is this person's real bad side going to emerge." I was waiting for the erratic behavior, as described in the forum, to surface. In fairness, that type of behavior never did appear, at least not during my meeting. Yet, I must say that my *knowledge* about this person was definitely affected.

As I said above, from what I've seen of this type of employee/social web activity and from what I have shown in this example, most employee insidiously competitive activity appears chaotically organized and semantic in nature. But that doesn't mean that Employees could not organize cosmically, and with the intent of a cognitive attack. In doing so, they would use the same tools as in the chaotic attack, the tools of Mutant Conversation, Snark, and Hip Chat. Cosmically speaking, such social network discussions could be created to have an even greater effect than their chaotic cousins.

Of course, it could be that in this CafePharma.com example, the attack was in fact cosmically organized, with the attack class being cognitive and covert. Instead of these Employees being individuals who had worked with the targeted person at a prior company, as stated within the conversation, it could very well be that the persons in this conversation were current subordinates of the targeted person. The persons in that conversation could have been the same people who shared the room during my presentation.

This idea and the example illustrate the scenario where Employees organizing internally could "gang up" and move into social media as a group, a "wolf pack" if you will, to create discussions about superiors they despise in an effort to have them removed from the company. Perhaps they would anticipate that their comments on social networks, either general or professional, would be picked up by senior management at review time, creating some doubt in the reviewer's mind about the targeted manager's worth to the company. How would you like to be that targeted manager? That would be like dealing again with school yard shenanigans. The "cool" kids siding against the "nerds." But this time such an attack wouldn't have just social consequences. The actions would have effects on the personal finances of the targeted manager, as well as having effects on the targeted manager's family. But within the context of *Insidious Competition*, the actions could also have an effect on the *corporate image* of the company involved.

Envision that if enough employees of a certain company are cosmically and cognitively targeted by a wolf pack of employees, casual readers obtaining this information via web searches may think, "Wow. This must be a horribly-run company. If they have so many managers that their own employees view as 'idiots,' maybe I should decrease or eliminate my purchases from that company."

Was this the situation in this example? Was this example one of cosmic organization with a covertly cognitive objective? I really don't know. What I do know is that in this example, the attackers employed very well one of the principles of propaganda – Societal Basics. Here they used the value of work to denigrate the individual, giving readers the idea that the targeted person's work skills would not contribute to the support of work and, as a result, would not contribute to larger societal values. Very well played. And it did work on me, at least a little.

Activist Stockholders

This type of "friendly" insidious competitor is known by various names: stockholder activist, activist shareholder, or activist investor. The key word to keep in mind here is "activist." You have seen this word before in this book, and we should keep the ideas found in the previous discussion of Activists in mind as we talk about this type of insidious competitor.

I see basically two different sub-types of Activist Stockholders. There are those who are "activists," as noted above, whose goal is to cause a corporation to change its behavior in support of a political, social, or cultural objective chosen by the Activist Stockholder, and then there is a sub-type of Activist Stockholder whose goal is to have a person of their choosing elected to the board of directors of the corporation in order to have better control over the business direction of the corporation, with a financial motive underlying.

In this book, we will be concerned only with the first type, the activist sub-type. We will limit this discussion to that activist sub-type because it is that sub-type that will cause the most change to the corporate image. Their activities call in players from outside the corporation in order to garner support for their agenda, and in doing so affect the corporate image. While the second sub-type, the financial sub-type, that which is concerned primarily with financial and business matters within the corporation, represents activities that are primarily internal to the corporation, and as such would not play upon the corporate image to the extent that the activist sub-type does.

Why They Are a Threat

We may tend to think of this insidious competitor, this "activist holding a share of stock," as "friendly" because they are a stockholder, a part owner of the company in question. But to do so would cause us to proceed from a false assumption. A rose by any other name, Activist Stockholders are individuals, usually working as independent groups or within a larger activist organization, who become stockholders of a targeted public company in order to impose a political, social, or cultural agenda on that company, forcing the company to take an action it otherwise would not have taken absent the activist shareholders' influence.

In discussing The Friendlies classification of insidious competitors, we learned that neither the Customer/Client/Consumer nor the Employee, have an agenda objective to put a company out of business. For these two types, doing so would be counter-productive. This limitation of counter-productivity also applies to the Activist Stockholder. The Activist Stockholder's goal is to create a political or social or cultural change. By driving the targeted company from the marketplace the Activist Stockholder would lose its vehicle for change. If that happens, an Activist Stockholder is re-classified only as an activist, by definition. Then there would be no advantage in holding the stock. The advantage this insidious competitor holds *is* the stock.

But, I believe that this type of insidious competitor is far more aggressively antagonistic toward their corporation than other insidious competitors within the classification of The Friendlies. I place them here in this classification because they are legal owners of their company and, thus, are a "part" of the company. By their title, "stockholder," friendly they are presumed to be, but their activist agenda is what makes them insidious, often acting at cross-purposes to the main corporate objectives.

It is this action toward their own goals, which is often against corporate objectives, that impacts the corporate image. The Activist Stockholder battles within social media to portray the *meaning* of the corporation in one way, while the corporation itself endeavors to take that *meaning* in a different direction.

In the following pages, we will come to understand how and why the

Activist Stockholder conducts their *battle for meaning* in order to accomplish their objective. But unlike other insidious competitors examined in this book, the threat from this insidious competitor, the Activist Stockholder, is twofold. Not only will the Activist Stockholder attempt to change the *meaning* of the *corporate image* externally in order to achieve its goals, but if the Activist Stockholder is successful in reaching its goal, the direct change that they seek, a change made to corporate governance, can also redefine the *meaning* of the *corporate image* from *within the corporation itself.*

How They Are Organized

What's the organizational form of the Activist Stockholder? What's the nature of their attack? This one should be easy. I think by now at this point in *Insidious Competition* you will understand that this class of insidious competitor is cosmically organized and that the nature of their attack is cognitive. No fooling around here. They're leaving nothing to the natural and uncontrolled ebbs and flows of chaotic organization, nor are they pulling any punches by mounting only a semantic attack. They're going full bore. They're going for the cognitive effect. They want a behavioral change. To achieve their goals, they're taking the tools of Mutant Conversation, Snark, and Hip Chat "by the horns," steering and applying those tools to their fullest effect. In this way, this type of activist is similar to its cousin insidious competitors, NGOs and Activists. But these Activist Stockholders differ from their factional cousins. Activist Stockholders have an "influence" augmenting their strategy; an influence that can be more effective than any strategic influence that can be conjured up by your ordinary garden-variety activist or NGO.

What do these Activist Stockholders use as their influence? Roses and chocolates? Nope. Charm? Hardly.

Activist Stockholders use a share of stock and the privileges that come with that ownership. The privilege that is key here is the proxy vote. These groups use the power of the proxy vote as the avenue to their desired political, social, or cultural change.

For readers unfamiliar with the proxy vote, here is a quick explanation using American laws and procedures to illustrate. To abide by U.S. Securities and Exchange Commission (SEC) and state corporation regulations, each year public companies must put up for a vote, certain issues among the shareholders who, as you know, are the owners of the company. Two of the common issues voted upon are the election of the members of the board of directors, the group that is responsible for setting general policy and direction for the company, and the election of the company's financial auditors. Other general "housekeeping" issues may also be put to a vote, as well as other issues which may not be so mundane and quotidian. Be those issues mundane or even extraordinary, the shareholders may cast their votes in one of two ways. Shareholders may attend the legally required annual meeting of the corporation and cast their votes in person. Or, by the more commonly used method, shareholders may cast their votes via the "proxy." The proxy is the instrument by which shareholders "vote their shares" remotely, each stockholder having one vote for each share owned. Proxies may be cast by mail, by telephone, or online.

Although shareholders vote their shares, which seems "democratic," the shareholders are not the only people who determine what issues will go to vote. Many of the issues placed on the annual ballot are determined by the board of directors or officers of the corporation. So, the process is not really "democratic" or representative of the positions and concerns of the larger corporate ownership. Even though the process is not truly democratic, since the early 1940s, the power of *all the owners* of a corporation has been progressively unleashed.

Since 1942, in an effort to improve the democratization of corporate ownership, SEC regulations have provided for shareholder initiatives, meaning that after meeting certain criteria stockholders may create, and have placed on the annual ballot, issues upon which all shareholders will vote.[116] Many of those shareholder initiatives have been created by the so-called activist investor and contain calls for action that the corporation's management perhaps would have never considered undertaking if left to their own choices. Such activist stockholder initiatives are often of the variety that would involve changes to existing company procedures or the creation of new strategic pursuits. Currently, in many cases of stockholder initiatives, Activist Stockholders seek "remedial" type actions from the company aimed at "sustainability" issues which are of the type that are intended to impact the environment (local or global) in the manner which is desired by the activist investors.

Activist investors bringing such initiatives to the ballot are often motivated by politics and social causes, not by good business practices. For example, activist investors may often remain unswayed by the fact that the company may already be complying with all environmental regulations within the jurisdictions in which the company operates. These activist shareholders, often not engineers or manufacturing experts, are sometimes ignorant that their initiatives: 1) may run the risk of causing harmful impact to the very environment that they believe they are trying to protect; and, 2) may jeopardize manufacturing plan synergies of the company, causing inefficiencies, raising costs, hurting workers, and negatively impacting other corporate stakeholders. In other words, there is a distinct likelihood that Activist Stockholder initiatives "don't see the forest, just the trees." In only considering the politics of their issue, their initiatives may be counterproductive to their own larger goals as well as the corporation's goals, and of course could have a negative impact on profits and therefore the economy, and society, at large.

On the proxy ballot itself, notation is made as to whether the board of directors recommends a "yes" or a "no" vote. More often than not, the board of directors recommends a "no" vote on shareholder initiatives. Are you surprised that there is gambling at Rick's?

Standard management thinking on the recommendation of a vote is that shareholders will follow the guidance of the board, and vote per the board's recommendation, on any issue. So, if corporate boards of directors frequently recommend a "no" vote on stockholder initiatives, is all the concern about Activist Stockholders just "much ado about nothing?" Are shareholder initiatives effective? Would these initiatives have an effect on boards to act as the activist shareholders request?

In the academic and professional literature, there is quite a bit of controversy over this matter. Study conclusions point in both directions. Some studies have shown that when shareholders collectively organize to "just vote no" on the election of specific corporate officers, or other ballot issues not of their creation, that such action *does* appear to have some effectiveness in defeating the officer or the issue.[117] Other studies show that the spread of Activist Stockholder tactics remains in question, with some legal opinions suggesting that the ability of activists to gain power from such initiatives may be limited in the future.[118]

While the debate over the effectiveness of stockholder initiatives goes on, and academics attempt to figure it all out, the Activist Stockholders continue to practice and perfect their art. Indeed, the current winds of political change, in the United States, may give Activist Stockholders a setting more favorable to their pursuits. With the current shift in the American government from a Republican-controlled, "business friendly," federal government to a Democrat-controlled, "not as business friendly," government (including a Democratically appointed majority at the SEC), one could make a case that efforts to increase shareholder governance of corporations may increase.[119] Should shareholder governance of corporations increase, the role of social media in the actions of Activist Stockholders will be invaluable to their efforts.

Their Tools

As I have previously pointed out, social media are inexpensive and pervasive. More people are using them each day. The existence of social media, and their availability and applicability to the cause of the cosmically organized Activist Stockholder, is especially crucial in our analysis of this insidious competitor.

Social media provide a venue, and ready access, to the ordinary shareholders at-large, who are generally chaotically organized, but who do have a common interest (i.e., the profitability of the same corporation). Through that common interest, these ordinary shareholders can develop into somewhat of a crowd, particularly if they are exposed to the right "spark," like that of the cosmic Activist Stockholder. Under such conditions, social media can act as a tying domain, through which activist shareholders can reach the ordinary shareholders at-large. One easily accomplished approach is for the Activist Stockholder to search the social web, looking for existing conversations about the target corporation, or looking for opportunities in which to start such conversations.[120] Particularly fertile ground might include general financial discussion sites, such as Yahoo Finance. Activist Stockholders may employ the tools of Mutant Conversation, with its elements of mutated truth, and Snark, with its elements of entertaining attraction, to bring attention to the activist shareholder agenda which is to identify, place, and pass "their" stockholder initiatives in the annual shareholder vote. They may even toss in a dose of Hip Chat here and there. Remaining grounded in the principles of propaganda and taking advantage of the Five Factors of Insidious Competition can improve the success rate of the Activist Stockholder in using social media to advance their cause.

As of this writing, it is not typical for corporations to participate in social media, especially on financial issues. One reason for this may be SEC regulations on corporation to investor communications. Public companies, in the U.S. at least, are regulated on what they may say regarding financial issues. And from what I have gathered through client discussions, there is confusion in corporate ranks as to how these regulations apply within the new venue of social media.[121] This means that, in today's world, on corporate ballot issues, the ordinary shareholder at-large may not hear directly from the corporation in social media regarding certain issues. This situation may provide an unprecedented opportunity to the Activist Stockholder to present *its* agenda, within social media, relatively unopposed by the corporation and in effect "total." This "total" exposure, a leveraging of the Totality principle of propaganda, can favor the Activist Stockholder.

In this scenario, Activist Stockholders may enjoy, like their NGO and Activists cousins, the availability of a chaotically organized group. The Activist Stockholder may then co-opt ordinary stockholders at-large in favor of the Activist Stockholder agenda. Depending upon the strength of their issue, coupled with the effectiveness of Mutant Conversation and Snark through social media, successful co-optation may well lead to the *de facto* creation of additional, cosmically organized, Activist Stockholders from the ranks of the ordinary, and now formerly chaotically organized, stockholders at-large. In other words, "more" may spring from "few." This is how revolutions get started.[122]

And what would be the nature of their attack? The Activist Stockholder would definitely be oriented toward a cognitive attack. They seek a vote in favor of their own shareholder initiative. This requires a cognitive action, or a "call to action," which they solicit via social media. Would that cognitive attack be overt or covert?

Like their NGO and Activist cousins who would use the moral shield to gain legitimacy, and who would definitely want their identity known as a way to gain strategic advantage, the Activist Stockholder is likely to take the same approach. They would seek the support of the "moral legitimacy" they believe their initiative communicates, and base their campaign on it. Therefore, the Activist Stockholder attack would definitely be overt.

An Example

Launched on November 20, 2009, ironically as I was writing this section of this book, MoxyVote.com is a social network intended to link activist organizations, known on MoxyVote.com as "advocates," with individuals who wish to exercise their corporate proxy.[123,124] MoxyVote.com allows, and encourages, corporate shareholders not only to vote their proxy via the site, but the site also creates a social environment where activists/advocates can state their cases in the hopes of swaying individual investors' votes.

Individual investors and advocates register to use MoxyVote.com. When individuals register they choose advocate organizations to support. Each individual registered on the site has a "wall" (similar to that as on Facebook) where individual users may view "updates" and comments from the user community . . . er, uh . . . crowd regarding advocate campaigns, and other events occurring, within the crowd. Also shown on the individual's wall are updates from the various advocate organizations that are supported by that individual. When I reviewed this site, most of the advocate updates I saw addressed different campaigns in which the advocate organization was active. The updates addressed such things as a particular targeted company's involvement in human rights issues, executive compensation, or climate change. The advocate updates are intended to sway individuals' votes on upcoming proxy fights. In fact, MoxyVote.com makes proxy vote results, as voted by the individuals, "viewable" so that others may see how MoxyVote users voted on various corporate resolutions. Posting of results is, in itself, another method of influence that is active on the site.

On the day of my review, MoxyVote.com had only 18 registered advocacy organizations and 36 corporate ballots available for voting. But the day I reviewed the site was only the site's second business day of operation. So, it remains to be seen how successful this attempt at social media-based stockholder activism will be. But MoxyVote.com may gain in influence by its debut in social media at this particular time, if by nothing else. Let me explain.

In a Wall Street Journal article about MoxyVote.com, it was reported that in January 2010 the New York Stock Exchange will ban brokers from voting shares on behalf of clients who don't file their proxy and vote those shares themselves.[125] As I write this section, brokers who hold clients' shares in "street name" (i.e., in an electronic account in lieu of the client holding physical shares) may vote those shares if the client does not vote them by a specified date. Generally, brokers vote along with management's recommendations.

So, after this process has changed, I can foresee that the influence of sites like MoxyVote.com may increase. Here's how.

The Activist Stockholders who roam social media financial sites, as I mentioned previously, may direct the conversation to sites like MoxyVote.com. And there, these new MoxyVote.com users may come under the influence of the advocates pleading their campaign on that site. In fact, it may be that Activist Stockholders roaming the general social web in search of a specific corporation's ordinary stockholders at-large will work in concert with some of the advocates registered on a site like MoxyVote.com.

Sites such as MoxyVote.com afford the Activist Shareholder yet another tool in their quest for control of the *corporate image*. There, on sites such as this, the cosmically organized Activist Stockholder can gain even more organizational force by directing general social web users to that site. And after arriving there, users will enter into the conversation on that site, which will be supported by "updates," and perhaps at least a touch of Snark, from the site's registered advocates.

Labor Unions

Another "friendly" group that can act as insidious competition is Labor Unions.

Labor Unions. Some companies can't live with them and other companies . . . well, other companies can and do live very well without them. But labor unions exist and, to be complete in our review of insidious competition, they need to be considered. In the companies that must live with them, there is often a love-hate relationship between management and labor. And it's the "hate" side of that relationship that can give rise to Labor Unions becoming insidious competition from within social media.

How They Are Organized

Of course, members of labor unions are also employees. Like Employees, Labor Unions, as insidious competitors, would not have on their agenda the destruction of the company for which they work.

As we saw previously, Employees are generally chaotically organized with their attacks being of the semantic type, for the most part. This characterization is largely due to the fact that "employees" tend to act individually. But members of labor unions, although they are also employees, act as a group.

That's why they are called a "union." In considering Labor Unions as insidious competitors, we must recognize that they act as a *united* group. And in acting as a *united* group, they are definitely cosmically organized. By definition, a labor *union* cannot be chaotically organized within social media, or anywhere else for that matter.

Like Activist Stockholders, there is no fooling around here. Labor Unions always have an objective and as insidious competitors in social media, the same will also be true. The objective of labor unions is to get someone to do something. That something is usually some sort of contract concession, such as a pay raise or an increase in benefits. That concession requires a behavioral change and by definition that means that the attack class of the Labor Union would be cognitive.

Why They Are a Threat and Their Tools

Labor Unions are similar to Activist Stockholders in that both groups attempt to affect corporate governance.

Similar to Activist Stockholders, Labor Unions may also attempt to gain this influence via the proxy vote. There is evidence in the academic literature to suggest that union proxies vote against the election of corporate directors when there is a level of management-labor discord at a targeted company.[126] It seems reasonable to expect this. Once again, are you shocked that there is gambling at Rick's?

So Labor Unions seeking to amplify votes against "corporate objectives," would act very similarly to Activist Stockholders, using similar social media approaches and tools. Unions could jump into social media, find ordinary stockholders at-large and make a case. Mutant Conversation could be allowed to seek its own natural level, supplemented by Snark and a dose of Hip Chat thrown in, via which the Five Factors of Insidious Competition can take full effect.

Snark would be especially effective here, given the fifth of the Five Factors, institutional disdain. Snarky comments by union members would tend to capitalize on peoples' general feeling about the "domineering and impersonal" corporate giant. Those same snarky comments would also attract sympathetic followers through the hip nature of the comment, playing, as we've discussed before, on the Totality and Temporal Focus principles of propaganda. Conversely, Hip Chat would talk up how relevant the union's agenda is and, using the moral shield and calling upon the Societal Basics principle of propaganda, say that the union's only goal is to provide a "decent" living for its members and their families. Once the Societal Basics are brought into play, with the Five Factors "fanning the flames" of emotion, then it is that Mutant Conversation kicks in, with audience members forwarding only the pieces that mean the most to them, disintegrating contextual meanings, and leaving your company's corporate image to suffer in the iterative mutations.

In other ways as insidious competitors, Labor Unions may share characteristics similar to those discussed previously for Employees. As I observed in that section, Employees are largely chaotically organized and their attacks are mostly semantic in nature and such an approach could be similarly mounted by Labor Unions. Although this would depart from the cosmic and cognitive nature of Labor Union competitive attacks, it could be looked upon as an ancillary approach. Just as in the case of Employees, individual Labor Union members could take up snarky trash talking directly on a social network site, independently and not at the suggestion of their union leaders. And the effects of the trash talk could be further leveraged by making it available, by way of reference, to ordinary stockholders located on other social sites. Individual efforts are often chaotically organized (Howard Beale being an exception along with some others) and, as such, would generally have semantic, rather than cognitive goals. But this approach could also have collateral consequences of a cognitive nature through its semantic influence. Such influence may sway the ordinary stockholder at-large subliminally, at least, and in similar fashion to the way I was influenced in my opinion of the pharmaceutical director, per our discussion back in Employees section of this chapter. In fact, just such a sway may cause the ordinary stockholder to vote the annual proxy in a manner that would delight the labor union members. Although this independent method is not one which the Labor Union would likely consider as their main focus, it is however possible and therefore should be considered by anyone wanting to analyze the potential power of any insidious competitor.

But, let's not forget the obvious, however, which would be for the Labor Unions to directly take its "case to the people." Or should I say "stage their drama for the people." Unions are notorious for portraying themselves in a David and Goliath battle. We touched on this strategy back in the NGO and Activists section. We discussed how assuming the role of David in a story exploits one of the Four Myths/Values, that of Hero. And we saw how that role of Hero acting against incredible odds, plays into the dramatic elements of a story that all humans love. Labor Unions as insidious competitors, primarily cosmically organized and primarily cognitive in their attack, may play out their drama, publicly, not using the "Anonymous" screen name, and attempt to gain favor with the social media audience who loves an underdog. On the part of the Labor Union, this underdog tactic would be hard to ignore, so I believe this is the most common scenario. Thus, their cognitive attack would be overt.

The cognitive objective to such a social media play would be for union members, via very well-crafted Snark messages, to portray the company as an overbearing, inhuman Goliath and to ask audience members to apply pressure directly to the company's management by sending messages in favor of the union's objectives: "Send an e-mail to the CEO of XYZ Company and tell him to award union members a living wage." Or to ask social media audience members to cast their economic votes by boycotting the company's products or services until a contract settlement is reached. Everyone loves an underdog.

If, in all of these scenarios, the messages are well-snarked, and well-organized, their effect in the *battle for meaning* against the corporation which employs them can be devastating to not only the *corporate image* being assailed, but also to management's future efforts to control that image and with it, the company. In other words, in the *battle for meaning* with the Labor Union as the assailant, the *corporate image* can become collateral damage as a result of the Labor Union's pursuit of their own goals.

An Example

Yes, cognitive and overt their attacks would most often be, and performed usually within a cosmic format. A prime example of a labor union using social media to attack the corporate image in this way is shown in the blog GlennTilton.com.

Glenn Tilton is, at this writing, the Chairman, CEO, and President of United Airlines. But GlennTilton.com was not set up by Glenn himself. No. The blog was set up and is operated by the Airline Pilots Association, United Airlines Master Executive Council. The blog is copyrighted accordingly. That is to say, the pilot union of United Airlines runs this blog.

In the "About" section of this blog, the pilots of United Airlines announce:

> *This Web site was developed by the Air Line Pilots Association, United Airlines Master Executive Council. As professional pilots, we believe in accountability. Glenn Tilton, Chairman, CEO, and President of United Airlines, has failed all of us... costing shareholders, employees, and the travelling (sic) public billions of dollars. This Web site bears the name GlennTilton.com as a daily reminder to everyone invested in a positive future for United Airlines exactly where the source of our problems lies. (sic) This Web site is not owned, endorsed, or in any way sponsored by United Airlines or Glenn Tilton. For all of us, Glenn Tilton must go.*[127]

Okay. Spelling is not their strong suit, or maybe it's just accurate typing that challenges them. Nevertheless, this blog is definitely an example of a cosmically organized effort by a labor union to attack a *corporate image* from within social media. Now, let's talk tools.

The articles on the blog are filled with snarky comments, one of the tools of the Labor Union insidious competitor. For instance, in a post dated October 21, 2008 and titled "Further Hedge Losses Further Proof of Misdirection of Airline . . . ," the question "How is it that an oil man such as Glenn Tilton can't figure out how to stem losses from hedging jet fuel?" is posed.[128] Although a question, the line stands as a bit of a snarky statement. This question cum statement functions as a snide remark, addressed at a "knowing" receiver. The receiver is one who should agree that any person who is an "oil man" should know how to hedge oil prices. I don't know if Glenn ever was an oil man; that is not necessarily at issue here. What matters in this discussion is reality *perception* for the average reader.

Since I don't know if Glenn Tilton was ever an oil man, I'll assume the position of the average reader and say it's likely that the average reader would not know if Glenn was ever an oil man, but would accept the assertion on its face. Okay. Let's say the average reader just believes that Glenn was, at one time, an oil man. The average reader has no reason not to believe that. In such a situation, the snarky remark, disguised as a question, would tend to lower the average reader's view of Glenn's skills and with it the image of the airline he runs. To the average reader, since Glenn is the CEO of the airline, his image is the airline's image. They are one and the same. This *experience* leads to a *perception* which yields *knowledge.*

This oil man reference is not the only example of the tool of Snark appearing on this social site. Other examples of Snark appear in the section entitled "Your Emails to GlennTilton.com." One particularly snarky e-mail is titled, "What If Glenn Tilton Was Your Banker?" The e-mail briefly alludes to the low performance of the airline and blames it on Glenn. The e-mail asks would you want your banker, presumably with your money, to act in a similar fashion. Its Snark is especially effective given the e-mail's date, August 11, 2008, which was before the banking crisis of Fall 2008.[129] Perhaps the e-mail would not have been as snarky if it had been dated after the banking crisis was revealed? Maybe. But the e-mail was dated prior to that time. And in a temporal environment where banking was not commonly seen as under undue stress, such snarky articles would not do wonders in promoting the image of Glenn and, along with it, the *corporate image* of United Airlines.

Also appearing on the site are stories from customers and employees. In one letter from a customer, which is noted as being posted with permission, the customer writes an open letter to Glenn Tilton explaining a problem in being able to achieve the seating he needs on a flight that he is about to take with his six year-old daughter. The letter leaves the issue unresolved, yet the writer's point is clear. The writer complains about the customer service he received from the airline and shares his anguish by saying, "So, here I am, frustrated, anxious and stressed out that I might have to ship my six-year-old little girl cross country with two strangers next to her and her mother a couple of rows back." [130] Brilliantly played.

In this letter the writer employs, probably unintentionally, the Societal Basics principle of propaganda. This letter calls upon one of the four daily values, "the value of protecting youth." By doing so, in allowing the reader to have this experience and this perception of the writer's thoughts, the writer's propaganda can be successful in changing the reader's *meaning* of the United Airline *corporate image* and, perhaps, it may even help achieve the stated cognitive goal of the labor union, the removal of Glenn from the United Airline's executive suite. It could be that letters such as this, involving the safety and comfort of children, may incense other readers to pass the letter along within social media. Letting it "digitally drift" and mutate along its way, just waiting for the inevitable influence of the Five Factors to propel it along a journey, resulting in a public outcry for the ouster of Glenn.

The writer of this letter also calls upon the social value of work when he says, "What happened to customer service?," [131] an implication that can be interpreted by the reader that the company in question does not work hard enough to satisfy its customers. Comments of this sort can further degrade the image of the company in the eyes of the average reader, altering the reality in which the company wishes to have itself portrayed.

Regarding what I mentioned above when I said that the union could ask social media audience members to send emails to company management, within the navigation bar of the Glenn Tilton blog are two provided links which readers may use to e-mail either Glenn himself or the United Airlines board of directors. To increase their chances of success, the Labor Union must make it easy for the audience to help them successfully attain their cognitive goal. The pilot union does exactly that by providing that e-mail link.

At the time of this writing, judging by the posts' dates on the site, it appears that the GlennTilton.com blog has only been active for about a year and one-half. So, it remains to be seen how effective this blog will be. Yet, no matter what level of effectiveness can be attributed to any possible future attainment of the pilot union's goal, it is plain that the existence of such a blog does not help maintain the image of the company as its management would likely prefer.

Take-Aways from Chapter Thirteen – The Friendlies

1. The Friendlies are people who are seen as "part" of your company. These are people who don't wish to harm your company to the extent that would drive it from the marketplace, but they wish to influence the corporate image of your company so as to put pressure on it to change the company's behaviors.
2. There are four types of Friendlies:
   a. Customers/Clients/Consumers
      i. Tools: Mutant Conversation, Snark, and Hip Chat
      ii. Attack: All classes apply. Semantic, Cognitive Covert, and Cognitive Overt.
      iii. Organization: Chaotic
   b. Employees
      i. Tools: Mutant Conversation, Snark, and Hip Chat
      ii. Attack: Primarily Semantic
      iii. Organization: Primarily Chaotic
   c. Activist Stockholders
      i. Tools: Mutant Conversation, Snark, and Hip Chat
      ii. Attack: Cognitive Overt
      iii. Organization: Cosmic
   d. Labor Unions
      i. Tools: Mutant Conversation, Snark, and Hip Chat
      ii. Attack: Primarily Cognitive, primarily overt
      iii. Organization: Primarily Cosmic

Following is Figure 13-1, Reality Benders, Nasties, & Friendlies, a graphic representation of the insidious competitors that we have discussed so far.

Figure 13-1, Reality Benders, Nasties, & Friendlies

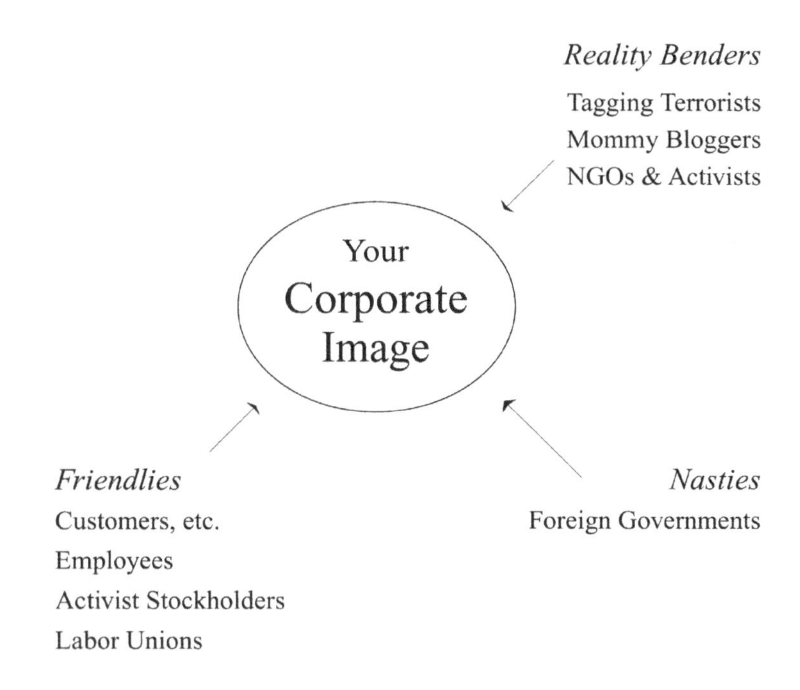

CHAPTER FOURTEEN: The Digital Pirates

The Reality Benders, The Nasties, The Friendlies. Each class of insidious competitor which we have so far discussed has had very different characteristics. The class we are about to discuss now is also differently characterized. The Digital Pirates.

The term "digital pirates" is, in the vernacular, taken to refer to people who "borrow" corporate intellectual property and pass it around, often forgetting to give it back. These folks got their start back in the early 1990s when they began forwarding via the Internet the work of others. Remember that digital drift problem? A good example of this is shown by the Dave Barry column story that we discussed back in Chapter Six. A more well-known example of this "digital piracy" is in the way Napster.com got started.

Napster.com was started as a filing-sharing service for individuals to pass around music MP3 files. Essentially it was a way of getting songs onto your computer without paying someone for them as you would if you downloaded them from a site like iTunes.com. Because, as I pointed out earlier in this book, digital content travels easily, the actions of digital pirates were enabled. And many folks came to believe that because the process of digital piracy was so easy, then it must be legal, enabling the process further. False logic. Once an individual has a gun in his or her hand, murder becomes easy. But its ease of accomplishment doesn't make a task legal.

In this chapter, we aren't going to examine the ways of the Digital Pirate from a standpoint of appropriating files of information. Remember that in this book we aren't concerned with the issue of the theft of information. We are, instead, concerned about the *theft of meaning.* That's the type of Digital Pirate at which we'll look. What you and I will examine here is a form of digital piracy that steals meaning from those who create meaning. Specifically, the type of Digital Pirate with which we are concerned in *Insidious Competition* is called a Culture Jammer.

Culture Jammers

Michael Strangelove, the author of *The Empire of Mind*, defines culture jamming as "the destruction of commercially produced meanings." [132] Now, yes I hear what you are thinking. Isn't the destruction of commercially produced meaning what we have been discussing throughout this book? It certainly is. So, is Michael's definition a bit too broad to be applied to our exact discussion about Culture Jammers? Yes. So, let me take the definition a bit further. Will I consult Webster's Dictionary again? I already did. The term is not covered by Webster's. Shucks. I'll turn to UrbanDictionary.com instead:

> *Culture jamming, is the act of using existing media such as billboards, bus-ads, posters, and other ads to comment on those very media themselves or on society in general, using the original medium's communication method.*[133]

Okay, good. What's different here, compared to our other insidious competitor types, is that culture jamming is visual, not textual. But what about the meaning angle? Let me take Michael's definition further.

Culture Jammers, alternatively known as subvertisers or ad busters, are primarily concerned with the re-rendering of corporate advertisements or corporate logos in such a manner that the new version of the artwork produces a message which contaminates that intended by the ad's or logo's owner. Or as Michael characterized them, Culture Jammers appropriate and alter ad images and change the original, intended messages.[134] Through culture jamming, the intended message is corrupted into a new message which is based on social or political activism. Indeed, Culture Jammers are often affiliated with activists or are activists themselves. Their culture jamming is an artistic expression of their activism.

Culture jamming as defined here is nothing new. As Michael points out, culture jamming has been around for quite a while.[135] But what I am pointing out here, the same as that to which Michael alluded in *The Empire of Mind*,[136] is that the Internet, and social media in particular, allows culture jamming to become much more pervasive and pernicious.

Why do culture jammers do what they do? Well, as Michael puts it, culture jamming is a "protest against the aggressive take-over of our shared mental landscape by commercial messages and a direct attack on corporations' claims of sovereignty over the meaning of their intellectual property and cultural products." [137] In other words, culture jammers do this because they regard private meaning as public. They compete, insidiously, with your company message, your image, your ephemeral image and the essence of your company's well-being and, by extension, your own personal livelihood.

Why They Are a Threat

Culture jammers, ad busters, subvertisers are a threat to your company's corporate image because, as we discussed above, they subvert the message intended to be communicated and change the message to something the jammer feels is more relevant. By this behavior, Culture Jammers redefine the *meaning* of the *corporate image*, costing the owners of the corporate image revenue and, with that revenue, jobs. Perhaps your job.

The visual work and accompanying message of the Culture Jammer is passed around within social media. Digital drift. Drifting makes passing around the culture jam very easy. Prior to the success of the social web, culture jamming did exist but its degree of pervasiveness was confined by time and space. But today, as we have previously observed, with social media those boundaries of time and space are broken down.

The product of the Culture Jammer, the visual form, is what I classify as "pop art." It is artistic expression based on the icons, flows, and timeliness of popular culture and it is on that propaganda principle of Temporal Focus that the jammer relies to send its message. The jammer digitally appropriates the corporate image and then reinterprets and digitally alters that image. The ease of the process now in the digital world makes it "feel" oh so much more legal. There often is a sense of irony, whimsy, or drama in the reinterpreted image, which makes its appearance curious and something which people will want to view. We want that drama. We need that drama.

That image, reinterpreted as pop art, may be seen by social media users as a "fun" interpretation of a corporate image. It is the "fun" element that attracts viewers, and it is that same insidious element of fun which can carry the changed meaning to the audience and infect that audience like a virus on an ice cream cone passed around in a group of sneezy third-graders. Yes. Culture jamming is a threat. Culture jamming is a threat because of its insidious "fun" nature, which disarms its hostility, encouraging the jam's dispersion across the social web, picking up the Five Factors along the way, and propelling it forward.

Their Tools

And is art the tool? Well, from our perspective here in *Insidious Competition* the tool is actually Snark. But instead of the snarkiness being in text, in the case of the Culture Jammer as an insidious competitor, the snarkiness is embodied visually. The visually altered work of the Culture Jammer is worth a thousand snarky words.

Just as written Snark is intended to attract a certain segment of the social media population and in that action form a crowd, with crowd behaviors, against the target of the written snark, so does the visual snark. The pop art tends to attract a segment of the social media population that is young and considers itself liberal, "right-thinking" (not the political right, of course), and with a certain self-defined hipness. Just the kind of persons who, we would expect, pride themselves on institutional disdain.

But this segment would not be the only segment to view the snarky culture jamming. The culture jam would be visible to all in the world with access to a computer and the Internet. Under those conditions, the alteration of the company's corporate image would spread throughout the social web and the Internet in general.

How They Are Organized

Generally, Culture Jammers are chaotically organized and their attacks are semantic in classification. Culture Jammers act independently and are what I characterize as "fringe activists," meaning that they are usually not part of a larger activist organization and their dedication to an activist cause may be casual or even of a passing, periodic nature.

There could be exceptions to this categorization, of course. An example of such a possible exception may be seen at the site AdBusters.org. This site, which also has a companion magazine claiming a circulation of 120,000, acts as a central organizing point for Culture Jammers worldwide. On their site, AdBusters.org lists its mission as being:

> *. . . a global network of artists, activists, writers, pranksters, students, educators and entrepreneurs who want to advance the new social activist movement of the information age. Our aim is to topple existing power structures and forge a major shift in the way we will live in the 21st century.*[138]

Now, on the surface this might seem like an organization that is cosmically organized and with an attack class that is cognitive. Well, AdBusters.org themselves might be cosmically oriented, thus an exception to the rule as noted above. But AdBusters.org is not an ad buster or subvertiser themselves. AdBusters.org simply serves as a central repository, "a global network," for the chaotically organized Culture Jammers out there. And, as stated in the quote above, AdBusters.org's goals are so general, and not specifically focused on one activist problem, that they cannot be classified as being cognitively oriented.

So, for the most part, Culture Jammers are chaotically organized and semantically oriented in their attacks.

Some Examples

You already have the example of AdBusters.org, and you may go to that site to experience ad busting. In the course of this conversation it would seem logical to display some of their work here. To do that I would, of course, need their permission. I contemplated doing that. They would probably have agreed. Yet, I was concerned about the legality of that which AdBusters.org displays on their site. Although I would have probably gotten the permission of AdBusters.org, I was concerned about the need for permission from the owner of the original corporate image being altered. The law of copyright, satire, and parody can become quite complex. Frankly, I just didn't want to become involved in the tussle given that you can access Adbusters.org quite easily on your own.

But consistent with what we discussed above, AdBusters.org does not represent the true characterization of how I see Culture Jammers being insidious competition. I see AdBusters.org as more of an art site, a museum, rather than as a statement, or re-statement, of corporate image meaning. An art site such as this doesn't fit the definition that we hashed out above. We discussed above that the true Culture Jammer was chaotically organized and semantic in orientation. So, let's stick to that definition as we explore some examples of culture jamming. And what I find best on the social web that fits that definition and is the best place to go fishing for culture jamming is Flickr.com, the Web's top photo sharing site.

Because of the legal concerns, to which I alluded above, I won't be showing you any copies of examples here. From the people who posted the culture jams on Flickr.com, I'm sure I could get the rights to reproduce those as examples in this book. In other projects, I've gotten reproduction rights from people who post on Flickr.com. It was easily done. Many Flickr.com posters are very cooperative. But in this case of culture jamming, it's the underlying rights about which I'm concerned. How do I really know if the culture jammers posting on Flickr.com have the rights to the corporate images they're mangling? Duh. Should that even be a question?

Let's move on now to discuss Flickr.com and what's going on there in the practice of jamming culture.

The Flickr.com photo sharing site is the most popular photo sharing site on the web. It is by definition a social site (i.e., photo sharing). The social sharing is augmented by a comments function which accompanies each photo display page. So not only is the site social, because of the exchange of images it facilitates, but Flickr.com is also social because it enables conversation about the photos that are shared on the site. The site is rich with examples of culture jamming.

The Subvertising Flickr Reach Example

To find some examples for you, I went to Flickr.com and searched on the terms "ad busting," "subvertising," "culture jamming," and variants of those terms. I found five groups I thought relevant. Actually, it was quite easy to find photos that were relevant to culture jamming because Flickr.com is rich with this type of artwork. It's an ad busting target-rich environment. Although there are probably more groups of the ad busting type on Flickr.com, these five groups shall serve well as examples.

On Flickr.com, members have the option to pool their photos within "affinity groups" organized around various topics. There I found the following photo group pools related to culture jamming named: Ad Busters, Subvertising,

Ad Busting, and Culture Jam. A related group I found is named the Anti-Mc Donald's Group. Their addresses at Flickr.com are as follows:

Ad Busters Group	http://www.flickr.com/groups/adbusters/pool/
Subvertising Group	http://www.flickr.com/groups/subvertising/pool/
Ad Busting Group	http://www.flickr.com/groups/21753757@N00/pool/
Culture Jam Group	http://www.flickr.com/groups/culturejam/pool/
Anti-McDonald's Group	http://www.flickr.com/groups/anti-mcdonalds/pool/

Flickr.com is an important site in terms of the amount of insidious competition that it can help spread. Alexa.com, a Web site ranking company and a part of Amazon.com, ranked Flickr.com the 33rd most popular Web site on the day that I researched culture jamming on that site. So, due to the worldwide Internet traffic that Flickr.com attracts, Flickr.com can help pass around a lot of snark that can contribute to the meaning change of a company's corporate image. One of those companies snarked on Flickr.com might be your company, infecting its ability to gain revenue, decreasing its ability to protect your job and, by extension, your children's well-being. That worldwide traffic can help create a lot of "views" of culture jamming.

What's a "view?" On Flickr.com, a view is simply each instance of when a photo is seen by a user. Among these five groups of culturally jammed images there are many, many views. Unable to find any function on the site, or off the site for that matter, that would automatically measure the total views of all the photos within one group pool, I elected to average the number of views among all the photos within a group pool. Now, there's some controversy over the way that Flickr.com counts photo views. If you Google in "how does flickr count views," you will experience what I mean. Then you can perceive and have some knowledge on this subject.

(Don't forget. Experience >>> Perception >>> Knowledge.)

What I'm after here is just an estimate, an order of magnitude, as to how many views the photos in each group have totaled. We want to have that estimate so we can continue our discussion as to the impact and level of insidious competition that can be anticipated from the Culture Jammer.

I went through each group pool and reviewed a relevant sample of the individual photos in that group. In my review, I assessed the subject and theme of these photos and found that most, if not all, placed a particular company, or even just business and commerce in general, in an unfavorable light. For the relevant sample of my review, I recorded the number of views for each photo. (On each photo's Flickr.com page, the number of views for the photo is listed near the bottom of the page.) After totaling the number of views and averaging the views for the sample, I multiplied the average views per photo by the total number of photos, or items as Flickr.com calls them, that were within the group pool. This product gave me the estimated number of views by group pool. My findings are shown in Table 14-1, Flickr Findings, which I have included below.

Table 14-1, Flickr Findings

Group Pool	View Estimate for Group Pool
Ad Busters	854,720
Subvertising	133,078
Adbusting	484,008
Culture Jam	79,764
Anti-Mc Donald's	68,892
Total View Estimate	**1,620,462**
Adjusted Estimate	**1,458,416**

The Adjusted Estimate represents a corrected number because some of the photos appeared in more than one group pool that I examined. To me, it looked like about a ten percent overlap within the studied groups, so I adjusted the View Estimate down by ten percent.

The Adjusted Estimate is approximately 1.5 million views of negative business messages. Some were pointed directly at specific companies; some were directed only at business in general or at the concept of capitalism.

Specific companies, in no order of occurrence, that were among the more common targets of the Culture Jammers, were: Disney, Mc Donald's (so popular, that they had their own group), Nike, Microsoft, Geico, Sony, Pepsi, Coca-Cola, and BMW.

But are 1.5 million anti-business impressions significant? Do those 1.5 million impressions hurt the *meaning* of the *corporate image* generally or specifically? Absent market research directed at answering that question, I suppose the answer depends upon your perspective. Considering that there are many more millions of positive impressions put into various media daily, perhaps these 1.5 million negative impressions aren't an item for concern. But considering that Flickr.com and sites like it have only been around for a few years (as of this writing), these 1.5 million negative impressions represent attempts at *meaning change* that did not exist a short time ago and which are now broadly accessible through the global Internet. I'm sure that business marketers would rather not have these impressions out there at all, than to have to deal with them, even at least to some degree. These 1.5 million insidiously negative impressions represent the vanguard of what may multiply both now and in the future on Flickr.com or other photo-sharing sites. These 1.5 million negative impressions may be forwarded in a digitally drifting manner from Flickr.com, within a medium that is uncontrolled, at the fingertips of just about everyone in the developed world, and which is used by more and more people daily.

Culture jamming, as a class of insidious competition, is likely to increase. I say that because Culture Jammers are successful in getting their snarky message viewed. Of the photos I observed, I saw that the more highly viewed photos had two things in common - "hot" looking women and large, prominent, blatant corporate logo manipulation. (You expected me to say something else, didn't you?) These are two success factors, sex and "boldness," that serve the Culture Jammer seemingly as well as they do Madison Avenue. If the visually snarky, culture jamming insidious competitor wants to increase its success rate, then they'll use these two factors as a way to get more eyeballs to watch them hammer away at the corporate image, gaining some converts in the process.

Then with each new eyeball comes intensification and expansion of the *mangled corporate image* as new converts can jump on the culture jamming bandwagon by using relatively inexpensive and available tools, like Photoshop, to add their own snarky and negative view of the corporation. Combine this "ease of culture jamming" with the enabling of the Five Factors of Insidious Competition, and the corporate image becomes even more susceptible to damage from an expanding sea of chaotically organized insidious competitors.

The "Eat Shit" Example

Sorry for the profanity, but I didn't create that title, as you'll see in a moment.

So, in culture jamming, the tool of Snark is not used "textually," but "visually." An example of the employment of visual Snark in culture jamming is given with the photo at this address: http://www.flickr.com/photos/greenwood100/3386320914/in/pool-anti-mcdonald's.[139] This photo, entitled "Eat Shit," is simple in its snarkiness. The image shows a group of pigeons atop an awning ostensibly leading into a Mc Donald's restaurant. The name "Mc Donald's" is covered with pigeon poop. The individual who took the photograph, the culture jammer, has made their opinion quite clear. The remark is obvious. The statement is snide, derogatory in an indirect manner, and uses invective in a "knowing" way; the viewers know what the pigeon poop on the name implies. As we discussed back in Chapter Eight on the Four Tools of the Insidious Competitor, snark "appeals to a knowing audience that shares the contempt of the snarker." This image's message fits perfectly the definition of snark. The message defines the meaning of Mc Donald's corporate image in a way that is *not* one that they would prefer back at Mickey D's corporate HQ.

The Revolution Example

Culture Jammers are always about revolution. If it wasn't for the word "revolution," I don't know how they could get out of bed in morning.

Another photo from the Anti-Mc Donald's group is one entitled "The Revolution. LIVE Tonight. (sponsored by Global inc.)." This culture jam may be found at http://www.flickr.com/photos/raze_165/2947506643/in/pool-anti-mcdonalds.[140] The image is a montage consisting of a modified Ronald Mc Donald holding a red can which bears a logo that looks much like the Coca-Cola logo. Ronald is modified in such a way that he looks like Ché Guevara, complete with a black beret that sports a Mc Donald's double arches logo. The Ronald Ché mash-up is placed in front of a television which shows a burning car on the screen. Snarkily, "The Revolution" "appeals to a knowing audience that shares the contempt of the snarker." The contempt, the disdain for institutions, is aimed at the multinational corporation, represented by the Coca-Cola and Mc Donald's logos. This culture jam communicates to the viewer a pervasive coldness of the multinational corporation, which is thought by some to "own" the daily lives of all on the planet. The comments accompanying this image, all effectively anonymous, echo this disdain and run contagiously through the comment progression. Not one comment dissents with the message presented. The Five Factors play heavily here and contribute to the changing of what the corporate image means.

The Slogan Example

This image relies on textual snark, but it would not make its points as strongly if the textual snark was not shown within the context of an image. The image is entitled "The Slogan."

This subvertisement may be seen in the Anti-Mc Donald's Group at http://www.flickr.com/photos/adijr/2851305136/in/pool-anti-mcdonalds.[141] "The Slogan" depicts the front of a Mc Donald's restaurant. Next to the door is handwritten the "slogan," "Get Fat or Die Trying." The slogan itself is a take-off of many more positive adages such as "Get Rich or Die Trying," etc. The adaptation and employment of the slogan is "knowing." It calls upon a certain sector of the popular culture who understands the irony intended within the humor. The usage of the slogan exploits the very essence of Snark by being sly and condescending. And the slogan is funny because it calls upon irony. The slogan is snarky and textual, but yet would not work unless it was paired with a visual. Thus, "The Slogan" makes use of both visual and textual snark tools.

Attack Class, Organization, & Use of Propaganda Exemplified

Consistent with what we previously discussed about the attack class and the organization of the Culture Jammer, the attacks on corporate meaning described in these examples are of a semantic nature. The messages make no attempt to change a behavior; the images don't ask you to do anything.

The organization displayed by the group picture pool individuals is chaotic. There is no organized group with an intended action. These are merely individuals submitting images to a "group pool." They don't appear to have an organized agenda among themselves.

Do these three images make use of the principles of propaganda, presented via the tool of Snark? Absolutely. Each image conveys a message grounded in the principles of propaganda.

These images address the "individual and the masses," the Person & People principle of propaganda. The masses because the iconic images of the Mc Donald's and Coca-Cola logos are recognized by all, not just those who are attracted to this group picture pool on Flickr.com. The individual because as Jacques Ellul said, and as we earlier explored in Chapter Seven, these images target individuals in a group, persons connected by common interest and who are bound together by emotionalism. The individuals attracted to this group picture pool are attracted for a reason, to see advertising subverted, to see corporate images besmirched, or to have their own opinions about corporations reinforced. In addition to the individuals who are attracted by, and who directly view, the Flickr.com group pool, other casual viewers on Flickr.com, can view these same images outside of the group pool and be similarly affected, spreading the *insidious competition* of the negative image.

The propaganda principle of Veracity is at work within these images, or should I say that these images conveniently leave out truth per se, instead relying on opinion based on a truth, as we discussed in Chapter Seven. As I said in that chapter,

> *The interpretations to be made by the audience are dependent upon the effectiveness of the intended innuendo and the intended suggestions contained in the one-sided propaganda. That is what packs the punch. So, it is in the implicative language that the value of really good propaganda lies.*

In these images, the innuendo is quite well communicated. The innuendoes are made well visually in "Eat Shit" and "The Revolution." I don't think that their points would have been driven home nearly as well in these two images had the Culture Jammers tried to communicate using only words. The visual form provides the amusement and wit to attract an audience which is then slyly exposed to the message that insidiously competes for the corporate image.

Take-Aways from Chapter Fourteen – The Digital Pirates

1. Digital Pirates "borrow" intellectual property from those who create it.
2. There is one type of Digital Pirate with which we are concerned in this book: the Culture Jammer.
3. Culture Jammers appropriate and alter corporate ads and logos so as to change the meaning of those visual images.
4. Culture Jammers are business threats because of the insidious, "fun" nature of their "pop art," which disguises its underlying hostility, encouraging viewers to further disperse it on the social web.
    a. Tools: Snark
    b. Attack: Semantic
    c. Organization: Chaotic

Following is Figure 14-1, All Insidious Competitors, the final graphic in the series that represents the insidious competitors that you and I have discussed in this book.

Since we are now at the end of Section Three, Attack Classes and Types of Insidious Competitors, I have included for your convenience Table S-3, Insidious Competitor Profiles. This table summarizes the organizational types, attack classes, and tools for each insidious competitor that we have discussed.

Figure 14-1, All Insidious Competitors

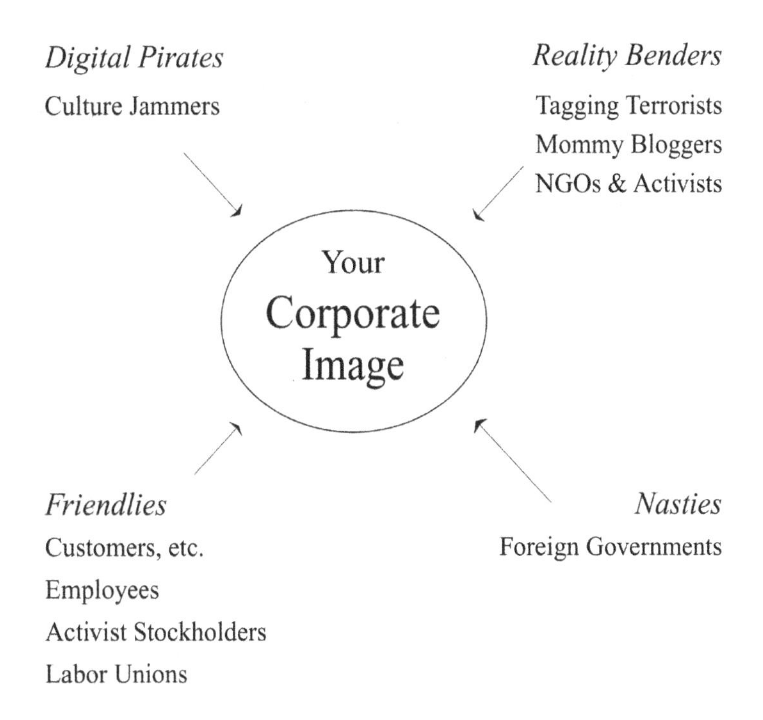

Table S-3, Insidious Competitor Profiles

	Organization		Attack			Tools			
	Cosmic	Chaotic	Semantic	Cognitive		Mutant Convo.	Snark	Hip Chat	Soc. Eng.
				Overt	Covert				
Reality Benders									
Tagging Terrorists	X	X	X				X		
Mommy Bloggers		X	X	X		X	X		
NGOs/Activists	X			X		X	X	X	
Nasties									
Foreign Agents	X				X	X	X	X	X
Friendlies									
Customers, etc.		X	X	X	X	X	X	X	
Employees		X	X			X	X	X	
Activist Stockholders	X			X		X	X	X	
Labor Unions	X			X		X	X	X	
Digital Pirates									
Culture Jammers		X	X				X		

Section Four:
Strategies and Tactics Against Insidious Competition

Chapter Fifteen: Suggested General Strategies & Tactics Against Insidious Competition

We've come through a lot in the preceding pages.

We've discussed how social media sets up an environment that is ripe for the development of a new type of competition, non-traditional and *insidious competition*. We've seen how that environment is very much like a crowd and how crowd behaviors can take hold, providing fertile ground for the Five Factors of Insidious Competition. We've talked about how those Five Factors can mess with the essence of reality and repackage it to the advantage of the insidious competitor, who has little fear of liability. And then we've come to understand how that repackaging of reality can damage The Ephemeral Image on which the success of the corporation depends, not to mention your own *personal* success. The threat was, at that point, clear. The threat still is clear. As business people, once we realize a threat we owe it to our shareholders, to the preservation of our own jobs, and to our families who look to us for support, to understand that threat and work to eliminate it, or at least to mitigate it. Toward this end, we started to learn about the process of knowledge and how people come to know what they know or think that they know. There we learned about solipsism and epistemology. It was a heady discussion, but we came through with flying colors and now have a better understanding as to how the insidious competitor does what they do.

To get to that understanding we found that through the solipsistic and epistemological process, the system of knowing, the insidious competitor employs the principles of propaganda. We studied the principles of propaganda so that we could comprehend not only how some of those principles were found in and supported the world of social media, but also how other of those principles were applied, both consciously and unconsciously, by the insidious competitor within social media. We learned about how insidious competitors organized and then, from that knowledge, we dug deeper and learned specifically how principles of propaganda were brought to bear on their targets through the use of various tools. But learning about their organization and their tools is not enough to combat them and at that point in our story we still needed more information. So toward our goal of eliminating, or at least mitigating, their effect, we learned about the classes of attacks that could be made by insidious competitors using the tools we discussed. Then we kept on going.

Our discussion moved on to learn about the specific types of insidious competitors, how to identify them, specifically what made them a threat, how they operate, how they organize, what tools they use, and what motivates them.

Our journey was considerable, but given that we went through philosophical and social theory that took about one hundred years to evolve, our journey was completed in a relatively short period of time.

We learned a lot about a new type of competitor who threatens our businesses, our livelihoods, the well-being of our children, and the attainment of the happiness for which all of us strive. Learning for learning's sake is good. But in business, in commerce, nobody eats until somebody actually does something. And doing, to be effective, must be preceded by knowing.

Now we know.

And now that we know, we can do something.

Section Four teaches us to apply what we learned.

Here's how we'll accomplish that.

First, here in Chapter Fifteen, I will discuss some parameters. Second, also here in Chapter Fifteen, I will discuss suggested general strategies and tactics. The parameters are the conditions under which the strategies and tactics may be applied. That's what Section Four is all about, strategies and tactics. And for business people, that's the payoff for getting through this book, practical suggestions. These strategies and tactics are suggested stepping off points in tackling the problem of insidious competition for your own company. Yes, you know what's coming next. Here comes the disclaimer, and some precautions.

Since I don't know who you are, or what company you work for, or what your company's specific problems are, or anything about your company's business environment, there is no way that I can determine if any or all of these suggested strategies and tactics would be applicable to, or appropriate for, your company's insidiously competitive situation. As they say in medical and pharmaceutical advertisements, "These statements are not meant to diagnose or cure any disease." The suggested strategies and tactics I will discuss are given here with the understanding that they are "food for thought." They are suggestions. Use them to germinate and create strategies and tactics specific to your own particular business situation. Regarding our discussion of the suggested strategies and tactics against insidious competition, as you create your strategies and tactics seek assistance from qualified professionals in areas such as competitive strategy, corporate communications, public relations, law, human resources, competitive intelligence, social media, and marketing, as well as other business disciplines.

The strategies and tactics we are about to discuss will be organized into two categories: proactive and reactive. The proactives are those that would be undertaken to prevent or minimize insidious competition from taking place in the future. You would use these to short-circuit problems before they arise. And, of course, the reactives are those that would be undertaken when you haven't, or until you have, mastered your proactive strategies and tactics. It's my guess, that at this point in the evolution of insidious competition, most of you will be applying the reactives. Hopefully, *Insidious Competition* will help you get to a point where you will no longer need to be in the reactive position.

Third, after we discuss general strategies and tactics in this chapter, we'll move on to the remaining chapters to discuss each competitor type as it relates to the proactives, the reactives, or to both. At that point, using our understanding of each insidious competitor's type of organization, its attack class, and its tools, we will look at how we might be able to combat each insidious competitor type through the suggested strategies and tactics that we just discussed.

Parameters

In order for your strategies and tactics to be effective, you must attend to the concepts that we learned earlier in this book.

The Five Factors of Insidious Competition

Back in Chapter Three, we found that insidious competition is enabled by the Five Factors of Insidious Competition - anonymity, power, contagion, instinct, and disdain. The Five Factors are there, present in social media, and there is little that we can do to change their existence. So, we must learn to operate knowing that they exist. When creating your strategies, and the supporting tactics, you must realize that social media users can always be anonymous if they choose. With that anonymity comes a feeling of power and, with it, a tendency to corrupt the rules and procedures of society. This feeling spreads contagiously throughout the crowd that is social media, calling upon instinctual behaviors which tend to support the behavior of the crowd. With disdain of institutions being a common characteristic of crowds, *the battle for the meaning* of The Ephemeral Image, *your corporate image*, becomes your key concern.

You can't and won't stop any of The Five Factors. You can't change them. But what you can do is realize their presence and their immutability, learning to work with them, turning them more to your favor.

The Seven Principles for Successful Propaganda

After discussing propaganda generally, we focused on the Seven Principles for Successful Propaganda in social media:

1. Person & People (individual and masses),
2. Totality (the idea of "propaganda by choice"),
3. Organizational Unit (the orientation of the group or individual that creates or propagates the message, e.g. cosmos vs. chaos),
4. Goal Orientation (an orthopractic outcome),
5. Societal Basics (knowledge of the sociological presuppositions and myths, i.e., values of daily life),
6. Temporal Focus (timeliness of the message), and

7. Veracity (containing elements of truth).

From our discussion we learned that some of these principles are created by, are supported in, and fortify the environment of social media, while other principles are those that must be applied, via tools, within the social media environment in order to make a propaganda bid successful.

Whether they are principles that support social media or whether they are principles that can be brought to and applied within social media, your understanding of these principles is essential if you are to fight in the *battle for the meaning* of your *corporate image* against this new type of competitor, in this new type of battleground called social media. Again, you can't change this situation. The principles of propaganda are like The Five Factors, at once both a force and condition of human nature.

Just as the insidious competitor uses principles of propaganda, either consciously or unconsciously, then so too must the company understand and employ those same principles of propaganda in order to protect The Ephemeral Image.

Solipsism & Epistemology

How do people know what they know? How do they acquire *meaning*? We explored this process in our discussion of solipsism and epistemology. We saw that process broken down into the following steps:

Experience >>> Perception >>> Knowledge

From this process we know that to control the social media user's *knowledge* of your company's corporate image as *you* define it, you must aim to control the *perception* of that image *within the sphere of social media*, working to ensure that your image is *experienced* as *you* intend. And, in the new world of insidious competition, this means you must be actively engaged in fighting against misperceptions (both intentional and unintentional), while controlling, or at least increasing the likelihood, that the social media user experience of your company's corporate image is a positive one.

The solipsistic and epistemological process is a flow of human nature. Again. You can't change this. You can only go with the flow. So, your strategies and tactics must be created to operate within this flow.

Use Drama

"Never let the truth get in the way of a good story."

Because humans love drama and because it's engrained in our psyches, I shouldn't need to go into further explanation on this topic. We covered it quite well, already.

You simply need to know that, when proceeding into the *battle for meaning*, using drama will help you greatly in your quest for success.

Strategies & Tactics

Before the construction of any strategy, or its supporting tactics, you must have a goal. The strategy is the roadmap and if there is no goal you wouldn't know which roadmap to choose.

In the *battle for meaning*, you will have one of two goals:

1. to control or minimize the redefinition of your corporate image by the insidious competition within social media, or;
2. to regain your company's corporate image once altered (or repackaged) in reality by the insidious competition within social media.

The first goal is one that can be met by using proactive, or preemptive, strategies and tactics. The second goal is one that can be met by using reactive strategies and tactics. Let's take a closer look.

Proactive Strategies & Tactics

Against chaotically organized insidious competitors, and in some cases against cosmically organized ones, use proactive strategies and tactics before the meaning-mangling begins, if you can, or at least before it becomes less subtle and moves to a higher level of attack. You would want to insert yourself into the battle early, at the point where you have a better chance of minimizing the redefinition of your corporate image.

Strategy: "Immunize" the social media crowd against "infectious memes." Infectious memes are those that will propagate readily within an environment like social media, where contagion reacts to the power and institutional disdain that exists within.

Tactic: Anticipate negative memes that attackers might create. Provide information nullifying the claims made by the attackers. Address the "issue" before it becomes an issue.

Tactic: Take immunization strategy into relevant epistemic communities across several different media.

Tactic: Craft your message strongly within the Societal Basics, the four values of daily life and the sociological presuppositions.

Strategy: Use search engine optimization (SEO) procedures to push the appearance of insidious competitor conversations lower in search engine results page rankings (SERPs) by pushing your pages higher.

Tactic: Don't perform in-house. Use third-party contractors. (Don't worry. We're going to get a chance to learn more about SEO and SERP when we discuss specific strategies and tactics for Mommy Bloggers. Having an example will make this easier to understand.)

Strategy: Reposition social media.

Tactic: Run public service announcements (PSAs) stating that the "facts" shared in social media are not always true and are usually unvetted, and that the false and misleading information in social media is a disservice to the public. In the PSAs note that online fact-checking software exists and that individuals should make use of it. Put some research behind these statements demonstrating that social media, with its unvetted commentary, disguised as facts, puts reality at risk for all of us. Run PSAs through multiple channels, including via trade organizations.

Strategy: Encourage third-party sources of information, strengthening your company's corporate image along the issues that insidious competitors may likely attack from within social media.

Tactic: SEO them up in SERPs by creating company information sites linking back to the third-party information site.

Tactic: Have company social media staff enter into problematic discussions with links back to the third-party sources.

Reactive Strategies & Tactics

Assuming that your proactive strategies haven't been implemented, or that they have not been implemented effectively, and you are under an image attack from within social media, then you are playing defense. That means reactive strategies and tactics will be necessary.

Reactive strategies and tactics should be used aggressively. But don't fear alienating the very people you are trying to reach through your social media counter-strategy. Aggressiveness does not mean obnoxiousness. What I mean is this. You need to be aggressive in your efforts to "right the wrong" that has been done to your corporate image. Pursue your strategy and tactics with great energy and purpose, while keeping your company positioned as calm, but assertive. It is important here that your social media squad has the attitude that they can, and believes that they will, retake control of the *meaning* of ***their** corporate image*, not just "the company's corporate image." They need to believe, and act, knowing that it is their livelihood, as well as that of their co-workers, that is at risk and that the company needs their help. After all, it is a "company" of people.

Strategy: Attack the attacker. In the social media environment of today, without fear of liability, insidious competition has very little to lose. It's a one-sided battle when only one side has anything to lose. And in one-sided battles, the loser never can win. That's no way to conduct a battle, and it is indeed a battle. Insidious competitors are battling to redefine what your company means. It's your job to make sure that doesn't happen. Change the balance.

Tactic: Identify the attacker as mistaken. Present information within social media discussions countering image-damaging claims. Link back to the third-party sources created in the proactive strategies.

Tactic: Make alliances with other organizations to have them help present your case.

Tactic: Radicalize the attacker. Through social graphing software, look for connections to the attacker which will weaken their case or associate them with questionable sourcing. Look for ways to separate the attacker's supporters, in the social media crowd, from the attacker. Cut the psychic shareholding. Sever the emotional supply lines and weaken the influence of the Five Factors.

Tactic: Dilute the insidious competitor's message. Go to targeted social sites where insidious competition is operating against your corporate image and talk about other issues. But don't take conversation too far afield.

Tactic: Make your counter-attack across different media, not just social media, and within relevant epistemic communities in all media targeted.

Tactic: Hold the attacker to liability laws. Frame your argument in "the truth" stating that the attacker is disseminating misleading information. Where it makes sense to do so, take the position that the misleading information (i.e., repackaged reality) is against the "public interest," especially that of "the children."

The Next Step

Now that we have had a broad look at some suggested general strategies and tactics, let's take a look at each of the insidious competitor types we have discussed and see how we might apply these general strategies and tactics in a more specific way.

First up . . . Tagging Terrorists.

Take-Aways from Chapter Fifteen - Suggested General Strategies & Tactics Against Insidious Competition

1. In countering insidious competition, keep in mind that you must operate within unchangeable parameters. Those parameters are some of the most important concepts we have discussed in this book: The Five Factors, the Seven Principles for Successful Propaganda, the solipsistic and epistemological process, and the desire for drama.
2. Before battling the insidious competitor, have a goal in mind. General goals are: minimizing company image damage before a specific attack appears, and regaining company image after a specific attack occurs.
3. Proactive strategies are directed at precluding an attack. Reactive strategies are directed at defending against a specific attack.

CHAPTER SIXTEEN: Suggested Strategies & Tactics Against The Reality Benders

In the following chapters, we are going to look at each of the insidious competitors we have discussed. You and I will look at them with regard to what strategies and tactics could be used against them as you *battle for the meaning* of **your** *corporate image.*

Here in Chapter Sixteen, we will discuss strategies and tactics for the group of insidious competitors labeled as The Reality Benders, followed in the next chapters by strategic and tactical discussions for those groups labeled as The Nasties, The Friendlies, and The Digital Pirates.

Please note that, as I mentioned in the previous chapter, regarding our discussion of the suggested strategies and tactics against insidious competition, as you create your strategies and tactics seek assistance from qualified professionals in areas such as competitive strategy, corporate communications, public relations, law, human resources, competitive intelligence, social media, and marketing, as well as other business disciplines.

To implement strategies and tactics, your organization must be ready, able, and *willing* to do so. Your company must not only have the personnel ready to devote to these tasks, but those personnel must be knowledgeable and experienced in both the unique environment of social media ***and*** in the process of knowledge acquisition as we have learned here in *Insidious Competition*. Companies can staff up to this level of demand. Groups can be assembled to address insidious competition, and those groups can be put together in a relatively short time period. What your company will need in this *battle for meaning* is a social media squad tasked to monitoring and entering into "conversations" within the social web. You will need this squad in order to be prepared to deal with this new environment that serves as a new battleground for your corporate image. Making these preparations is not difficult. Not difficult, that is, as compared to what I said in the first sentence of this paragraph. What I said there is that a company must be "*willing*" to carry out strategies and tactics against insidious competition. Being "*willing*." That's the really difficult part.

Being "willing" means that top management is "on board" with the idea of fighting back. And management being "on board" means not only having the resolve to confront this problem, but it means also having the resolve to secure and dedicate the appropriate resources, both personnel and funding, to effectively fight back. In my almost two decades as a business consultant, I have found that many American corporations are not "willing" to fight back, against anything. What they are willing to do is to "satisfice," a portmanteau of satisfy and sacrifice, meaning to make the best of a bad situation rather than to change the situation that is causing the "bad" to begin with. To appease. To concede. History has shown us where that type of behavior gets us.

If you are not willing to fight back, if you don't have the resolve, if you're content to pull a Chamberlain at Munich, well, then just stop reading this book right now. The remainder of these pages is not about concession. The following pages are about fighting back. Fighting back against an insidious foe that isn't going to get any nicer just because we leave them alone. The remainder of these pages is about fighting a foe that is not only attacking your company's *corporate image*, but is also one that is attacking your own personal livelihood and your own personal pursuit of happiness.

If you think all of that is worth defending, then read on.

Tagging Terrorists

I'm glad you decided to continue the fight. Let's examine each insidious competitor strategically and tactically. We start here with the Tagging Terrorists.

Recapping from Chapter Eleven, we saw that the profile of the Tagging Terrorist looks like this:

Tools: Snark
Attack: Semantic
Organization: Cosmic or Chaotic

Let's discuss these characteristics from the perspective of strategic and tactical approaches that may neutralize, or even reverse, their insidiously competitive effects on your corporate image.

Organization: Cosmic or Chaotic

The best place to start a strategic and tactical assessment of an insidious competitor is with their organizational structure. The Tagging Terrorist, as we discussed, can be either cosmically or chaotically organized, but at this point in their evolution, it is the chaotic form of organization that appears to be most prevalent. So for now, at least, let's assume that it's more likely that if your company's image is being negatively "tagged," it is not being done from a centrally organized entity pushing tags with the intent of destroying your corporate image. But let's keep in mind the line in the Jackson Browne song, "The Road and The Sky." "Don't think it won't happen just because it hasn't happened yet." Cosmic can happen.

Remember what we said earlier in discussing Tagging Terrorists? The playground, or venue, of the Tagging Terrorist is social bookmarking sites and the function of these sites is to allow members to "bookmark," or "tag," websites which they consider to be significant, helpful, cool, interesting, educational, etc. Social bookmarking site members classify their lists of sites by using "tags," better known as keywords, by which other members may search and receive a list of common Web site bookmarks. The sites that are bookmarked by members are ranked in popularity, based upon how many other members have also bookmarked the same sites. The ranking of the sites is intended to help other members to determine which sites are worth visiting.

It's pretty easy to create numerous, hundreds, or thousands of member accounts, each having a distinct screen name, on a social bookmarking site for the purpose of "tagging" a specific company's Web site(s) to less-than-flattering keywords. And the way it works in social bookmarking sites is that more "tags" lead to higher popularity ranking of specific sites. So, don't look to the cosmically organized attacker to be truthful about the size of its organization. Instead realize that the high number of distinct screen names is a way for the cosmically organized Tagging Terrorist to "look big" and to be more effective in its "tagging" effort.

At this point in our discussion, some guiding principles based on the "state of the art" of *today's* Tagging Terrorist may help you determine the most likely type of organizational structure of the Tagging Terrorist that is attacking your company.

- Smaller number of "tags" means the insidious competitor is more likely chaotically organized.
- Larger number of "tags" means the insidious competitor is either chaotically or cosmically organized. Further refine chaotic or cosmic by looking for:
  - Larger number of "tags" linked to *a small number of distinct* screen names OR linked to *a large number of "anonymous"* screen names means the insidious competitor is most likely chaotically organized.
  - Larger number of "tags" linked to *a large number of distinct* screen names means the insidious competitor is more likely cosmically organized.

By way of graphical summarization for the above, and for your convenience, I have included Table 16-1, Tagging Terrorist Organizational Structure, below.

Table 16-1, Tagging Terrorist Organizational Structure

	Number of Tags	Distinct Screen Names	Anonymous Screen Names
More Likely Chaotic	Small		
	Large	Small	Large
Chaotic or Cosmic	Large		
More Likely Cosmic	Large	Large	

Also helpful in your strategic and tactical selection will be knowledge of the insidious competitor's attack class and tools. For the Tagging Terrorist, we will discuss those next.

Attack: Semantic

Continuing our strategic and tactical assessment of Tagging Terrorists, we remember that the attack class of the Tagging Terrorist is semantic. A semantic attack is the less egregious of the two attack classes we discussed. Tagging Terrorists are generally only out to diddle with the meaning of your corporate image and generally they aren't counting on people to respond to their attack. There is no obvious effort to change the behaviors of social media users by employing this type of attack. Tagging Terrorists are only targeting the social media user's *knowledge* (i.e., the meaning) of your company's corporate image, perhaps with the hope that behaviors may change serendipitously at a later date.

A tagging semantic attack, generally chaotically organized, is relatively speaking not a high level threat. Nor is this type of threat highly difficult to combat as compared to threats from some other insidious competitor types. Your social media squad faces a relatively high probability of success in this attack class. Entering into social bookmarking sites and countering attacks on your corporate image may require some time, but it is doable. It is doable especially when considering that this insidious competitor is usually chaotically organized, while your social media squad will be cosmically organized and motivated with purpose, such as the preservation of their own livelihoods. As long as your social media squad gets in there and "slugs it out" with these taggers, your company's efforts should go far against countering their attacks.

Tools: Snark

The Tagging Terrorist uses the tool of snark. And, the Tagging Terrorist's use of snark is very dependent upon humor, a sarcastic humor, to ridicule and demean the targeted company. In countering the effects of the snarky Tagging Terrorist, don't forget to use the attractiveness of humor to your own advantage, just not the sarcastic variety. Tags, created by your social media squad, can be associated with witty and humorous sites that reinforce your desired image of your corporation.

Proactive Strategies & Tactics

So, now let's discuss our *generally* described and suggested proactive strategies and tactics, as applied to the case of the Tagging Terrorist.

***Strategy**: "Immunize" the social media crowd against "infectious memes." Infectious memes are those that will propagate readily within an environment like social media, where contagion reacts to the power and institutional disdain that exists within.*

> ***Tactic**: Anticipate negative memes that attackers might create. Provide information nullifying the claims made by the attackers. Address the "issue" before it becomes an issue.*

In the case of combating the chaotically organized Tagging Terrorist, cull through the tags that are made to your corporate image. Get a feel for the general ideas and concepts that the taggers are associating with your company. Anticipate how those memes might be extended and modified into other memes. Once you have a better understanding of both today's situation and what the forecast for tomorrow might be, put tactics in place designed to counter those negative associations with positive messaging, grounded in the real truth about your company or its products.

For example, when we first discussed the Tagging Terrorist, we discussed some sites to which the name "KFC" was tagged. To counter some of the negative or less than positive tag associations, a company like KFC might tag their own name to sites involving partying, fun food, quick meal ideas, or simply articles about comfort food and its popularity during an economic downturn. If there are tags existing that may imply food from companies like KFC is unhealthy, have the social media squad tag to third-party sites citing the benefits of the sorts of foods offered by companies like KFC. And take care to be sure that such benefits are not exaggerated. The science or economics etc. must be sound here. For example, use tags to Web sites with credible information that's "on the side of KFC" to address "issues" before they become larger issues, and "anticipate future issues" before they become "issues." Make sure that your squad tags your product to the same competitive advantages that you highlight in your existing advertising programs. Pre-emptive tagging can only help to negate, or diffuse, the strength of an argument that an organized foe may make at a later date.

A cosmically organized social media squad can mount a counter-attack through the creation of multiple account profiles, and screen names. (Of course in the creation of any profiles, the squad should take care to be sure that no fraudulent behavior is performed.) These numbers of screen names and accounts can, in time, in your cosmically organized counter-attack, overwhelm the numbers of tags created by the chaotically organized insidious competitor. This method would employ a Search Engine Optimization (SEO) type strategy to help push negative tags down in the tagging popularity list so that they are seen by fewer people. (Don't worry, we are going to discuss SEO and SERP strategies more completely when we talk about Mommy Bloggers in the next section.)

Tactic: *Craft your message strongly within the Societal Basics, the four values of daily life and the sociological presuppositions.*

Remember when I asked you to think differently about propaganda? Well, now is the time to remember that propaganda is a set of principles which *influence a process*, the solipsistic and epistemological process, the system of knowing. Propaganda is not a **negative** process; it's just a process.

So, be sure to bring in some principles of propaganda to help you. Look for opportunities to tag to sites that support the daily values of life, such as "work." In our KFC example, a squad could tag to sites with ideas about how busy working parents can balance their work schedules with the responsibilities of home by getting a helping hand with food preparation.

Can you also see, how carefully selected tags might relate our KFC example to one of the four sociological presuppositions, the search for happiness? That happiness could be that which comes from being able to spend more time with family, even after a busy day at work. Credibly tagging your company's corporate image to sites with messaging grounded in the Societal Basics principle of propaganda can only strengthen your position within social media. And don't forget to take a page from the snarky playbook of the Tagging Terrorist. Create tags linking to witty and humorous sites that bolster the image of your company, using the element of humor to attract social media user eyeballs.

Tactic: *Take immunization strategy into relevant epistemic communities across several different media.*

Have your social media squad enter into conversations immediately relevant to your company's products or services. But take care not to "sell." That is not your intent. Your intent here is to immunize social media users against future attacks from the Tagging Terrorist. Extend your reach by tagging epistemologically related sites. Using our KFC example again, tagging to sites devoted to organizing parties would extend KFC's reach as they mention these "tagged" (or bookmarked) sites in their social media conversations about KFC's products. The goal here is to spread the word about tags to sites with positive imagery and messaging that then become associated with your corporate image and that provides a countering, or softening, of any future negative memes from the Tagging Terrorist.

* * *

Discussion: Against the Tagging Terrorist, proactive strategy, with its supporting tactics, is grounded in the solipsistic and epistemological process.

Experience >>> Perception >>> Knowledge

Conceptually, this strategy is basic to any marketing communications vehicle, but what makes this strategy *entirely* different in social media is that, in social media, this strategy is performed on both an individual and a mass communications basis at the same time.

Through engagement within the epistemic communities, uh . . . I mean crowds, through the tags that your squad has created, you are influencing the *experience* stage of the process. You are offering an experience to social media users other than that they would receive from the insidious competitor. And that different *experience* leads to a *perception* that is different than that desired by the Tagging Terrorist. Separately, by creating tags to your company or brand name which are more favorable than those created by the Tagging Terrorist, you are competing *within the perception stage* of the process. In both cases, your intent is to *change* the knowledge stage of the process, or the *meaning.*

Reactive Strategies & Tactics

Okay. Now, let's assume that your company, which has either not implemented a proactive strategy, or the proactive strategy has not yet been effective, is under a Tagging Terrorist attack. And since the attacker seems to be taking big chunks out of the *meaning* of your *corporate image*, let's just assume that this is something more than a chaotically organized attack. Let's assume the attacker here is cosmic. With that as backdrop for our learning, let's discuss our *generally* described suggested reactive strategies and tactics, as applied to the case of the Tagging Terrorist.

***Strategy**: Attack the attacker.*

> ***Tactic**: Identify the attacker as mistaken. Present information within social media discussions countering image-damaging claims. Link back to the third-party sources created in the proactive strategies.*

As shown above in the Proactive Strategies & Tactics for Tagging Terrorists, we saw that in the first tactic we should, "*Provide information nullifying the claims made by the attackers.*" In a reactive strategy against a cosmically organized Tagging Terrorist the same basic principle applies. We would want to tag our brand or company name with links to third-party, objective sites providing information which counter the claims being made. And again, you must be sure that the information to which your social media squad is tagging is sound and is based on good science, economics, etc. To do otherwise will only weaken your case on the social web.

* * *

Discussion: In using this reactive strategy against a Tagging Terrorist, there are not many tactical options. About your only option here is to modify with accurate information the perception step of the solipsistic and epistemological process of:

Experience >>> Perception >>> Knowledge

You might be thinking that you would want to direct your social media squad to enter the epistemic communities across the social web and reference these tags leading to the more accurate information about your company's products or services. But, under a tagging cosmic attack, consider that such a move might be seen as too defensive.

Mommy Bloggers

Among all the insidious competitors that we have looked at in this book, the Tagging Terrorists are probably among the least lethal to your corporate image. I say that because social bookmarking sites simply aren't one of the most popular venues within the social web today. (Though I don't think you should dismiss them, as they can be a bellwether for future memes that might compete for your corporate image in other areas of the social web.) Social bookmarking sites are certainly not as popular as are the venues of social networks and blogs. Blogs. That brings us to Mommy Bloggers.

Recapping from Chapter Eleven, we saw that the profile of the Mommy Blogger looks like this:

Tools: Mutant Conversation and Snark
Attack: Semantic or Cognitive Overt
Organization: Primarily Chaotic

Let's discuss these characteristics from the perspective of strategic and tactical approaches designed to neutralize, or even reverse, the Mommy Bloggers' insidiously competitive effects on your company's corporate image.

Organization: Primarily Chaotic

Let's start our analysis by taking a look at the way the Mommy Blogger is organized.

As you and I previously discussed, it seems that Mommy Bloggers can be sometimes cosmically organized, but for the most part they appear to be chaotically organized. For Mommy Bloggers to be cosmically organized and have an overwhelming effect upon The Ephemeral Image of any corporation, they would need to be organized by an online publication, advocacy group, or retailer (indeed this has happened), and would need to be in very great numbers. As it stands now, these types of organizations have gathered Mommy Bloggers to blog about different topics, but the number that have been gathered under one banner remains relatively small as compared to the number of independent, chaotically organized Mommy Blogger journalists that exist on the social web. To have an effect from one blog site that is greater than that of the chaotically organized Mommy Bloggers collectively, the cosmically organized group would need to be so large that their presence on that one blog site would look almost ridiculous, possibly negating their credibility. So, for our strategic and tactical implementation illustration purposes, we'll go with an organizational profile of Mommy Bloggers that is chaotic, as we discuss both proactive and reactive strategies and tactics against this insidious competitor.

Attack: Semantic or Cognitive Overt

As we discussed earlier when we were learning about the Tagging Terrorist, the semantic attack tends to be the less egregious of the two attack classes that we have discussed. As we know, semantic attacks aren't orthopractic. And while Mommy Bloggers participate in semantic attacks, they also take it a step farther. They diddle with the meaning of the corporate image and then they often move in for a cognitive change. They can do this easily because of the venue in which they appear; the blogosphere. Moving from semantic attack to cognitive attack is not nearly as easy for the Tagging Terrorist.

Making this quick switch in attack classes is very easy for the Mommy Blogger which makes their potency of attack very high. What also makes their attack potency, whether the attack is semantic or cognitive, very high is the fact that they leverage to very good effect the principles of propaganda. This leverage, as discussed, is affected by using the Societal Basics principle of propaganda (i.e., the four values of daily life and/or the sociological presuppositions). And it all manifests, as we saw, in the moral shield. So, when we consider our strategies and tactics in the *battle for meaning* against the insidious competitor of the Mommy Blogger, we must adequately consider that their attack classes are protected by that moral shield and that they may quickly turn from semantic to cognitive.

Tools: Mutant Conversation and Snark

In the case of the Mommy Blogger, it may be possible to turn the tool of Snark around on them.

Remember from Chapter Eight, we saw that:

(David Denby) . . . says that like political correctness (PC), snark "refuses true political engagement, the job of getting at the truth of things." [142]

Then you and I discussed . . .

. . . if that's true, I suppose we could say that snark is less about its style and more about its message which is the obfuscation of facts. And if Snark is about the obfuscation of facts, if it's about innuendo, then it's a direct

application of the shading of the truth . . . as we discussed in the propaganda chapter.

For the Mommy Blogger relying heavily on Snark, a counter-attack that highlights the inaccuracies of the Mommy Blogger's position and demonstrates how the position relies on innuendo and how the Snark relies on the obfuscation of facts, can help to set the record straight. Everybody likes a mom. But no one is going to like a mom that can be shown to be misrepresenting facts. Mommy blog readers might not end up "hating" the mom. The reader's deeply engrained respect for motherhood probably won't let that happen, and that should not be your goal anyway. But the reader may lose at least some respect for the Mommy Blogger shown to be relying on innuendo, instead of facts. That loss of respect for a specific Mommy Blogger can mean a decrease in her "blogging" audience, which means a reduction in the number of *experiences* in the system of knowing and thereby a reduction in the threat level to your company.

What about their usage of Mutant Conversation? Can the tool of Mutant Conversation also be used to combat Mutant Conversation? In our example of the Mommy Blogger who dealt more in innuendo and less in fact, Mutant Conversation can be used to broadly share the negatives associated with incorrect (non fact-based) blog reporting. A word of caution is needed here, however. Integrity is paramount in this process and no company wants to be seen as the source of discrediting a Mommy Blogger to the extent that she is made out to be a flat-out liar. Remember that your mission is to discredit any and all "reporting" (not just the content but also the process, e.g., the previously mentioned use of Snark) that does not accurately represent the facts. Your mission is not to personally discredit a particular Mommy Blogger or Mommy Bloggers in general. You will only want to discredit their innuendoes as it relates to your corporate image. Be sure to monitor the situation, as it relates to your company, regularly. It might be a good idea to step in to correct any unfair attacks *against* the Mommy Bloggers who have attacked your corporate image in the past. An attacked company that takes the high road might reap greater rewards and, in the end, it is simply the fair thing to do.

Counter-attacking or preempting Mommy Bloggers, as in dealing with all insidious competitors, is about the truth. It's about operating on a higher level than the opponent. Because of their moral shield, in competing against the Mommy Blogger, this rule is imperative.

The truth sets everyone free.

Proactive Strategies & Tactics

As we considered before, in the battle for meaning ideally you will want to insert yourself into the fray before things have gotten out-of-hand. That means pre-emptive actions. That's what proactive strategies and tactics are. So, now let's discuss our suggested proactive strategies and tactics as applied to a case of a semantic attack from the "morally shielded" Mommy Blogger.

***Strategy**: "Immunize" the social media crowd against "infectious memes." Infectious memes are those that will propagate readily within an environment like social media, where contagion reacts to the power and institutional disdain that exists within.*

***Strategy**: Encourage third-party sources of information strengthening your company's corporate image along issues that insidious competitors may likely attack from within social media.*

> ***Tactic**: Anticipate negative memes that attackers might create. Provide information nullifying the claims made by the attackers. Address the "issue" before it becomes an issue.*

Spend time analyzing just how Mommy Bloggers discuss your company, its products or services, and its image. Understand how they use the principles of propaganda, see if they use drama in their stories, and observe how well-arrayed the Five Factors are in their favor.

Once you have a good understanding of the recurring negative memes that target your ephemeral image, have your social media squad move to establish connections with sites providing independent, objective information that refutes the negative memes.

Or, if indeed the Mommy Bloggers tend to point out something that is an actual problem within your company or with its offerings, then by all means ***correct*** that problem – and make sure that the blogosphere becomes aware that you have done so. Swiftly taking such action will help mitigate the immediate situation while further preventing the issue from escalating into a crisis at a later date.

Tactic: *Take immunization strategy into relevant epistemic communities across several different media.*

This tactic follows nicely from the one above where we discussed that you should make sure that the blogosphere becomes aware when your company has corrected any actual problems with your products or services. If your company corrected an actual problem with its offerings, as discovered in your Mommy Blogger analysis as shown in the previous tactic, your social media squad would deploy into the relevant epistemic communities, er uh . . . crowds within the blogosphere and social networks and announce that news. Yes, Mommy Bloggers will "declare victory" and "take the credit." Let them and congratulate them for it.

Tactic: *Have company social media staff enter into problematic discussions with links back to the third-party sources.*

Similar to the usage of this tactic against the Tagging Terrorist, your social media squad would go into epistemologically related social media venues, having conversations on topics related to the issue at hand, referencing links to objective, third-party sites that contain nullifying information. By implementing this tactic you are not "avoiding" the issue raised by the Mommy Blogger. The objective here is to "discuss" the issue, presenting the facts and providing links to objective third-party sources to back them up.

It may also be beneficial that in these discussions your social media squad mentions, if applicable, that the Mommy Blogger's "reporting" process (Snark) precluded debate on the issue and thus did not present an accurate view of the issue.

Tactic: *SEO the third-party sites up in SERPs by creating company information sites linking back to the third-party information site.*

I briefly mentioned SEO previously and we're going to discuss SEO and SERPs in more detail very soon. Just let me say here that since I've mentioned third-party sites supporting your company image, your social media squad would want to help those sites get noticed as much as possible. To help them get noticed in search engine results, create links from your own company sites back to those third-party sites. Search engines love inbound links and reward sites having them with higher search page rankings.

***Tactic**: Craft your message strongly within the Societal Basics, the four values of daily life and the sociological presuppositions.*

Remember. What makes this competitor especially insidious, and especially competitive, is that moral shield. The messages that your squad takes into the social web must be those that express concern for solving the problems of others. Now, this should really not be very difficult. We talked about this previously. One of the purposes of business is to solve problems for people.

If your squad members truly believe that their company is dedicated to solving the problems of individuals, as it should be, then that attitude will come through genuinely in their social media conversations. That will be their truth, a critical principle in propaganda. And with that truth, grounded in the Societal Basics principle of propaganda, your social media squad may very well just be able to "out moral" the moral shield. Or, at the very least, the squad may be able to approach parity with the moral shield of the Mommy Blogger.

While paying attention to the principles of propaganda, while having a conversation based in truth, daily values, sociological presuppositions, and morality, the social media squad should use the elements of story effectively. In other words, they need to format their conversations into dramas. The Mommy Bloggers dramatize. Your social media squad must dramatize even better.

Let's go back to the example of The Motrin Incident, from earlier in the book, to see how this drama tactic might work.

During The Motrin Incident there were many allegations from Mommy Bloggers that the Motrin marketers didn't check with moms when in the process of creating the ad. Well, the makers of Motrin, Mc Neil Pharmaceuticals, a Johnson & Johnson company, are a bunch of sophisticated marketers. They didn't get to where they are by being a bunch of marketing dolts. For me, it's hard to believe that they didn't run at least the concept of the ad, if not the actual copy, by some moms prior to going into production and then distribution. And, I wouldn't be surprised to learn that at least some of the marketers are moms, themselves. It's also hard for me not to believe that there were probably many marketing meetings about this video ad before it saw the light of day; that there were probably supporters for the ad and detractors thereof; that there were probably internal politics which held the birth of the video ad in the balance; that there were the usual internal conflicts and office politics in delivering this ad to the public. It's also hard for me to believe that the Mommy Blogger reaction to the ad didn't cause at least a small stir on the McNeil home front, resulting in the apology that was to follow.

So, why not just say that? In the form of a story? A drama. What I just described is a drama. Why not relate the tale? In so doing, they could have employed the Societal Basics principle of propaganda and let every Mommy Blogger know just how committed the Motrin staff really is to mommies and their babies and *then* apologize for the "misunderstanding," which was surely not the intent of a corporation with a reputation for caring about families. But be sure to say it in a dramatic format.

Did they not do this because Mc Neil Pharmaceuticals did not, and may still not, have a social media squad? Or was it afraid to use it?

Instead, Mc Neil did what so many other companies do when faced with insidious competition. They caved. They apologized. I'm still not sure what for, and removed the video ad from their site, although it will in all likelihood live in perpetuity on sites like YouTube.com. They did what they did because it is what big companies know to do. But in the long run doing what big companies know to do runs the future risk of leaving them unprepared for engagement with this new type of insidious competitor we now find in social media. Yes, their "apology" likely "stopped the bleeding," but telling their story, *as a story crafted within the Societal Basics*, might have helped them "win points" with Mommy Bloggers. Telling their story, attracting readers with drama, seizing the opportunity to "out moral" the moral shield, and gaining sympathetic converts in the process, would have gone a long way to precluding any future "anti-mommy" type attacks against the Motrin makers.

I can tell you from my past experience as a competitor intelligence analyst, that relating that "dramatic" tale would not have revealed any direct or indirect competitive intelligence that would have been of much value to a competitor. But the tale itself, and the fact that Motrin wanted mommies to know their side, would have been loaded with opportunity to maintain and grow Motrin's relationship with its valued "mommy" customers.

Strategy*: Use search engine optimization (SEO) procedures to push the appearance of insidious competitor conversations lower in search engine results page rankings (SERPs) by pushing your pages higher.*

Tactic: *Don't perform in-house. Use third-party contractors.*

What is this exactly? What's all this SEO and SERP stuff? I mentioned this before. Thanks for being patient.

SEO has as its goal the concept of optimizing the keywords that appear on a site, such that Internet searches for those keywords are more likely to return that site on the top of the search engine results page (SERP). The SERP is the page with the returned list of results for a particular keyword search. As an example, if someone Googled the word "mommy," and your company makes products for "mommy," wouldn't you want your company Web site to appear high on the first page of the list of search results? Of course, so you would be sure that "mommy" appeared as many times as possible, in strategic locations, on your site. The idea behind this tactic is to use SEO in such a way that your site appears closer to the top on the SERP than do pages containing the insidious competitor conversations.

You may even use SEO principles in helping support third-party sites to rank more highly in the SERP, so that they too will appear higher in the SERP than the insidious competitor conversations. Search engines rank Web sites that have many inbound links more highly than those that have fewer inbound links. So, give those third-party sites a chance at a higher SERP rank by creating links to them from your SEOd Web sites. You may also create new Web sites specifically for the purpose of linking to the supportive third-party sites, although you would want to be sure that such sites contain legitimate and helpful content. But don't go "crazy" with the number of links. You don't want your insidious competitor running a link trace to find that a high proportion of inbound links to the third-party sites are from your company. Yet, always remember, higher rankings for your, or your identified third-party, Web sites mean possible lower rankings for the insidiously competitive Mommy Blogger site(s).

When you perform these SEO procedures, contract them out. You have seen me say several times, "Don't perform in-house. Use third-party contractors." Why use contractors? Because this SEO process is detailed, laborious, and time-consuming. You don't want your social media squad spending time on a task of this type. Your social media squad time is better spent in conversations engaged in the battle for meaning. You hired the people in your squad for their skill in the art of online conversation. Don't bog them down with SEO programming tasks.

A more detailed explanation of SEO procedures, including SERP, is beyond the scope of this book. But what's important to our discussion here in *Insidious Competition* is that we need to realize that the SEO tactic is intervening in the *experience* step of the system of knowing. If you can be successful in *reducing the number of experiences that have negative perceptions* attached to your *corporate image* (or conversely *increasing the number of experiences that have positive perceptions*), well then, the audience's *knowledge,* their reality, their definition of the *meaning* of your corporate image has a greater chance of not being repackaged.

Strategy: *Reposition social media.*

> ***Tactic***: *Run public service announcements (PSAs) stating that the "facts" shared in social media are not always true and are usually unvetted, and that the false and misleading information in social media is a disservice to the public.*

In these PSAs note that online fact-checking software exists and that individuals should make use of it, even if they are checking "facts" from a "trusted" blogger that they read regularly. Since a PSA is of a general nature, perhaps you shouldn't single out Mommy Bloggers in particular, but simply bloggers in general. However, by using this tactic you could give special emphasis to topic issues on which you anticipate Mommy Bloggers may write about your company in the future. With this approach you could still give attention, albeit indirectly, to the insidiously competitive problems generated for your company by this competitor type.

Stress in the PSAs that fact-checking software is downloadable by individuals and can help social media users determine what's "true" from "false" on blogs and other websites.[143] Also stress in these PSAs that *all bloggers* should be using such software so that they can make better decisions on the information they put into their blog posts. This plays on the Veracity principle of propaganda.

Put some research and examples behind these statements demonstrating that social media, with its unvetted commentary, disguised as facts, puts reality at risk for all of us. Run PSAs through multiple channels, including via trade organizations.

Reactive Strategies & Tactics

All right. You've likely come to this section because your company is now under an attack from Mommy Bloggers. That attack is likely cognitive. And remember, we said that cognitive Mommy Blogger attacks are likely to be *overt.* They have no reason to hide their identity. The strength of their attack lies in their identification as Mommies and the Mommy Blogger strength is wrapped in their moral shield. Cognitive attacks, especially cognitive overt attacks, are the ones that really grab the attention of the victim because the attackers are trying to enlist their audience in a business-damaging behavior against the victim, like a boycott.

Possibly, now due to that attack you are reading about reactive strategies and tactics against the Mommy Blogger. Maybe you are in this situation because either: 1) you didn't perform proactive strategies and tactics via a dedicated social media squad; or, 2) you didn't implement them effectively. (Didn't I recommend that before creating and implementing strategies and tactics for your specific situation that you should consult a professional?)

Mommy Bloggers can be tough competitors for all the reasons we've discussed in *Insidious Competition*. They can also be tough competitors because of another reason we've touched on in these pages, your own reticence to take on a Mommy. Get over it.

Don't think of them as Mommies. They are competitors.

Period.

Mommy Bloggers are competing for your corporate image. They are impacting your company's revenue stream and its ability to pay your salary. Mommy Bloggers have the potential to affect negatively your life and the lives of **your** children. Don't let them.

Game on. Let's discuss our suggested strategies and tactics as applied to the case of the chaotically organized Mommy Blogger.

Strategy*: Attack the attacker. Change the balance in the battle for meaning. Give them something to lose (e.g., their legitimacy, their reliability, and/or their integrity as "trusted" writers).*

> ***Tactic****: Identify the attacker as mistaken. Present information within social media discussions countering image-damaging claims. Link back to the third-party sources created in the proactive strategies.*

If you have implemented some proactive strategies, then you may already have the previously mentioned third-party links established. If not, get started. Right now! It takes some time to identify these sources, and if you are currently under attack, well, then time is of the essence.

In the proactive tactics, I discussed having your social media squad enter into epistemic crowds for the purpose of participating in relevant conversations and mentioning these third-party links. Do the same here and do it blatantly. You are reacting. Do it with purpose and intention. Change the balance. Use the veracity of an independent source, *one which Mommy Bloggers will also see as being credible*, to counter the Mommy Bloggers. Use the objective source to disseminate the truthful message, which will result in readers questioning the original Mommy Blogger information. Perhaps you may even be able to get the objective source to comment on the Mommy Blogger's attack blog post, right on her blog.

Overall, your goal here is to oppose and defeat the Mommy Blogger attack by using objective, independent sources to counter her *untruth,* while informing readers of the *truth*. In doing so, you want to be objective, making sure that Mommy Bloggers are confronted on the facts of the issue, without confronting the Mommy Blogger personally. Yes, you want to damage the legitimacy of the Mommy Blogger claim, the reliability of her writing, and the integrity of her sourcing, but you do not want to damage the Mommy Blogger herself. Don't make it personal; keep it strictly business.

Just one comment before I move on to the next tactic. With regard to the objective, third party sources, you must be absolutely certain that those sources have no connections to your company. Because if they do, any good blogger, Mommy or otherwise, will "sniff out" those connections, negating any benefits sought through this tactic and perhaps making the overall attack even more painful.

> ***Tactic**: Radicalize the attacker. Look for ways to separate the attacker's supporters in the social media crowd from the attacker. Cut the psychic shareholding. Sever the emotional supply lines and weaken the influence of the Five Factors.*

Remember that here, as in the prior tactics, you are in reactive mode and you want to change the balance. But don't get carried away by the excitement of the battle, the "fog of war," because this tactic needs special skills in diplomacy.

This attack will likely be cognitive and overt, so you will probably know the identity of the Mommy Blogger(s) attacking your ephemeral image. So, do some good competitor intelligence. Have your social media squad use social graphing software to determine any links between the attacking Mommy Blogger(s) and others (organizations or individuals). Look to see if those links go to credible sources. Also, using software specific for this function, look to find the primary source of the misinformation or inaccuracies.

Remember, this tactic is about correcting the false message being heard by other social media users, while eliciting some deserved sympathy as the "injured party." (And if your company **doesn't** deserve sympathy, you need to be thinking **differently** about how to correct the problem and make it public that you have done so, all while showing how you have been listening.) Appeal to other Mommy Bloggers on the basis of wanting them to have accurate information.

As we saw with the negation of celebrity back in Chapter Five, here in this tactic cut the psychic shareholding by bringing the truth to light, while remaining mindful of the critical necessity for diplomacy. Take care not to find fault with the Mommy Blogger personally, but instead find fault with the reliability of her information. Other Mommies won't want to keep backing a Mommy Blogger in whose blog they lose confidence. As the psychic shareholding is decreased, so should support for this Mommy Blogger wane. The fourth of the Five Factors, instinct to follow group interests, will be weakened. You will be working the system of knowing, perhaps without even realizing it, because the number of experiences associated with her negative perception of your company will decrease.

Tactic: *Dilute the insidious competitor's message. Go to targeted social sites where insidious competition is operating against your corporate image and talk about other issues. But don't take conversation too far afield.*

Using web monitoring software and social media search engines, seek out other blogs and social sites where the attack on your company is being discussed. On those sites, look for other salient topics and attempt to move the attack conversations toward the other topics. In doing this, you are changing the numbers of experiences that the audience can have with an issue that you are trying to quiet. For every one conversation that you dilute, you will have prevented many others being born from it. But don't do this fraudulently and do this carefully. If you can't steer the conversation in an appropriate direction of your choice, then don't overdo it. The repercussions might be more severe than the original attack.

***Tactic**: Hold the attacker to liability laws. Frame your argument in "the truth" stating that the attacker is disseminating misleading information. Where it makes sense to do so, take the position that the misleading information (i.e., repackaged reality) is against the "public interest," especially that of "the children."*

If there is a Mommy Blogger attack that is so severe as to present as facts things that are libelous and actionable in court, state within social media, and other media, that their attack is totally out-of-bounds, unfair, and untrue. Be sure to be on solid ground here and, of course, check with your company's legal department before proceeding.

Frame your argument in the truth, using links to independent third party sources to back up your position. Assuming you can do so, show objectively how their misleading information is actually doing a disservice to all mothers who only want the best for their children. Show, with data, how your company is also committed to the welfare of mothers and their children. This is a battle. You need to be sure that you are on solid ground to change the balance effectively.

Let's not leave this tactic without re-stating the obvious. You will need your company's legal department if you want to really get serious about holding Mommy Bloggers to liability laws. So, make sure you have a good, on-going relationship with your legal department.

* * *

Discussion: In both the proactive and reactive modes, we see examples of attempting to control or influence the solipsistic and epistemological process:

Experience >>> Perception >>> Knowledge

Most of the tactics that you and I just discussed attempt to adjust *perception,* while some attempt to modify the number of *experiences*. Successfully affecting a change in either experience or perception will change *knowledge,* which is, after all, your real goal in *the battle for meaning*. Your main objective is to ensure that the knowledge, or image, that the Mommy Blogger reader has about your company is your company's image, as your company has defined it.

It should go without saying, but I will say it again anyway. Dealing with a Mommy Blogger attack, either semantic or cognitive, requires skill, diplomacy and great caution. Most of you reading this probably already know that. And knowing that, if any of you have suffered a Mommy Blogger attack in the past, you have probably shied away from counter-attacking. But if you are reading this section and if you are considering what can be done about this insidious competitor, well, then this insidious competitor must be doing serious damage to your corporate image. If that is indeed the case, then you owe it to your shareholders, your employees, their families, and well, yes, your own children, to fight back.

NGOs and Activists

Of all the insidious competitors we have studied in this book, Mommy Bloggers can be the most treacherous. A misstep in combating them can not only be counterproductive, but it can downright make matters worse. And a misstep is easy to make. Yet, Mommy Bloggers can be battled.

Other insidious competitors that can be treacherous are NGOs and Activists. Missteps can be made here, too, yet like Mommy Bloggers, NGOs and Activists can be engaged. NGOs and Activists are probably the most effective in their anti-corporate image campaigns and, except for Customers/Clients/Consumers, the ones against which you will most often run up.

Recapping from Chapter Eleven, we saw that the profile of the NGOs and Activists looks like this:

Tools: Mutant Conversation, Snark, and Hip Chat
Attack: Cognitive Overt
Organization: Cosmic

Let's discuss these characteristics from the perspective of strategic and tactical approaches designed to blunt or negate the insidiously competitive effects that NGOs and Activists can have on your corporate image.

Organization: Cosmic

There are many similarities between the Mommy Bloggers and NGOs/Activists as insidious competitors. They use their tools in a similar manner and they share an attack class. Where NGOs and Activists differ from Mommy Bloggers is in their organization. The organization of NGOs and Activists is cosmic whereas Mommy Bloggers are primarily chaotic. But if Mommy Bloggers became more organized, if there was a "central Mommy Blogger," if those Mommy Bloggers changed their organizational status to cosmic, then they would essentially become activists. Mommy Bloggers are so close to NGOs and Activists in many ways, and chief among those is the moral shield.

So, because of these similarities, many of the proactive and reactive strategies and tactics which we will discuss next will be much the same as those discussed earlier for Mommy Bloggers.

Attack: Cognitive Overt

Using their tools similarly and sharing a moral shield, NGOs and Activists share an attack class with Mommy Bloggers, cognitive overt. Yes, much of the time the attack class for Mommy Bloggers will be semantic, but they have the capability to go cognitive in a heartbeat. NGOs and Activists are after an orthopractic outcome. As we discussed, they have an agenda. Their attacks are cognitive and overt. You will know who is attacking you and you will know what they want. And their actions will be embedded in that moral shield.

Tools: Mutant Conversation, Snark, and Hip Chat

The key to battling the NGO and Activist in social media is to use their own principles of propaganda against them. The principles of propaganda support the moral position. Know this and you may be able to "out moral" them and dissolve that shield.

Just as in the case of the Mommy Blogger relying heavily on Snark and Mutant Conversation, a counter-attack that highlights the inaccuracies of the NGO/Activist position can be used. What is critical in this maneuver is to portray their use of Snark as closed-minded, one of not inviting debate, and as a method of relying upon innuendo rather than truth. But, just as with the Mommy Bloggers, truth must be steadfastly on your side in order to pull these strategies off effectively.

NGOs or Activists who persist in making their case through innuendo, versus facts, should be considered irresponsible. Your job, as a reputable company, is to call attention to the truth while discrediting reporting that is not grounded in the facts. Don't let the falsehoods of NGOs and Activists stand "uncorrected," particularly if their false assertions have already broadly mutated. Challenge their assertions in the social web. By framing their assertions as being misleading and by declaring the importance of responsible reporting, readers will, by extension, question the responsibility of the NGO/ Activist reporting. Causing social media users to lose faith in the integrity and validity of the message from the NGO or Activist will break the psychic shareholding.

Just as with Mommy Bloggers, counter-attacking or preempting NGOs and Activists in social media is about the truth. It's about operating on a higher level than the opponent. The truth sets everyone free. Just be sure the truth is on your side before you proceed.

Proactive Strategies & Tactics

NGOs and Activists are always in action against companies. It's what they do. Unlike Mommy Bloggers who don't always have companies in their sights, NGOs and Activists do. Having companies in their sights is part of their process of "private politics." If you work at a company that manufactures something and you work in corporate communications, investor relations, marketing, R&D, government relations, or a similarly-named department, you know that these people poke their noses into your business on a regular basis. And they are quite aggressive when they do so.

What does that mean relative to our conversation here? That means proactive strategies and tactics. You know that if they aren't bothering you now, those NGOs and Activists will do so soon. So, proactive strategies and tactics can help mitigate, or possibly eliminate, those future attacks and may assist in making your job easier down the line, not to mention helping to preserve your job.

***Strategy**: "Immunize" the social media crowd against "infectious memes." Infectious memes are those that will propagate readily within an environment* *like social media, where contagion reacts to the power and institutional disdain that exists within.*

***Strategy**: Encourage third-party sources of information strengthening your company's corporate image along the issues that insidious competitors may likely attack from within social media.*

***Tactic**: Anticipate negative memes that attackers might create. Provide information nullifying the claims made by the attackers. Address the "issue" before it becomes an issue.*

***Tactic**: Take immunization strategy into relevant epistemic communities across several different media.*

"Know your enemy." Sun Tzu, an ancient Chinese general, is credited with that adage. This adage applies here in dealing with NGOs and Activists in social media. Unlike Mommy Bloggers, some of whom might be your present customers or clients or consumers or even future ones or at least people who can possibly be made into friends, NGOs and Activists will never be made into your friends. They have plenty of other friends. They aren't interested in making you into a friend, even though they may sometimes seem to be. NGOs and Activists are indeed opponents and should be considered as such.

Have your social media squad, along with your corporate communications people, spend time isolating what issues are hot buttons for various NGOs and Activists. Look to the past to see on what issues they have confronted you. Given your current macro-business environment, extrapolate to what they may hit you with next. Identify the hot memes they have concentrated on in the past, offline as well as online. Discover what issues are salient in the mainstream news, especially as they might impact your industry or company. Become expert on how NGOs and Activists use the principles of propaganda. Determine if they use drama in their stories. See if they take advantage of the Five Factors within social media and, if so, how well they exploit them.

Also, know how well specific NGOs and Activists are represented within social media. Some use social media very heavily while others are only just scratching the surface of this new medium. If they Twitter, follow them. If they are on Facebook or LinkedIn, "friend" or "network" them. Be sure to do so within your company's identity. No social engineering here. You want to do everything above board. But don't talk to them in those networks. Just "listen" for those negative memes.

After your squad gets a handle on the negative memes that NGOs and Activists targeting your company like to propagate, then, have your squad set up links with objective and independent sites that provide information supporting your company's position on the issues.

For instance, going back to the Carrotmob.org example that we previously discussed, the social media squad of a business not offered the "carrot" would most likely isolate the meme of "product sustainability" as the issue working against it. If applicable, the squad might then work to find third-party sites offering information showing that their company's products did indeed qualify as "sustainable." Proceeding further, the social media squad would enter the relevant epistemic social media crowds (i.e., those concerned with product sustainability) and enter into conversations with the objective of sharing information showing that their own products do measure up to the "carroted" products.

But as always, caution would be advised here.

Like in the Mommy Blogger strategy discussion above, if the NGOs or Activists point out an actual problem with your products, one with which you agree and one by which any objective standard of measurement would support the NGO and Activist claim, well then, there is one thing that you must do. **Fix it !** And do so before engaging in the social web with these strategies and tactics.

***Tactic**: Have company social media staff enter into problematic discussions with links back to the third-party sources.*

Have your company's social media squad spend extra time in epistemic communities where there are very specific discussions involving the issues that the NGOs and Activists use as hot buttons, using the third-party links as ammunition.

Then, and only then, can your squad go into the social web, discussing these memes, with relevant crowds, and pointing to third-party links which have objective information that supports your company's position. Doing so can help preclude future NGO or Activist attacks.

Again, going back to the Carrotmob.org example, can you see how the social media squad can be used under this tactic? The social media squads of companies that are being "indirectly propagandized," in other words, those whose reputations are being indirectly affected because they do not carry the products "authorized" by Carrotmob.org, should have information on relevant third-party sites providing objective information in support of their own products. The squad should also identify other social media sites where Carrotmob.org product recommendations are heavily discussed. These sites perhaps provide a good opportunity for point-to-point discussions that make the reader aware of the positive features and benefits of not only your product, but perhaps also for other products not supported by Carrotmob.org. And where the superiority of your product, vs. the Carrotmob.org recommendation, can be shown, do so.

Tactic: *SEO the third-party sites up in SERPs by creating company information sites linking back to the third-party information site.*

As in the Mommy Blogger discussion previously, help SEO those third-party sites which support your arguments by having your company create links to those third-party sites from your SEOd websites. But don't overdo it. When your adversaries start to check out those objective sites to which you refer in your social web conversations, when they run the list of sites linking into those third-party sites you recommend, you don't want your company sites to represent too high a proportion of the total inbound linking sites. Don't give these NGOs and Activists more ammunition to use against you. It's your job to get more ammunition to use against them.

Tactic: *Craft your message strongly within the Societal Basics, the four values of daily life and the sociological presuppositions.*

Review the principles of propaganda from Chapter Seven. Craft your messages using these principles, remaining especially grounded in Societal Basics. Wherever your social media squad goes on the social web they must remember that their opponents, the NGOs and Activists, in the minds of the reader, have the moral shield, or a layer of protection in the presumed morality of their "do-good" approach. Conversely, you and your squad must remember that, precisely because your company doesn't have a "carrot," you may be presumed to be the antithesis of "moral." Work hard to overcome this perception by getting readers to see your company as the "hero" in the story, or the one altruistically interested in others having access to correct and truthful information. Elevating the importance of your message will help reduce the importance of the NGO's and Activist's message. As we discussed earlier in *Insidious Competition*, expressing a true concern for helping others, for *solving their problems,* should be the main goal of the company. Make sure that you believe this. If you do, chances are that your squad will believe this, as well.

Don't forget the power of a good story to get people engaged and listening, as you hit hard on those four daily values and sociological presuppositions. Take the time to relate how your company has made changes that address NGO and Activist issues. Tell it like a story. In the Carrotmob.org situation, for example, can you legitimately document how your products might be better for children? Maybe they are safer around the house than the Carrotmob.org endorsed products. Maybe they are equally, or even more, environmentally friendly and make work easier allowing for greater productivity. Point to how through use of your product "happiness" may be realized, perhaps because it's more efficient, therefore providing the user with more free time. "Out moral" the moral shield.

***Strategy**: Use search engine optimization (SEO) procedures to push the appearance of insidious competitor conversations lower in search engine results page rankings (SERPs) by pushing your pages higher.*

***Tactic:** Don't perform in-house. Use third-party contractors.*

I covered this in the discussion on Mommy Blogger proactive strategies and tactics. The application to NGOs and Activists should be the same.

Reactive Strategies & Tactics

So, are you now actually under an overt cognitive attack? That's probably why you are reading this section. Maybe you didn't implement any proactive strategies or maybe you did but they haven't been successful yet. Regardless, you're under attack and it's probably a heavy one. First, before we go any further, there is one thought I want to put into your head.

Don't think of the NGOs and Activists attacking your good company image as societal do-gooders. They are not that. They are your competitors.

Period.

They'll take market share from you just the same as a conventional competitor would. So, don't treat those NGOs and Activists gingerly just because they aren't a traditional, or regular, competitor. Although atypical, they are a competitor just the same.

In this pursuit, don't wimp out.

If you find yourself feeling sorry for this insidious competitor, then you don't belong in your current position at your company. If you feel sorry for this competitor or sympathize with their cause, you aren't doing your co-workers or your stockholders any favors. If you feel sympathy for this opponent, perhaps you should be working instead for the NGO or the Activist.

Take a deep breath.

Are you ready now? Okay. Let's discuss our suggested reactive strategies and tactics as applied to the case of the very cosmically organized NGO and Activist.

Strategy: *Attack the attacker. Change the balance in the battle for meaning. Give them something to lose (e.g., their legitimacy, their reliability, and/or their integrity as trusted advocates).*

> ***Tactic***: *Identify the attacker as mistaken. Present information within social media discussions countering image-damaging claims. Link back to the third-party sources created in the proactive strategies.*
>
> ***Tactic***: *Make alliances with other persons or organizations to have them help present your case.*

NGOs and Activists make a lot of mistakes. One of the mistakes they make is that they will often enter into an anti-corporate campaign from an emotional standpoint; they will rely on the principles of propaganda very heavily to make their case. A result of that approach can be that their data is often skewed or incomplete. Many times NGOs and Activists deal in what I would call "do-it-yourself science" or "do-it-yourself economics" to make their cases. This is especially true of NGOs or Activist organizations that are not particularly well-funded. Many NGO and Activist organizations are under-funded, so many of this insidious competitor type will have data that are "full of holes."

Given this weakness, in *the battle for meaning* with this insidious competitor, it is imperative to have the best objective information. That means having impeccable data from completely independent third-parties. We talked about the importance of that independent information before. Here, in battle with the NGO or Activist, having that high quality supporting information is critical. Your battle can be won or lost on the caliber of that information.

Take your high quality, information-based, response directly into the social sphere. Look for venues where the attack is specifically mentioned. Deploy your social media squad to those areas. Have the squad make your argument forcefully – and with facts quote the links to supportive, independent, backing information. Make your argument high quality, high quantity, and high visibility. Have the squad make repeated visits to the same social sites in order to make the same arguments over and over. This is what the NGO or Activist will not expect. They will not expect you to hang-in for the long-haul. Surprise them.

Grab every opportunity to ask other social media users to help you spread your information. Leverage the contagion aspect of the Five Factors. Seek out assistance from trade organizations and even ordinary people. Call upon the principles of propaganda to help you enlist these independent champions. Ask these would-be champions to help you because the success of your "joint effort" will help maintain truth. Show them that in this case the attacker is not David. Show them that the David in this drama is your company because your company relies on truthful information and not the inaccurate or incomplete truths, the innuendoes, of the NGO and Activist Goliath.

Doing this successfully will alter the perception element in the solipsistic and epistemological process that the NGO or Activist wants the social media user to experience. By doing this successfully you will change the very experience - perception - knowledge system that the attacker wants the user to have. By gaining the advantage of new knowledge for users, through their new perception of truth and through their new perception of the NGO and Activist "untruth," you will succeed in discrediting the misleading information of the NGOs and Activists. And in doing so, they will look weak and unreliable in their position about your corporate image. As their arguments lose support, so will they.

Just be sure, of course, that you are correct and they are not.

> ***Tactic****: Radicalize the attacker. Through social graphing software, look for connections to the attacker which will weaken their case or associate them with questionable sourcing. Make the attacker's supporters in the social media crowd separate from the attacker. Cut the psychic shareholding. Sever the emotional supply lines and weaken the influence of the Five Factors.*

Although we discussed the use of this tactic against a Mommy Blogger attack, this tactic is even more appropriate against an NGO or an Activist. Why?

In all likelihood, the cosmically organized NGO or Activist attacking your company will contain persons who are associated with a political agenda that leans heavily either left or right. Most NGOs and Activists I have observed lean left; only a small percentage leans right. With leanings in either direction often come connections, by the members of the NGO or Activist group, that can be considered "radical," extremist, outside the mainstream of society, or highly politically-motivated. Due to the very political nature of their organization, there will likely be more of these connections with NGO or Activist staff than there will be with Mommy Bloggers. Using social graphing software, discover these individual connections, primarily for the NGO or Activist personnel who are leading the attack within social media, the "campaigners" that I mentioned back in Chapter Eleven. And, oh yes, as I said. These attacks are overt. You will know who is attacking you. The identity of the individual attackers will be clear. Use it to research their connections.

Use those same social graphing software and search engine link searches to find what groups or individuals link to the NGO or Activist that is attacking you. There might be some connections there that can also be considered "radical."

For American NGOs and Activists, examine the organization's Form 990. This is the form that tax exempt organizations file with the Internal Revenue Service annually and is publicly-available. This report will give you an idea of from where the attacker gets their funding. Look for politically-motivated connections.

Documenting these highly-political connections, on Web sites used by relevant epistemic crowds, might just grab the attention of readers who weren't aware of these deeper connections and who might find such connections objectionable, or at least unsettling. Here is where having an experienced and savvy social media squad is especially important. Your squad not only needs to be capable of following the political connections, but they also need to know what those connections mean, and be experienced and savvy in the ways in which they should make those connections public. Remember, your goal is to cut the psychic shareholding between social media readers and the NGO or Activist, meaning sever the emotional connection that the reader has with that NGO or Activist group. Care is needed and you may need experts in this area to assist you, but if you have framed your case well, the truth behind the connections may serve your case nicely, with a boost from Mutant Conversation that could propagate and mutate the story in your favor.

If the attacker uses Snark, have your squad remind the reader in social media that the attacker's snarky tone is closed-minded, because it is. Remember. You and I discussed that Snark cuts off debate and casts its user in an elitist light. If there is anything activists and campaigners hate to be called it's closed-minded and, although they may think of themselves as elitist, they don't want to be seen as elitist because it weakens any case they try to bring to the public (i.e., the "common man"). Characterize them as elitist. Make the opponent overreact. Make them lose their "cool." That blown cool will show up in social media discussions and further cut the psychic shareholding.

> ***Tactic**: Dilute the insidious competitor's message. Go to targeted social sites where insidious competition is operating against your corporate image and talk about other issues. But don't take conversation too far afield.*

As in the Mommy Blogger section on this tactic, look for ways to dilute negative conversations about your company. Essentially what you're doing here is *reducing the experience* portion of the solipsistic and epistemological process. Give the attacker fewer developed points of conversation to hijack. In this tactic, you would want to look for conversational topics other than those about the attack and encourage those conversations, creating more conversations that are not about the attack. Again, as I said in the Mommy Bloggers section, you should not do this fraudulently and you must do this carefully. If you can't gently steer a conversation away from the topic of the attack, then don't overdo it because the results may be counterproductive.

> ***Tactic**: Hold the attacker to liability laws. Frame your argument in "the truth" stating that the attacker is disseminating misleading information. Where it makes sense to do so, take the position that the misleading information (i.e., repackaged reality) is against the "public interest," especially that of "the children."*

This one is straight-forward and, of course, should always be approached in consultation with your company's legal department. In the application of this tactic toward the Mommy Blogger, you needed to proceed adroitly, applying some of the principles of propaganda along the way. When dealing with

NGOs or Activist organizations, you are basically dealing with a "business." They look at their campaigns with an eye on the cost to benefit ratio. If you make a campaign too expensive for them, they'll back off.

If in social media they're saying things about your company that simply aren't true, first warn the attacker. If they persist in circulating that type of information, then a lawsuit is always an available course of action.

Far too often companies being wrongly accused will not do this. They'll just wait for "things to blow over." Oh, yes. The pain will stop after a while. But in that while your reputation will be damaged. Revenue will be lost, so will jobs. One might be yours. As in the Mommy Blogger application of this tactic, be sure to have a good relationship with your company's legal department.

* * *

Discussion: Here in the strategic and tactical discussion for NGOs and Activists we have seen suggestions for action on the solipsistic and epistemological process:

Experience >>> Perception >>> Knowledge

In both a proactive and reactive mode, we discussed examples of how you might reduce the number of experiences of negative memes or increase the number of positive memes. We also discussed how perceptions in the process could be changed to your favor. These actions will in the end affect the knowledge about your company image that is gained by social media users. Yes, you can impact reality.

Chapter Seventeen:
Suggested Strategies & Tactics Against The Nasties

This chapter is the shortest chapter in this book. And the reason behind its brevity is personally the most disappointing for me.

The Nasties.

Back in Chapter Twelve, I made you aware of the incipient threat from this insidious competitor. We discussed the likelihood of their existence and I supported my theory that they do exist. We talked about how dangerous they could be and about how difficult it would be to identify them. And that's the genesis of my disappointment.

I can't identify them. Neither can you.

At least not presently.

One reason would be that this insidious competitor is using the tool of Social Engineering. They are disguised. We can't recognize them. They may be there, but we think that they are our friends or business colleagues. This insidious competitor is the only one in this book that I cite as using the tool of Social Engineering. And if they used it, they would use it quite well. Why? Because they have had similar past experience in doing so.

This competitor is, for me and probably you as well, an educated guess. And as such I can't provide a concrete example of their existence. I wish I could.

But their attack class is cognitive covert. Covert. That is the key behind the problem. Very covert.

For if this insidious competitor is outfitted with current or former national security personnel as in my theory, then there is very little chance that we are going to sniff out their identity.

The only thing that I can think of which may tip their hand is the use of vernacular. If you see negative conversations in social media that just don't add up in terms of your company's national vernacular, this may indicate a Nasty. Then again, it might just indicate a customer, or employee, or Mommy Blogger, or activist who is foreign-born and is "vocabularily-challenged" (if I may coin that term).

So, given these conditions, if I can't identify a Nasty, then I can't make any strategic or tactical suggestions against them.

But I'm continuing work in this area, and someday may have a breakthrough.

CHAPTER EIGHTEEN: Suggested Strategies & Tactics Against The Friendlies

In this chapter we will discuss strategies and tactics for the group of insidious competitors we labeled as The Friendlies. Our discussion will be about implementing strategies and tactics against the insidious competitors of Customers/Clients/Consumers, Employees, Activist Stockholders, and Labor Unions. And this application must be made very carefully. If you thought the discussion of implementing the strategies and tactics against the Mommy Bloggers was delicate, wait until you read further in this chapter.

Please note that, as I have mentioned previously, regarding our discussion of the suggested strategies and tactics against insidious competition, as you create your strategies and tactics seek assistance from qualified professionals in areas such as competitive strategy, corporate communications, public relations, law, human resources, competitive intelligence, social media, and marketing, as well as other business disciplines.

"Friendly" is this class of insidious competitor. But the fact remains that they are diddling with the meaning of your company's image. And much of that diddling is undeserved. That is the theme of *Insidious Competition,* to assist companies in defending their good corporate image, which is being wrongfully wrecked.

If you think that's a worthwhile pursuit, then read on.

Customers/Clients/Consumers

Let's examine strategies and tactics for each insidiously competitive Friendly. We start here with the Customers/Clients/Consumers.

Recapping from Chapter Thirteen, we saw that the profile of the Customer/Client/Consumer looks like this:

Tools: Mutant Conversation, Snark, and Hip Chat
Attack: All classes apply. Semantic, Cognitive Covert, and Cognitive Overt.
Organization: Chaotic

Let's discuss these characteristics from the perspective of strategic and tactical approaches which may neutralize, or even reverse, their insidiously competitive effects on your company's corporate image.

Organization: Chaotic

As we discussed earlier, Customers/Clients/Consumers are for the most part chaotically organized. They have problems and they buy your goods and services to solve those problems. When their expectations are not met, they are dissatisfied. If that dissatisfaction is not resolved in a manner they deem to be fair, then they get angry. That anger can build. If that anger is injected into the social media sphere, it is subjected to the Five Factors and the anger can become a fury. The fury moves individuals to become crowds. This is a classic example of chaotic organization.

What this form of organization (i.e., chaotic) means for your company is that your company needs to stay continuously connected to its customer, client, consumer base via social media. You need to be constantly listening to what they are saying. And you need to be reacting, constantly, as well. You are probably already doing this with customer comments and complaints that come in through your company's toll-free number. Hopefully your company has a process for ensuring that these comments and complaints are regularly reviewed and action taken, as appropriate. You should be doing the same thing in social media. Always watch for the earthquake, the individual act, and then the resulting tsunami, the chaotically organized result. The power has shifted away from you and toward them. Social media has enabled this change.

You just have to keep up with it.

Keeping up with it is what most social media marketing programs are about. In essence they are about listening, conversing, reacting, resolving, and satisfying. And that's basically what we are discussing here in dealing with this particular insidious competitor.

Attack: Semantic, Cognitive Overt & Covert

I mentioned previously that semantic attacks are usually the less egregious of the two types of attacks we are considering in *Insidious Competition.* That thought applies here in our discussion of Customers/Clients/Consumers. A semantic attack created by Customers/Clients/Consumers can be a low threat level compared to a cognitive attack. But, remember we learned earlier how a semantic attack conducted by a chaotically organized insidious competitor can support later cognitive attacks. So, we wouldn't want to ignore semantic attacks. Leaving a semantic attack hanging out there just doesn't help your corporate image and can later create more and far worse problems. I make this point more strongly here because I believe that for the Customer/Client/Consumer the most popular attack class will be semantic. Because it is the most common type of attack that the Customer/Client/Consumer will perpetrate, there may be a tendency for companies to ignore this assault as a "cost of doing business." Well, as pointed out in various places in this book, in our social media world, that particular cost of doing business has risen.

But perhaps because semantic attacks present a lower level of threat and perhaps because these attacks are the more common, they provide a good starting point from which to build your new, relatively inexperienced social media squad into an experienced, savvy, squad ready to take on more dangerous cognitive attacks both from this type of insidious competitor as well as from the other insidious competitors we've been discussing. The semantic, chaotic Customer/Client/Consumer attack is a good place to start learning, because there is simply more known about this type of attack. It has been going on since before social media debuted. And the years of knowledge and the learning we've gained from long before the Internet was invented are directly transferrable here. You and your social media squad should expect to be dealing more with proactive strategies and tactics, than reactive. You can probably take a guess as to why.

Unlike the other "Friendlies" we will soon be discussing, Customers/Clients/Consumers are generally not organized to form a crisis type of attack, an attack demanding an orthopractic action. Even though Customers/Clients/Consumers can make a cognitive attack, it seems reasonable to expect that most such attacks would tend to be fragmented and on an individual basis, such as asking for a refund or other specific performance relative to an individual purchase. Such individualized "controversy" (with the exception perhaps of attacks created by well-known personalities as exemplified in the "Dell Sucks" example shown earlier) is generally of lower interest to the social media public than say, for example, a cognitive NGO attack asking a company to cease discriminatory hiring practices. For that type of crisis attack, reactive strategies and tactics are clearly required. However, given the likelihood of Customer/Client/Consumer attacks to be mostly semantic and chaotically organized, first focusing on proactive strategies and tactics makes good sense. That's not to say that reactive responses should not be made. Reactive responses should be made, but I expect that they would be made mostly from the perspective of resolving specific complaints and not from the broader perspective of the counter-attacking techniques related to the reactive strategies and tactics suggested in this book.

Tools: Mutant Conversation, Snark, and Hip Chat

This insidious competitor uses three of the tools from the insidious competition tool box. And they use them well. But unlike the previous strategic analysis of some insidious competitors, I don't suggest that you try to turn these tools around on this competitor. I believe doing so would be injurious to your case.

I do suggest that your social media squad understand how these tools are used and make their best effort to counter their effectiveness. For instance, when a customer has complained in social media repeatedly about the same problem, the social media squad member needs to recognize this and know when to step in, correcting the record, halting the mutation, and preserving reality.

Or in the case of Snark, the social media squad member must be skilled in recognizing snarkiness and how it precludes debate on particular issues. The squad member must then skillfully enter the conversation, deftly bringing up the issues about which debate has been precluded. The squad member must do so without making the Customer/Client/Consumer feel and look like a jerk.

This is a delicate balancing act, requiring personnel with great skill. Choose your social media squad personnel carefully.

Proactive Strategies & Tactics

All right, I think we're ready. Let's discuss the suggested proactive strategies and tactics and apply them to the case of the Customer/Client/Consumer.

***Strategy**: "Immunize" the social media crowd against "infectious memes." Infectious memes are those that will propagate readily within an environment like social media, where contagion reacts to the power and institutional disdain that exists within.*

***Strategy**: Encourage third-party sources of information strengthening company's corporate image along issues that insidious competitors may likely attack from within social media.*

> ***Tactic**: Have company social media staff enter into problematic discussions with links back to the third-party sources.*
>
> ***Tactic**: Anticipate negative memes that attackers might create. Provide information nullifying the claims made by the attackers. Address the "issue" before it becomes an issue.*
>
> ***Tactic**: Take immunization strategy into relevant epistemic communities across several different media.*
>
> ***Tactic**: Craft your message strongly within the Societal Basics, the four values of daily life and the sociological presuppositions.*

In dealing with the insidious competitors of Customers/Clients/Consumers, it is important for the social media squad to be always "patrolling" the social media sphere. This patrolling action can be done via web monitoring software which specializes in focusing on blogs, social networks, microblogs, and other venues in the social web. A discussion of web monitoring software is outside the scope of this book, so I will just say here that there are many good web monitoring solutions from which to choose. Most of those software solutions can help the members of your social media squad spot problems. When a squad member does spot a potential corporate image problem in a social web discussion, the squad member will be able to jump into that specific conversation and ascertain information which will aid them in minimizing any damage.

This is exactly what happened in the example I gave about my encounter with the Geek Squad. When I could not get the Geek Squad to respond in the fashion that they had promised, I tweeted. I tweeted about how the Geek Squad was not, in my opinion, honoring their warranty. Geek Squad was monitoring Twitter and they caught my rants before I went crazy and let my tweeting effort cost me more of my time than the effort was actually worth. Geek Squad entered into my conversation and let me know, along with everyone else who saw my complaint and were perhaps redefining the Geek Squad company image in their own minds (and maybe passing that image along, for further mutation), that they were going to rectify my problem.

It is important that this patrolling action is performed on a regular and frequent basis and by the same squad members. By patrolling on a regular and frequent basis, the squad members will be able to interject themselves into discussions before Mutant Conversation has the ability to significantly redefine your corporate image. By having the same squad members patrol, they will become experienced and familiar with the problems being discussed in the social web and possibly even with some of the people who appear repeatedly in that social web, making it much easier for the squad to spot potential problems, predict negative memes, and take action quickly.

With these insights, squad members will be able to enter into non-problematic discussions, or those of a general nature, concerning your company. By entering into these "ambient" conversations about your company, and by particularly concentrating within epistemic crowds where company-related issues are most significant, squad members can steer the conversation, negating, and more ideally preventing, unfounded claims. Such preclusive conversations can center on what the company has done to eliminate commonly-raised problems, demonstrating a concern for the customer or client or consumer well-being, and raising psychic shareholding which can be plainly defined as respect and goodwill.

Framing the discussion within the Societal Basics will further strengthen the positive relationship between the company and Customers/Clients/Consumers. All of these actions taken together would be adapting the *perception* step of the solipsistic and epistemological process, to the favor of your company.

* * *

Discussion: In these strategic and tactical recommendations, we try to influence the solipsistic and epistemological process primarily in the perception step.

Experience >>> Perception >>> Knowledge

With Customers/Clients/Consumers, we discussed concentrating on changing perceptions, as opposed to centering on changing the numbers of experiences which are available to be had. For this competitive type, we focused on the proactive strategies and tactics with emphasis on positively affecting the meaning of the corporate image one semantic event at a time. Strong proactive efforts increase the odds of keeping the corporate image intact and defined as the company wants it to be defined.

Employees

In dealing with Customers/Clients/Consumers, much of the battle for meaning is about "hanging in there" and remaining vigilant on a daily basis. With Customers/Clients/Consumers there will always be problems to address and there will always be their attempts to diddle with your company's corporate image. I see a similar situation in dealing with Employees as insidious competitors. Just as there will always be dissatisfied Customers/Clients/Consumers, there will always be dissatisfied Employees.

Recapping from Chapter Thirteen, we saw that the profile of the Employee looks like this:

Tools: Mutant Conversation, Snark, and Hip Chat
Attack: Primarily Semantic
Organization: Primarily Chaotic

Let's discuss these characteristics relative to the strategic and tactical approaches which may neutralize, or even reverse, insidiously competitive effects that Employees may have on your corporate image.

Organization: Chaotic

Just as Customers/Clients/Consumers are chaotically organized, so are Employees. Customers/Clients/Consumers become angry and so do employees.

You either are or have been an employee. If you are like most people, you are surrounded by employees every day. You know what I'm talking about.

Because Employee anger rises and falls sometimes at random and sometimes in connection with distinct events, the social media squad must be on constant patrol, looking for possible damage to the corporate image. Just as Customers/Clients/Consumers will never be totally satisfied, neither will be Employees. So, the fragmented and sporadically occurring attacks of Employees should be addressed.

Attack: Semantic

Attacks by Employees are mostly semantic and, as I said earlier, a semantic attack is generally at a lower threat level than a cognitive one. Yet, if the semantic attack is not dealt with, over time that threat may accumulate and become quite a significant factor in redefining your company's corporate image. This can be especially true if more employees, or others, chaotically join to support the position of the initial Employee insidious competitor.

Tools: Mutant Conversation, Snark, and Hip Chat

Although Employees, as insidious competitors, apply similar tools as Customers/Clients/Consumers, their comparative effectiveness in the use of these tools is likely to be less because comparative effectiveness hinges on the expectation of satisfaction, as held by the audience.

Social media users not only assume that companies will want to satisfy their Customers/Clients/Consumers, but they also assume that companies will go to some lengths to do so. There is a different sort of mindset with Employees, however. Most companies have an "at will" relationship with most of their employees. This means that the company pays the employee and if the employee is dissatisfied, he or she is free to simply change employers. In other words, the employee always has the option to leave the company if dissatisfied with the employee/employer relationship. For the Customer/Client/Consumer, it is expected that the company will make every effort to ensure satisfaction of the relationship. Not so with the Employee.

Companies know that is impossible to satisfy all employees all of the time. And as most of us know, no employee is ever completely satisfied and griping is generally preferred to changing jobs. Griping is easier and most griping is done with no real expectation of company redress. These are commonly accepted notions.

So, there are differences in expectations for the level of satisfaction that companies should provide to Customers/Clients/Consumers for the average complaint, than to Employees for the average gripe. Because of these differences, social media attacks by Employees may not be viewed with the same level of legitimacy and, thus, are not likely to receive the same level of attention, or commitment to redress, from the company. Additionally, people reading the online gripe, or rant, or attack, regardless of which specific tool is used, may view it as just that; an average employee gripe, which is not expected to be addressed. Is the reader's image of the company likely to be changed significantly? Probably not, unless the gripe is particularly egregious and wasn't "average" in the first place, or if the griping continues, or escalates, or other employees join in great numbers. So, should the company simply ignore Employee attacks in social media? Although there is a reduced level of expectation for companies to address the "average gripe," objectively addressing Employee issues, as they would those of Customers/Clients/Consumers, goes a long way to showing social media users that the company cares. Not only will such actions help mitigate potential long-term damage that can accumulate within social media, but they also provide the opportunity for the company to remain attentive to overall employee issues.

* * *

Right here I should make some important points regarding law and regulation. Generally, the social media squad has two basic functions. To listen. And then to engage. These basic functions have been emphasized in the preceding pages of *Insidious Competition*. The first function, that of a "listening post," enables a company to decide where to be proactive or where to be reactive in its second function, engagement.

With regard to Employees, the listening function of the social media squad should not be about creating a "big brother" type of "listening post." Tattle-tales are never highly regarded in any organization. When listening to Employees, you don't want to have your social media squad regarded by other employees in this manner. And with particular attention to Employees, the engagement function is not about blundering into areas which may be better managed by the human relations (HR) or legal department. Employer

– employee relations must be appropriately addressed and there can be legal implications associated with any strategies and tactics, particularly these. So here, with Employees, perhaps some extra precautions, additional to those I have pointed out earlier, should be observed in your strategic and tactical process. Always the squad will want to engage with an eye on the legal restrictions that apply within the jurisdiction(s) in which the company does business. With Employees, as with some other insidious competitors, your social media squad may need to be made aware that legal restrictions apply to the manner in which companies interact with their employees.

These points are made to remind you to stay on the right side of the law relative to all of your involvement with insidious competition, and especially here with Employees. In other sections of this book, I have suggested having a good relationship with your company's legal department. In this section here, I also recommend having a good relationship with your company's human relations department.

Those good relationships can come in handy. Because this book is available globally, and because there are so many different regulations in the various countries in which this book may be read, and because I am not an attorney in any of those jurisdictions, I cannot possibly say what a legal approach would be in any of those jurisdictions. However, before creating and enacting any strategies and tactics, you should certainly check with your legal and/or HR department for the preferred method of handing social media interaction with Employees.

* * *

Proactive Strategies & Tactics

Ready? Set? Now, let's go.

Because this insidious competitor is chaotically organized and focused mainly on a semantic attack, we will focus only on proactive strategies and tactics. Reactive tactics, absolutely essential to defend against a cognitive, crisis-type of attack, have less immediacy for the discussion of this competitor.

Strategy*: Encourage third-party sources of information strengthening your company's corporate image along the issues that insidious competitors may likely attack from within social media.*

***Tactic**: SEO them up in SERPs by creating company information sites linking back to the third-party information site.*

***Tactic**: Have company social media staff enter into problematic discussions with links back to the third-party sources.*

I believe, from what I have seen in social media, that many of these Employee "gripes" would be signed anonymously. So, at a certain gripe level (to be determined by upper management) there may be value in having the social media squad address these gripes as saying that the gripes would be forwarded to upper management for their consideration. And then be sure that that happens. Don't just provide lip service. Be sure that the gripes found in social media are passed along to the appropriate manager within the organization. Perhaps HR might be a good starting point as the recipient for such gripes. But, as previously noted above, the social media squad should take care in this interface so as not to come across as appearing to other employees as a "big brother" unit of the corporation. The squad would want to have a caring approach in such an interface, and that attitude should be reflected in their social media conversation.

Take every opportunity to make sure employees are hearing the positive news about their company. Don't you want to work for a company that has a great employee environment? Don't you want to work for a company that's not only successful, but is known for treating its employees with fairness and respect? Well, most employees do. Show me one who doesn't. We not only want to be on "the winning team," but we want that team to be fair and equitable to its members. If there are news articles, written by independent organizations, or surveys, or rankings appearing online, describing the superior employee environment at your company, you will want your SEO experts to help optimize those online sources by setting links from your company sites. And don't forget to have your social media squad converse about those third-party sources on relevant blogs and social networks, with links back to the online news articles or rankings/surveys. Not only does this provide valuable communication to your employees, it also serves to raise your company's positives higher in SERPs.

* * *

Discussion: As with Customers/Clients/Consumers, strategies and tactics for Employees also focus on influencing the perception step of the solipsistic and epistemological process:

Experience >>> Perception >>> Knowledge

We do this because attempting to influence the experience step will be very difficult if the negative memes from Employees appear on highly trafficked sites such as JobVent.com. Efforts to try to SEO down a site like JobVent.com would be foolish and would be simply a misuse of time. No, in the case of Employees, addressing the perception step, would be the better choice.

Activist Stockholders & Labor Unions

In this section we will discuss strategies and tactics for implementation against both Activist Stockholders and Labor Unions. The reason for the concurrent discussion is that both insidious competitors have essentially the same tool, attack, and organization profile, and both insidious competitors have essentially the same goal against a corporation, which is to achieve policy actions. From a strategic and tactical implementation standpoint, each insidious competitor has only slight differences and you and I will discuss those below.

Recapping from Chapter Thirteen, we saw that the profiles of the Activist Stockholder and the Labor Union look like this:

For the Activist Stockholder,
Tools: Mutant Conversation, Snark, and Hip Chat
Attack: Cognitive Overt
Organization: Cosmic

While for the Labor Union,
Tools: Mutant Conversation, Snark, and Hip Chat
Attack: Primarily Cognitive, Primarily Overt
Organization: Primarily Cosmic

Between these two insidious competitors, I see the threats from the Activist Stockholders as being the greater. The reason is that the sophistication level of social media use by Activist Stockholders is fairly high. Whereas, by comparison, the usage and sophistication of social media by Labor Unions is relatively low.

Simply put, the Activist Stockholders know how to use effectively the venue of social media. The Labor Unions, as yet, by comparison do not.

This is not to say that Labor Unions are not making an effort to be insidious competitors within social media. They are. But, at the time of this writing, it appears that they have more of a learning curve to climb than do the Activist Stockholders. This is not to say that this situation will remain always so. Therefore, although the threat level from Labor Unions is currently somewhat low, it is better to learn about them now for the time when, and if, they move to a higher threat level.

Conversely, the threat from Activist Stockholders is becoming greater every day, and especially so even as I write this. Remember when I gave you the example about MoxyVote.com back in Chapter Thirteen, I mentioned that MoxyVote.com had just come online? Well, I am writing this section on that same day and another article, appearing in The Wall Street Journal, just popped up on my Google Alert for "activists." The subject matter of this article was very scary.

The article was titled "Capitalism By Proxy" and discussed the expectation that, in early 2010, the Securities and Exchange Commission would change corporate proxy rules allowing stockholders more liberal access to the proxy.[144] The article discussed how the rule changes could afford shareholders greater freedom to nominate board members, at the company's expense, and would allow competitive elections to occur, simulating, as the article observed, an election environment which would be similar to that of a standard political campaign. Such a proxy method change would allow Activist Stockholders, or read that as just plain "activists," to gain greater access to corporate decision-making via the democratic process. The proxy voting process would then lead, as the article pointed out, to companies who answer to constituents, rather than investors.

The article went on to say that companies have always had to deal with multiple stakeholders, but it pointed out that if this rule change comes about, due to differences in the macro-environment, dealing with multiple stakeholders would become much more complex than what has been known in the past. (Aren't things always more complex than what has been known in the past?) One of the differences in the macro-environment creating this complexity, as pointed out by the Journal article, was social media.

The article pointed out that now with social media, the new corporate governance activist will be able to assimilate and distribute information quickly, or instantly, and adjust campaigns on the fly. Yes. No kidding. To me, this was no surprise because that's just what you and I have been discussing here in *Insidious Competition*.

Organization: Cosmic

You may notice many similarities between the strategies and tactics as discussed for NGOs/Activists and the Activist Stockholders. They do pose similar threats, after all. And like the NGOs/Activists, Activist Stockholders are cosmically organized. Oh, yes. You may get some that are chaotically organized. You may have some individuals floating around the social web trying to promote one cause or another, perhaps some of them might even be hiding behind "activist stockholding" to disguise a pump-and-dump or short-selling scheme. But for the most part, based on what we have discussed so far, we can see the Activist Stockholder as cosmically organized political groups and your strategy will be to address them as individual groups and not as groups of individuals.

Just as there are similarities between the NGOs/Activists and Activist Stockholders suggested strategies and tactics, there are overlaps between Activist Stockholders and Labor Unions. Both are cosmically organized, with Labor Unions being at least primarily so. Because of this, your social media squad must address threats from either group as a threat that has resources behind it.

Attack: Cognitive Overt

Activist Stockholders will have a purpose. And that purpose will be to move votes their way. Some of those votes may be to get shareholder initiatives passed, others may be, as suggested by the Journal article mentioned above, to get a specific board of director member elected. The Activist Stockholder purpose must be addressed head-on and countered in your strategies and tactics. This opponent will be using the principles of propaganda, the Five Factors of Insidious Competition, and the solipsistic and epistemological process - and with intent! They will try to increase the numbers of exposures to their arguments (*experience*) and they will try to change the view of the information given in their arguments (*perception*) in order to change the reality that people see (*knowledge*). In these arguments, they will use a moral shield. So should you.

Not very different from this attack approach will be the Labor Unions. But where they will differ slightly from the Activist Stockholder will be in the target of their altruism. The Activist Stockholder may portray greater society as the beneficiary of their campaign. Labor Unions may portray the children of their membership as the beneficiaries of their campaign. Both approaches depend upon the Societal Basics. Watch for this.

Tools: Mutant Conversation, Snark, and Hip Chat

Based on their "altruistic" goals, the Activist Stockholders and the Labor Unions will get those Five Factors of Insidious Competition working in their favor, too. No slouches, these groups. They'll likely send out into social media their arguments of morality in the hope that others will pick them up and mutate them in the favor of the Activist Stockholders or Labor Unions. We've covered this idea before. After all, who isn't going to mutate a message that deals with greater society or with children? This is important subject matter, and it makes the mutators feel important by passing it along. From there, it just rolls. You have got to know the flow of Mutant Conversation and how it works for them. You will need to turn it back on them.

And Snark? Yes. Both insidious competitors will use it. Know how to reverse it. Know how to frame it for what it is - the rejection of an honest discussion. In those reversals, you'll need to show the threat that exists in their actions of denying a fair and open discussion.

The Hip Chat? The Labor Unions will use this more than the Activist Stockholders. Use this positive talk tool to strengthen your own position. But just be sure you have members on your squad who are comfortable in using the applicable vernacular. Use of incorrect slang or the wrong vernacular in applying Hip Chat will only be counter-productive and may make your company look like you "don't get it," which is exactly what these insidious competitors will be saying about you. Don't let them win this argument by shooting yourself in the foot.

* * *

Just as I paused in the Employee section to make some important points, I will pause right here as well in order to make similar points. The two basic functions of the social media squad are to listen and to engage. But when engaging with either Activist Stockholders or with Labor Unions some extra precautions, over and above those mentioned in these strategy chapters, may need to be observed in the strategic and tactical process.

In many legal jurisdictions, company interactions with stockholders are governed by securities regulations and company interactions with labor unions are governed by labor union legislation and employment law. As I mentioned previously, the social media squad will want to engage with an eye on the legal restrictions that apply within the jurisdiction(s) in which the company does business.

Again, these points are made to remind you to stay on the right side of the law relative to the insidious competitors of Activist Stockholders and Labor Unions. As before, always have a good relationship with your company's legal and HR departments. Those relationships can contribute to smooth strategy and tactic creation and implementation and keep your squad on solid legal ground.

Reactive Strategies & Tactics

Let's focus our discussion on only reactive strategies and tactics for these insidious competitors. It's not that I believe that proactive strategies are not applicable. Certainly proactive efforts would help. But Activist Stockholders and Labor Unions are mostly "event-focused" competitors, requiring reactive strategies and tactics.

These two insidious competitors will become very active in social media around the time of an event, such as a proxy vote or a contract negotiation. So, because of their focus, these two insidious competitors have tendencies to be temporally concentrated. Anticipate the timing of these events, if you can, and be ready to engage through reactive strategies and tactics.

And just as with NGOs and Activists, do not think of Activist Stockholders and Labor Unions as societal do-gooders, although they may try to frame themselves as such. They are not. They are simply competitors.

Again.

Period.

***Strategy**: Attack the attacker. Change the balance in the battle for meaning. Give them something to lose (e.g., their legitimacy, their reliability, and/or their integrity as advocates).*

> ***Tactic**: Identify the attacker as mistaken. Present information within social media discussions countering image-damaging claims. Link back to the third-party sources.*

Be sure that you are correct in the arguments that you will present. With an eye on the previously mentioned regulations that may apply, be sure that when you say that the Activist Stockholder or Labor Union is mistaken, that they really are. The same holds true for NGOs and Activists, remember?

These two insidious competitors, like their NGO and Activist cousins, tend to frame arguments from within a context of emotion and politics. Like their cousins, the Activist Stockholders and Labor Union arguments are sometimes weak from a logical business perspective. So, your social media squad, on behalf of upper management and with their supervision, may want to frame any counter-arguments, their rebuttals, their reactive attacks from within the strengths of logic and truth, such as solid economics and business discipline or well-sourced science.

As always, it is imperative to have third-party sources of information to which the social media squad may point in supporting their counter-arguments.

Call attention to how the use of snarky language overlooks important issues and limits essential debate. Call attention to how Mutant Conversation allows important facts to be deleted from the discussion. Have your squad follow through by presenting a balanced debate, grounded in the facts.

* * *

Discussion: In the case of the Activist Stockholder or the Labor Union, the audience that will be involved will likely be relatively small. Both your social media squad and Activist Stockholders or Labor Unions are likely to be competing for readership by the same audience on the same Web sites, so limiting *experiences* is not a strategic option. Attempting to limit the experiences of readers being exposed to your opponent's arguments will also limit their exposure to your own arguments. No, your only option is to modify perception by presenting your side of the story, backed by credible and accurate information.

Experience >>> Perception >>> Knowledge

With Activist Stockholders and Labor Unions, it will be a regular slugfest in the battle for meaning and reality. Just be sure that you are better equipped. Hopefully the ideas in *Insidious Competition* will help you.

CHAPTER NINETEEN: Suggested Strategies & Tactics Against The Digital Pirates

Although, in this next chapter, we will depart somewhat from our previous strategic and tactical discussion format, as I have mentioned before, as you create your strategies and tactics seek assistance from qualified professionals in areas such as competitive strategy, corporate communications, public relations, law, human resources, competitive intelligence, social media, and marketing, as well as other business disciplines.

For this last insidious competitor in *Insidious Competition*, the reason for our departure from the previous strategic and tactical discussion format is that this insidious competitor is totally unlike the others that we've discussed. This insidious competitor is leveraging special protections in its pursuit to mangle your corporate image. Those protections lie in freedom of speech.

Culture Jammers

Recapping from our earlier discussion, we saw that the profile of the Culture Jammer looks like this:

Tools: Snark
Attack: Semantic
Organization: Chaotic

With their chaotic organization, Culture Jammers come at your corporate image pretty much at random. They make their statements in an unorganized fashion, while pulling on the heartstrings, and hitting with great force on the Societal Basics, the daily values of life and the sociological presuppositions. They deal in emotion. They deal in the process of evoking emotion. And, in doing so, they are regarded as artists.

These artists use that snarky imagery they are so good at to play with semantics. In keeping with their artistic view, Culture Jammers reposition the essence of your corporate image meaning as *they* see it. Or, as they want *others* to see it. As they do so, they rely, perhaps even unknowingly, on some realm of societal expectation and legal protection. Artists enjoy certain expectations and protections within our society. There could be no artists without these expectations and protections.

Society expects artists to evoke emotions. We want the artist to dig down deep inside us and express the feelings that we don't even know that we have. And to allow the artist their ability to evoke emotions, we give them the societal protection of being outrageous in their endeavors. Would we have it any other way? Should we have it any other way?

Whether we should have it any other way is a matter of opinion. But here is one opinion which I would like you to take seriously.

The Culture Jammer is one insidious competitor that your social media squad should not touch.

Look, but don't touch.

Doesn't such an opinion seem to run counter to the philosophy that I have put forth in the preceding pages of *Insidious Competition*? Yes. So, let me explain.

Interaction with this insidious competitor should be left solely to your legal department, who in all probability will have had quite a bit of experience in the past with this particular foe. There are many legal issues that run for and against artists and, as such, that legal wrangling should be left exclusively to the professionals. Because it should be left solely to the legal professionals, I won't be taking the discussion of those legal issues much further in these pages, except for one concept which we can discuss as ordinary people. That is the concept of artistic protection.

The main protection under which artists like Culture Jammers operate, even as they mangle the meaning of your corporate image, is that expressed in the First Amendment to the United States Constitution, which may or may not apply to you depending upon the nation in which you live. When Culture Jammers as artists diddle with the meaning of your corporate image, they do so within the realm of opinion and they are constitutionally and legally, in the United States at least, protected. Culture Jammers are not the only insidious competitors protected by the legal tenet of freedom of speech. Certainly all of the insidious competitors in this book are also protected by the expression of opinion, as is your social media squad. But none of the others are regarded as artists and therefore don't enjoy a special expectation from society. The other insidious competitors don't enjoy the expectation to be outrageous. Those other insidious competitors don't get the same kind of social expectation "pass" that the artist does. Therefore, those *other* insidious competitors (and as we've learned, there are many) can, and should, be engaged.

So, there is a huge risk to having your squad engage the Culture Jammer artist, to whom our society extends, through its expectations, special privileges. Because they are viewed as artists, seeking to do art for art's sake, usually without an agenda, they are seldom taken seriously from a business perspective. For that reason, only under very specific circumstances would I advise an attack against the Culture Jammer. And that, as I said, should be via your legal department.

***Strategy**: Attack the attacker.*

***Tactic**: Hold the attacker to liability laws.*

As your social media squad performs its basic duty of listening post, when they find that the Culture Jammer's intent goes beyond simple artistic expression, then it's time to call in the legal team to take action. Direct and obvious attempts to change the meaning of your corporate image with work that makes a purely false statement, or where there is a profit motive to produce a work to meet the ulterior motive of another, require legal action. The diddling of meaning for art's sake is one thing, but the diddling of meaning by lying, or for profit resulting from ulterior motive, while behind the cloak of artistic expression, is quite different.

Conclusion: Your Battle Starts Now

So, now we have come to the end of this book. It's been quite a journey; one that many business books do not even attempt. In this book, the approach we have taken to this problem of insidious competition has been new. That is because the problem is new. Old-style approaches just won't apply. And as I have mentioned previously, to understand how to deal with this new competitor, we must first understand the foundations upon which they operate. This new approach has enabled us to understand those foundations.

Here in *Insidious Competition - The Battle for Meaning and the Corporate Image*, I have defined a new type of competitor, one that competes for the corporate image. Almost anyone now can compete for your company's corporate image. Almost anyone can do this because of the proliferation, ready-availability, and "ease of operation" of social media.

You and I have found that social media is a powerful new domain to which people, with an instinctive need for interaction, are flocking, seemingly relentlessly. We have found that this new domain is becoming a "seventh uncontrollable factor" in the business environment that we must manage daily. This newest factor is very dangerous because, essentially, it is a domain in which crowd behavior predominates, and where those crowd participants feel powerful, almost invincible. With that feeling of invincibility, crowd participants, some of them just like you and me, can and will behave instinctively and in a way that they believe supports the crowd's interests. For the corporate image, this does not bode well. The crowd comes first. Where does your corporate image come in? Well, probably not at the top of a list of crowd interests.

From our general discussion of crowd behavior, and most importantly how it applies to social media, you and I came to learn more about the characteristics of the crowd that lies in wait within social media, as well as the inherent dangers arising from those characteristics. This understanding will help us in our future work as insidious competition fighters, enabling us to better understand and navigate those dangers so as to help make our strategies and tactics more effective. Then we discovered something *really new* (as if what we had discussed prior had not been new enough already). I introduced you to the *Five Factors of Insidious Competition*, one of the "hallmarks" of this book.

We saw that the discovery of the Five Factors was a direct result of our discussion of the characteristics of a social media crowd. The Five Factors, a framework that contains the factors of anonymity, power, contagion, instinct, and disdain, would not have been discovered had we not made the connection between crowds and the social media "community;" discarding that "community" label under which many have been laboring erroneously. This Five Factor discovery enables us to see social media for what it actually is and, in the process, from a business perspective understand better just what is going on within social media. We know now that the Five Factors stand in social media like obstacles in a steeplechase; unmovable objects which must be considered and with which we must deal if we are to win the race.

If that wasn't enough to scare us, we jumped into learning about the construction of reality. We found that the "keepers of reality" were under siege and were disappearing before our eyes. We learned that those keepers of reality, those "agents of common knowledge," are being replaced by innuendo generators and opinion makers within the social media sphere. And, we saw that an increasing percentage of the general population is being attracted to social media and, by extension, to those who confuse and replace fact with opinion. You and I discussed how irresponsibility can run high in social media and how persons in the social web have lower fears of liability there than do the people who have been traditionally "tending to our realities." All of this, as we saw, contributes to a manipulation of meaning, to the "repackaging of reality," which we discussed as being a clear threat to corporations who are so dependent upon the *meaning* of their *corporate image*. You and I discussed that this threat to the corporate image, perhaps the corporate image of the company for which you work, could be repeated anonymously and infinitely on the social web. This was unsettling. We moved on to learn more.

From our knowledge of the construction of reality, we then took our understanding and applied it directly to business, with particular attention to brands. We saw that the brand was the foundation of the corporate image; there could be no corporate image without a brand. At this point it became very clear that since the brand was a collection of expectations by customers, social media users could, by the millions, influence those expectations in such ways as to change the meaning of the brand and, with it, the meaning of the corporate image. No corporate image is immune. Whether or not a company participates in social media marketing, with or without a "brandividual," a company is susceptible to such danger, that of a change in the meaning of their brand and, thus, their corporate image. To learn how to combat that meaning change, we had to learn about what "meaning" actually "means." So, we went deeply into the process of meaning creation, the system of knowing. We learned about solipsism and epistemology.

Solipsism and epistemology, we saw, are really what you and I came to call "the system of knowing." You and I found out that in knowing, in acquiring meaning about something, there are two steps that precede our knowledge. Those two steps are experience and perception. We saw the system of knowing represented as:

Experience >>> Perception >>> Knowledge

Related to this system of knowing, we came to understand that the agents of common knowledge, those central reference points of a common reality, the newspapers, were succumbing to economic forces beyond their control. Because of their dearth and death not only were the number of experiences for common knowledge decreasing, but the perceptions of truly vetted knowledge, responsibly published, the liability-fearing-if-I-get-it-wrong-I-will-be-sorry kind of knowledge, were also being affected. All of which impact our view of a common reality. We saw that with much of our "media day" moving toward online media, the integrity of our system of knowing was in doubt. Then we came to realize that along with that integrity can flee the meaning of the corporate image.

With a good understanding of the system of knowing, we pushed on to learn about four tools that the insidious competitor uses to influence that system of learning, the solipsistic and epistemological process. You and I came to discover how the insidious competitor influences the meaning of your corporate image through the usage of these tools. And we learned that the application of those four tools is based on the principles of propaganda (i.e. the tools are used to apply the propaganda created by the insidious competitor). Once we got our minds past the "jack-booted" reputation of propaganda, we could see that there were seven principles of propaganda which either supported or described the social media environment or described the characteristics of a propaganda message itself. We came to see how those principles of propaganda can be applied within social media.

When learning about the seven principles of propaganda, an important feature of insidious competitors surfaced. That feature was related to how those insidious competitors were organized. You and I talked about cosmos and chaos, formal and informal. We came to realize that, generally, social media users, a crowd of insidious competitors, were informally organized, chaotically, but could and would still be "organized" enough, thanks to the Five Factors of Insidious Competition, to create and spread propaganda through the social web. On the flip side of chaos, we saw that some insidious competitors could be cosmically, formally, organized and could, and probably would, try to co-opt those naturally ambient chaotic forces to advantage.

All of the knowledge to this point began to give us a very good idea of how to handle the insidiously competitive forces within social media, those which are mangling the meaning of our corporate image.

Moving on toward a practical usage of the knowledge we had gained so far, we learned then about how not only were insidious competitors classified as either cosmic or chaotic, but that the classes of the attacks these competitors would mount could also be classified as cosmic or chaotic. For further classification, we also discussed that the attacks of the insidious competitor could also be categorized as either semantic or cognitive, sub-classifying those as either overt or covert.

These classifications, that we discussed, we would later see to be of great use in determining the strategies and tactics that we could create in opposition to the insidious competitor.

Then we got even more specific. We saw four classes of insidious competitor. The first, The Reality Bender, contained the types which we discussed as Tagging Terrorists, Mommy Bloggers, and NGOs/Activists. Then we learned about The Nasties and about how they still need more "looking into." The Friendlies were Customers etc., Employees, Activist Stockholders, and Labor Unions. Our discussion of the classes and types of insidious competitors then wrapped up with the Digital Pirates, specifically the Culture Jammers, and we talked about how that type of insidious competitor should probably be handled very differently than those we previously discussed.

All of our discussions on how these insidious competitors operate and what makes them "tick," enabled us to progress away from the foundational and on to the more pragmatic discussions of this book

After we had a good understanding of the underlying concepts of insidious competition and of the specific kinds of insidious competitors up against which we might run, we then went on to what businesspeople want to know, some specific suggestions, some potential action items. This new approach, this foundational understanding, brought us to our well-prepared discussion of strategic and tactical alternatives that might be applied against the new and insidious competitor. We discussed some possible strategies and tactics for each insidious competitor about which we learned, taking into consideration the tools that each uses, as well as their individual attack classes and organizational forms.

So, from all of this, I believe you are now well-prepared. Having read this entire book, you are certainly more prepared now to deal with this new type of business threat than you ever have been before. It's now that I leave you to deal with this new threat to not only your company's corporate image, but also to your own livelihood and to your family who depend upon that livelihood.

Protect the integrity of meaning. Defend your company's corporate image. Safeguard your well-being and that of others. Do it honestly, and do it with character. This is an honorable pursuit. Don't forget that this is a battle, an information-age battle. This battle is one that is fought against lies and misrepresentations, and as such is likely never to cease because . . . "Workers of the world are uniting."

Notes

1. Arquilla, p 111.
2. Schneier 2000.
3. Universal Mc Cann
4. Evans & Berman, p 29.
5. "Follow the Herd."
6. Le Bon, p 6 - 7.
7. Toffler, p 343.
8. Ibid.
9. Li & Bernoff, p 6.
10. Denby interview.
11. Dezenhall & Weber, p 147.
12. Li & Bernoff, p 10.
13. Laermer, p 99.
14. Strangelove, p 162.
15. Gitlin, p 12 - 70.
16. Dezenhall & Weber, pp 27 & 39.
17. Klaassen
18. Newman
19. Garfield
20. Denby, *Snark*, p 12.
21. Strangelove, p 190.
22. Ruder Finn

23. "Why People Go Online"
24. Op. Cit.
25. Universal Mc Cann
26. Neumeier, p 2.
27. Ibid.
28. Levitt, p 116.
29. Telofski 2001, p 42-43.
30. Armano
31. Dezenhall & Weber, p 94.
32. Neumeier, p 2.
33. Hamlyn, p 184-185.
34. "The News Industry's Uncertain Future."
35. Richman & James
36. "Bad News for Newspapers."
37. Ibid.
38. Op. Cit.
39. Sass
40. "Bad for Newspapers."
41. Shirky
42. Bowles
43. Holzner, p 69.
44. Loechner
45. "Propaganda and the Internet."
46. Ellul, p 6-7.
47. Ibid.
48. Ellul, p 9.
49. Loechner
50. Ellul, p 21.

51. Snow, p 147.
52. Wheatley, p 143.
53. Ellul, p 9.
54. Ellul, p 27.
55. Snow, p 147.
56. Walton, p 396.
57. Op. Cit.
58. Walton, p 397.
59. Ellul, p 39-40.
60. Dezenhall & Weber, p 59.
61. Black, p 134.
62. Ellul, p. 43.
63. Hazan, p. 21-22.
64. Ellul, p 57.
65. Walton, p 398-399.
66. Black, p 133.
67. Wheatley, p 143.
68. For more on fractals, see Telofski 2001, p 43.
69. Schneier, p 266.
70. Mitnick
71. Hogben, p 3.
72. Hogben, p 13.
73. Ibid.
74. Hogben, p 14.
75. Denby, *Snark*, p 1.
76. Denby, *Snark*, p 4.
77. Denby, *Snark*, p 3.
78. Denby, *Snark*, p 24.

79. Denby, *Snark*, p 74.
80. Cybenko, Giani, Heckman, & Thompson, 2009.
81. Cybenko, Giani, Thompson, 2002.
82. Ibid.
83. Cybenko, Giani, & Thompson, 2009.
84. Cybenko, Giani, Thompson, 2002.
85. Li & Bernoff, p 30.
86. Denby, Snark, p 1.
87. Mitchell
88. Ibid.
89. French
90. Mitchell
91. Dezenhall & Weber, p 201.
92. Ibid.
93. Bowen
94. I don't agree with the reference to the Internet as a "tool" here. The Internet is an environment in which tools are applied as we have seen thus far. But I reference this quote to make the point about use of the Internet and its effectiveness in "slanging matches." And I find that many of those "arguments" are not complex, but are more often simple and superficial.
95. Diermeier
96. Ganor, p 408.
97. Carrotmob.org/about, Consumer Column.
98. Ibid.
99. Carrotmob.org/about, Activist Column.
100. Carrotmob.org/about, Business Column.
101. Neo
102. Nolan

103. Jolly
104. Ibid.
105. "The News Industry's Uncertain Future."
106. "The Big Smear."
107. Brahman, p 123-125.
108. Brahman, p 125.
109. Universal Mc Cann
110. "Social Network Marketing Expands Sphere."
111. Pohle
112. Jarvis, p 12-14.
113. Jarvis, p 14.
114. Telofski, 2009.
115. Source code analyzed on January 12, 2010.
116. Gillan & Starks.
117. Del Guercio, Cole, & Woidtke.
118. Sullivan
119. Bainbridge
120. Such searches are simple via the miracle of Google.
121. In meeting with clients at public companies, I have listened to their own internal arguments, both pro and con, on using social media to communicate the company's position on various issues. One of the biggest areas of confusion is in the area of investor relations. The managers I have spoken with don't see clear guidance from the regulations on how to use social media. Perhaps they are unwilling to interpret existing, and older, rules which are non-specific on the new medium. Given this risk averse position, they appear to "err on the side of caution" and choose not to participate within social media.

122. This is also how hurricanes and avalanches get started. One element becomes "organized" and then gathers up other "unorganized" elements around it.
123. Notification of MoxyVote.com came to me through a Wall Street Journal article captured via Google Alerts.
124. Tuna
125. Ibid.
126. Agrawal
127. GlennTilton.com, accessed November 11, 2009.
128. "Further Hedge Losses Further Proof of Misdirection of Airline."
129. "What If Glenn Tilton Was Your Banker?"
130. "Glenn: Why Can't I Sit Next to My Six-Year-Old?"
131. Ibid.
132. Strangelove, p 104.
133. UrbanDictionary.com, accessed November 4, 2009.
134. Strangelove, p 102.
135. Ibid., p 106.
136. Ibid., p 105-106.
137. Ibid., p 105.
138. Adbusters.org, accessed November 4, 2009.
139. Accessed November 9, 2009.
140. Accessed November 16, 2009.
141. Ibid.
142. Denby, p 3.
143. Gaylord
144. Judge & Torrenzano

Bibliography

AdBusters.org, accessed November 4, 2009.

Agrawal, Ashwini K. "Corporate Governance Objectives of Labor Union Shareholders: Evidence from Proxy Voting." *Social Science Research Network - SSRN.com - NYU Stern Working Paper Series No. Fin-08-006*. September 1, 2008, http://ssrn.com/abstract=1285084, accessed October 7, 2009.

Armano, David. "The Age of Brandividualism." *Experience Matters*. January 23, 2009, http://experiencematters.criticalmass.com/2009/01/23/the-age-of-brandividualism/, accessed October 28, 2009.

Arquilla, John, David Ronfeldt, and Michele Zanini. "Networks, Netwar, and Information-Age Terrorism." p 107 - 129. In *Terrorism and Counterterrorism: Understanding the New Security Environment*, edited by Howard, Russell D., and Reid L. Sawyer. Dubuque, Iowa: Mc Graw Hill Contemporary Learning Series, 2006.

"Bad News for Newspapers." *The New York Times*. March 12, 2009, http://www.nytimes.com/interactive/2009/03/12/business/20090312-papers-graphic.html, accessed July 22, 2009.

Bainbridge, Stephen M. "Shareholder Activism in the Obama Era." *Social Science Research Network - SSRN.com*. July 22, 2009, http://ssrn.com/abstract=1437791, accessed October 7, 2009.

Black, Jay. "Semantics and Ethics of Propaganda." *Journal of Mass Media Ethics*, Vol. 16, #2 & 3. p. 121-137.

Bowen, David. "Corporate Nice Guise." *The (London) Evening Standard*. December 9, 2003, p. 35.

Bowles, Jerry. "The Internet is Killing America's Free Press and Why It Matters." *Social Media Today*. May 10, 2009, http://www.socialmediatoday.com/SMC/92500, accessed September 14, 2009.

Brahman, Ori, and Rom Brahman. *Sway: The Irresistible Pull of Irrational Behavior*. New York: Doubleday, 2008.

Carrotmob.org, accessed August 27, 2009.

Cybenko, George, and Annarita Giani, Carey Heckman, Paul Thompson. "Cognitive Hacking: Technological and Legal Issues." *Semantic Hacking*. http://www.ists.dartmouth.edu/projects/archives/semantic-hacking.html, accessed October 30, 2009.

Cybenko, George, and Annarita Giani, Paul Thompson. "Cognitive Hacking: A Battle for the Mind." *IEEE Computer*. August 2002, Vol. 35, #8, p 50-56.

Cybenko, George, and Annarita Giani, Paul Thompson. "Cognitive Hacking and the Value of Information," *Semantic Hacking*. http://www.ists.dartmouth.edu/projects/archives/semantic-hacking.html, accessed October 30, 2009.

Del Guercio, Diane, and Laura Seery Cole, Tracie Woidtke, "Do Boards Pay Attention When Institutional Investor Activists 'Just Vote No'?" *Social Science Research Network - SSRN.com*. January 2008, http://ssrn.com/abstract=575242, accessed October 7, 2009.

Denby, David. Interview on *Charlie Rose*, PBS Television. February 3, 2009.

Denby, David. *Snark*. New York: Simon & Schuster, 2009.

Diermeier, Daniel. "Private Politics: Public Activism as an Alternative Regulatory Mechanism?" *Policy Research Initiative*. May 23, 2009, http://www.policyresearch.gc.ca/page.asp?pagenm=2009-0014_05, accessed November 2, 2009.

Dezenhall, Eric, and John Weber. *Damage Control: How to Get the Upper Hand When Your Business is Under Attack*. New York: Penguin Group, 2007.

Ellul, Jacques. *Propaganda: The Formation of Men's Attitudes*. Vintage Books Edition. New York: Vintage Books, 1973/1965.

Evans, Joel R., and Barry Berman. *Marketing*. 3rd Edition. New York: Macmillan Publishing Company, 1987.

"Europe: Disinformation; Old and New Information Tricks." *The Economist.* August 5, 2006, p. 37.

"Follow the Herd. How Behaviors and Stories Spread Through Online Crowds." http://veryevolved.com/2009/01/follow-the-herd-how-behavior-and-stories-spread-through-online-crowds/, accessed September 16, 2009.

French, Robert. "The Borg: Mommy Bloggers Assimilate Johnson & Johnson." *Infopinions: Public Relations: Marcom - Auburn Media.* November 17, 2008, http://www.auburnmedia.com/wordpress/2008/11/17/the-borg-mommy-bloggers-assimilate-johnson-johnson/, accessed October 1, 2009.

"Further Hedge Losses Further Proof of Misdirection of Airline." *GlennTilton.com.* October 21, 2008, http://www.glenntilton.com/home/2008/10/21/fuel-hedge-losses-further-proof-of-misdirection-of-airline-b.html, accessed November 11, 2009.

Ganor, Boaz. "Dilemmas Concerning Media Coverage of Terrorist Attacks." In *Terrorism and Counterterrorism: Understanding the New Security Environment*, edited by Howard, Russell D., and Reid L. Sawyer. Dubuque, Iowa: Mc Graw Hill Contemporary Learning Series, 2006.

Garfield, Bob. "Comcast Must Die." *Advertising Age.* November 19, 2007, Vol. 78, #46, p. 1 - 21.

Gaylord, Chris. "Making the Call on Web 'Facts'." *The Christian Science Monitor.* October 11, 2009, p 35.

Gillan, Stuart L. and Laura T. Starks "The Evolution of Shareholder Activism in the United States." *Social Science Research Network - SSRN.com.* January 28, 2007, http://ssrn.com/abstract=959670, accessed July 22, 2009.

Gitlin, Todd. *Media Unlimited: How the Torrent of Images and Sounds Overwhelms Our Lives.* New York: Metropolitan Books, 2002.

"Glenn: Why Can't I Sit Next to My Six-Year-Old?" *GlennTilton.com.* October 23, 2008, http://www.glenntilton.com/stories-from-employ-and-custom/2008/10/23/glenn-why-cant-i-sit-next-to-my-six-year-old.html, accessed November 11, 2009.

Hamlyn, D.W. *The Theory of Knowledge.* Garden City, New York: Anchor Books, 1970.

Hazan, Baruch A. *Soviet Propaganda, a Case Study of the Middle East Conflict.* New York: John Wiley & Sons, Inc., 1976.

Hogben, Giles, Editor. European Network and Information Security Agency. *ENISA Position Paper No. 1: Security Issues and Recommendations for Online Social Networks.* October 2007, http://www.enisa.europa.eu/doc/pdf/deliverables/enisa_pp_social_networks.pdf, accessed July 22, 2009.

Holzner, Burkart. *Reality Construction in Society.* Revised Edition. Cambridge, Massachusetts: Schenkman Publishing Company, Inc., 1972

Howard, Russell D., and Reid L. Sawyer. *Terrorism and Counterterrorism: Understanding the New Security Environment.* Dubuque, Iowa: Mc Graw Hill Contemporary Learning Series, 2006.

Jarvis, Jeff. *What Would Google Do?* New York: Collins Business, 2009.

JobVent.com, accessed November 2, 2009.

Jolly, David. "In French Inquiry, a Glimpse of Corporate Spying." *The New York Times.* July 31, 2009, http://www.nytimes.com/2009/08/01/business/global/01iht-spy.html?_r=1&scp=9&sq=david%20jolly&st=cse, accessed November 2, 2009.

Judge, Clark S., and Richard Torrenzano. "Capitalism By Proxy." *The Wall Street Journal Online.* November 22, 2009, http://online.wsj.com/article/SB10001424052970203440104574404780012592404.html, accessed November 23, 2009.

Klaassen, Abbey. "Microsoft's So-Bad-It's-Good Windows 7 Ad Goes Viral." *Advertising Age Online.* October 1, 2009, http://adage.com/digital/article?article_id=139350 accessed October 1, 2009.

Laermer, Richard. *2011 Trendspotting for the Next Decade.* New York: Mc Graw Hill, 2008.

Le Bon, Gustave. *The Crowd: A Study of the Popular Mind.* Mineola, New York: Dover Publications, Inc. 2002/1896.

Levitt, Theodore. *The Marketing Imagination.* New York: The Free Press, 1986.

Li, Charlene, and Josh Bernoff. *Groundswell.* Boston: Harvard Business Press, 2008.

Loechner, Jack. "Internet Accounts for One Third of Consumer Media Day." *Media Post.* June 29, 2009, http://www.mediapost.com/publications/?fa=Articles.showArticle&art_aid=108379, accessed July 14, 2009.

Mitchell, Michele. "Five Reasons Why Mom Blogs Are the Blogs to Watch." *Problogger.net.* April 30, 2008, http://www.problogger.net/archives/2008/04/30/five-reasons-why-mom-blogs-are-the-blogs-to-watch/, accessed July 22, 2009.

Mitnick, Kevin D., and William L. Simon. *The Art of Deception.* Indianapolis, Indiana: Wiley Publishing, Inc., 2002.

Neo, Hi Min. "Threat of Next World War May Be in Cyberspace: UN." *Information Policy.* October 8, 2009, http://www.i-policy.org/2009/10/threat-of-next-world-war-may-be-in-cyberspace-un.html, accessed October 9, 2009.

Neumeier, Marty. *The Brand Gap: How to Bridge the Distance Between Business Strategy and Design.* Indianapolis, Indiana: New Riders Publishing, 2003.

Newman, Rick. "Why Health Insurers Make Lousy Villains." *U.S. News & World Report Online.* August 25, 2009, http://www.usnews.com/money/blogs/flowchart/2009/08/25/why-health-insurers-make-lousy-villains.html, accessed October 1, 2009.

Nolan, John. "A Case Study in French Espionage: Renaissance Software." *U.S. Department of Energy Web Site.* October 3, 2000, http://www.hanford.gov/oci/maindocs/ci_r_docs/frenchesp.pdf, accessed October 9, 2009.

Pohle, George, and Jeff Hittner. "The Right Corporate Karma." *Forbes.com.* May 16, 2008, http://www.forbes.com/2008/05/16/ibm-cemex-google-lead-clayton-in_gp_0516claytonchristensen_inl.html, accessed August 31, 2009.

"Propaganda and the Internet." *The Mackenzie Institute.* July 1999, http://www.mackenzieinstitute.com/1999/Propaganda_Internet.html, accessed April 17, 2009.

"Protect Insurance Companies PSA," (video). *FunnyOrDie.com.* http://www.funnyordie.com/videos/041b5acaf5/protect-insurance-companies-psa, accessed October 1, 2009.

Richman, Dan and Andrea James. "Seattle P-I to Publish Last Edition Tuesday." *Seattle PI Business.* March 17, 2009, http://www.seattlepi.com/business/403793_piclosure17.html, accessed July 22, 2009.

Ruder Finn, "RFIntentIndex." http://www.ruderfinn.com/rfrelate/intent/intent-index.html, accessed October 28, 2009.

Sass, Erik. "Tucson Citizen Ends Print Era, Web-Only." *Media Daily News.* May 15, 2009, http://www.mediapost.com/publications/?fa=Articles.showArticle&art_aid=106203, accessed July 22, 2009.

Schneier, Bruce. *Secrets and Lies.* New York: John Wiley & Sons, Inc., 2000.

Schneier, Bruce. "Semantic Attacks: The Third Wave of Network Attacks." *Crypto-Gram Newsletter.* October 15, 2000, http://www.schneier.com/crypto-gram-0010.html, accessed December 7, 2009.

Shirky, Clay. "Newspapers and Thinking the Unthinkable." *Shirky.com.* March 13, 2009, http://www.shirky.com/weblog/2009/03/newspapers-and-thinking-the-unthinkable/, accessed July 22, 2009.

"Social Network Marketing Expands Sphere." *eMarketer.com.* August 31, 2009, accessed August 31, 2009.

Snow, Nancy. "Terrorism, Public Relations, and Propaganda." In *Media, Terrorism, and Theory: A Reader*, edited by Anandam P. Kavoori and Todd Fraley. Lanham, Maryland: Rowman & Littlefield Publishing, 2006.

Strangelove, Michael. *The Empire of Mind: Digital Piracy and The Anti-Capitalist Movement.* Toronto: University of Toronto Press, 2005.

Sullivan, Matthew F. "Certified Trouble Ahead for Activist Shareholders?: The SEC, Delaware Certification & Shareholder Bylaw Proposals after CA, Inc. v. AFSCME Employees Pension Plan." *Social Science Research Network - SSRN.com.* March 3, 2009, http://ssrn.com/abstract=1352691, accessed October 7, 2009.

Toffler, Alvin. *Powershift: Knowledge, Wealth, and Violence at the Edge of the 21st Century.* New York: Bantam Books, 1991.

Telofski, Richard. *Dangerous Competition.* Lincoln, Nebraska: iUniverse, 2001.

Telofski, Richard. "Geek Squad Not As Geeky As Expected, Or As Good." *Telofski.com*. April 28, 2009, http://www.telofski.com/blog/2009/04/28/geek-squad-not-as-geeky-as-expected/, accessed November 9, 2009.

"The Big Smear." *The New American*. October 20, 2003, p. 19.

"The News Industry's Uncertain Future." *The Economist*. May 14, 2009, http://www.economist.com/research/articlesBySubject/displaystory.cfm?subjectid=348963&story_id=13649304, accessed September 23, 2009.

"The Slogan." *Flickr.com*. http://www.flickr.com/photos/adijr/2851305136/in/pool-anti-mcdonalds., accessed November 16, 2009.

Tuna, Cari. "Proxy-Voting Advocates Pool Resources on the Web." *The Wall Street Journal Online*. November 23, 2009, http://online.wsj.com/article/SB10001424052748704533904574548051210200852.html, accessed November 23, 2009.

Universal Mc Cann. "When Did We Start Trusting Strangers?" *The Next Thing Now*. September 2008, p 34-35, http://www.universalmccann.com/global/knowledge/view?id=34, accessed March 8, 2010.

UrbanDictionary.com, accessed November 4, 2009.

Walton, Douglas. "What is Propaganda and What Exactly is Wrong with It?" *Public Affairs Quarterly* Vol. 11, #4, October 1997, p. 383 - 413.

"What If Glenn Tilton Was Your Banker?" *GlennTilton.com*. August 11, 2008, http://www.glenntilton.com/your-emails-to-glenntiltoncom/2008/8/11/what-if-glenn-tilton-was-your-banker.html, accessed November 11, 2009.

Wheatley, Margaret. *Leadership and the New Science*. San Francisco: Berrett-Koehler Publishers, p. 143, 2006. Quoted in John S. Burns book review of *Complexity and Creativity in Organizations* by Ralph Stacey as seen in *The Journal of Leadership Studies*, Vol. 4, #1, 1997, p. 168. at http://jlo.sagepub.com/cgi/pdf_extract/4/1/168, accessed September 24, 2009.

"Why People Go Online." *eMarketer.com*. July 17, 2009, http://www.emarketer.com/Article.aspx?R=1007184, accessed October 28, 2009.

About the Author

Thanks for reading *Insidious Competition - The Battle for Meaning and the Corporate Image*, and thanks for wanting to learn more about my background.

I am a competitive strategy and intelligence analyst. At my consulting practice, The Kahuna Content Company, Inc., I specialize in the analysis of non-traditional competitors, which I define as "irregular competition." Some of the insidious competition you have read about here in *Insidious Competition* are what I define as irregular competitors. By irregular competition, a term I coined, I refer specifically to NGO and activist organizations. In recent years, these organizations have begun to have a greater influence on not only the corporate image, but also on how corporations operate day to day. In my work, I specialize in critical and independent analysis of irregular competitors and how they impact businesses from within both Web 1.0 and Web 2.0 environments as well as from within mainstream media.

Before Kahuna Content, I performed similar work, but it concerned more "regular" competitors. I founded and headed The Becker Research Company, Inc., one of America's premier competitive intelligence consultancies. Working with Fortune 100 clients, I helped them predict competitive actions from their regular, "garden-variety" competitors, reducing surprises and assisting them in maintaining or increasing market share.

After Becker Research, but prior to my current consulting practice, I founded and operated eBusiness Analysts, a Web 1.0 strategy firm. When everyone was crazy for e-commerce, I advised various clients on a reasoned and measured approach to conducting business on the Internet. It was during that time that I wrote my second book which is entitled *Dangerous Competition*, available via major online booksellers.

Prior to Becker Research, my previous experience in strategic counseling came from my work in a U.S. Department of Commerce program, the Trade Adjustment Assistance Center (TAAC). As a Strategic Planning Officer in the

TAAC, I designed strategic plans and advised American manufacturers who were adversely affected by foreign competitors.

Before my work for the USDOC, I was a professor of economics and marketing at Monmouth University and at Georgian Court University.

My educational resume sports a B.A. in Communications & Sociology from Rutgers University, and a M.B.A. in Marketing from Rider University. Because of my unique experience and educational background, I believe in analyzing both the soft and hard sides of business. I believe this because without knowing both, I think that a business analyst is really just wasting your time.

If you would like to follow my work, please visit my blog at www.Telofski.com.

Your comments or questions about *Insidious Competition* are welcome. If you would like to make a comment or pose a question about this book, please go to www.InsidiousCompetition.com.

Thanks for reading *Insidious Competition.*

Index

C

D

E

F

G

H

I

N

O

P

R

S

T

U

V

W

Y